Understanding
Natural
Language

Understanding Natural Language

Terry Winograd

Massachusetts Institute of Technology
Cambridge, Massachusetts

ACADEMIC PRESS
New York and London   1972

A Subsidiary of Hartcourt Brace Jovanovich, Publishers

ACADEMIC PRESS, INC.
111 Fifth Avenue, New York, New York 10003

United Kingdom Edition published by
EDINBURGH UNIVERSITY PRESS
22 George Square
Edinburgh EH8 9LF

Library of Congress Catalog Card Number: 77-190108

Second Printing, 1974

Appeared in the journal, *Cognitive Psychology* 3, No. 1, 1972

PRINTED IN THE UNITED STATES OF AMERICA

CONTENTS

EDITORIAL NOTE vii

1. Overview of the Language Understanding Program 1
2. Comparison with Previous Programs 34
3. A Grammar for English 46
4. An Introduction to LISP 76
5. A Description of PROGRAMMAR 80
6. Deduction, Problem Solving, and PLANNER 108
7. The BLOCKS World 117
8. Semantics 126
References 169
Appendix A: Index of Syntactic Features 173
Appendix B: Sample Parsings 175
Appendix C: Sample BLOCKS Theorems 179
Appendix D: Sample PROGRAMMAR Program 183
Appendix E: Sample Dictionary Entries 186
Appendix F: PLANNER Data for Dialog in Section 1.3 . . . 190

EDITORIAL NOTE

When it was decided that *Cognitive Psychology* would not specify size limits for articles, and that we would publish relevant papers in artificial intelligence, we hardly anticipated devoting an entire issue to a single piece of work. However, Winograd's "Program for Understanding Natural Language" seems sufficiently general and important in its implications to warrant the experiment. Some readers will find sufficient the first two sections, which present, respectively, an overview of the system and what it does, and a first-rate evaluation of research in artificial intelligence on natural language processing, semantics, and theorem proving. Others will want to explore in detail the structure of the syntactic component, the treatment of semantics, and the programming language for specifying theories of problem solving. Each of these contributions is significant in its own right. Together they form a unique, integrated system capable of parsing, interpreting, and acting upon the information contained in complex natural language discourse.

Winograd's system is not a "simulation," but it incorporates important ideas about human syntactic, semantic, and problem-solving abilities, and, in particular, about their interactions in understanding natural language. Human intelligence goes far beyond this system, and human language comprehension may turn out to differ in major respects from the means employed here. At the very least, however, Winograd's system should prove an invaluable tool for thinking about what we do when we understand and respond to natural language.

We hope the paper is of interest, and as always we welcome comments and suggestions both about individual papers and about the general publication policies of the journal.

Understanding Natural Language

TERRY WINOGRAD[1]

Massachusetts Institute of Technology
Cambridge, Massachusetts

This paper describes a computer system for understanding English. The system answers questions, executes commands, and accepts information in an interactive English dialog.

It is based on the belief that in modeling language understanding, we must deal in an integrated way with all of the aspects of language—syntax, semantics, and inference. The system contains a parser, a recognition grammar of English, programs for semantic analysis, and a general problem solving system. We assume that a computer cannot deal reasonably with language unless it can understand the subject it is discussing. Therefore, the program is given a detailed model of a particular domain. In addition, the system has a simple model of its own mentality. It can remember and discuss its plans and actions as well as carrying them out. It enters into a dialog with a person, responding to English sentences with actions and English replies, asking for clarification when its heuristic programs cannot understand a sentence through the use of syntactic, semantic, contextual, and physical knowledge. Knowledge in the system is represented in the form of procedures, rather than tables of rules or lists of patterns. By developing special procedural representations for syntax, semantics, and inference, we gain flexibility and power. Since each piece of knowledge can be a procedure, it can call directly on any other piece of knowledge in the system.

1. OVERVIEW OF THE LANGUAGE UNDERSTANDING PROGRAM

1.1. *Introduction*

When a person sees or hears a sentence, he makes full use of his knowledge and intelligence to understand it. This includes not only grammar, but also his knowledge about words, the context of the sen-

[1] Work reported herein was conducted at the Artificial Intelligence Laboratory, a Massachusetts Institute of Technology research program supported by the Advanced Research Projects Agency of the Department of Defense under Contract Number N00014-70-A-0362-0002. The author wishes to express his gratitude to the members of the Artificial Intelligence Laboratory for their advice and support in this work.

Requests for reprints or further information should be sent to the author, at the Artificial Intelligence Laboratory, M.I.T., 545 Technology Square, Cambridge, Massachusetts 02139.

tence, and most important, his understanding of the subject matter. To model this language understanding process in a computer, we need a program which combines grammar, semantics, and reasoning in an intimate way, concentrating on their interaction.

This paper explores one way of representing knowledge in a flexible and usable form. Knowledge is expressed as procedures written in special languages designed for syntax, semantics, and reasoning. These languages have the control structure of a programming language, with the statements of the language explicitly controlling the process. The steps the system takes in understanding a sentence can be determined directly by special knowledge about a word, a syntactic construction, or a particular fact about the world.

We feel that the best way to experiment with complex models of language is to write a computer program which can actually understand language within some domain. For our experiment, we pretend we are talking to a simple robot, with a hand and an eye and the ability to manipulate toy blocks on a table. The robot responds by carrying out commands (in a simulated scene on a display screen attached to the computer), typing out answers to questions, and accepting information to use in reasoning later on.

We had three main goals in writing such a program. The first is the practical desire to have a usable language-understanding system. Even though we used the robot as our test area, the language programs do not depend on any special subject matter, and they have been adapted to other uses.

The second goal is gaining a better understanding of what language is and how it is put together. To write a program we need to make all of our knowledge about language explicit, and we have to be concerned with the entire language process, not just one area such as syntax. This provides a rigorous test for linguistic theories, and leads us into making new theories to fill the places where the old ones are lacking.

More generally, we want to understand what intelligence is and how it can be put into computers. Language is one of the most complex and unique of human activities, and understanding its structure may lead to a better theory of how our minds work. The techniques needed to write a language-understanding program may be useful in other areas of intelligence which involve integrating large amounts of knowledge into a flexible system.

The organization of this paper is as follows. Section 1 conveys a general idea of what the various components of the system do, and how they function together. It also provides a detailed sample dialog, as an extended example of the functioning of the system in a limited domain.

Within Section 1, different subsections cover the parts of the system. For example Section 1.4 introduces the syntactic theory employed in the model. It presents Systemic Grammar, a theory developed by Halliday (1967, 1970), which emphasizes the limited and highly structured sets of choices made in producing a syntactic structure, abstracting the features that are important for conveying meaning. These choices are represented in the grammar by the presence of syntactic features attached to all levels of syntactic structures. These features are chosen in accordance with a set of system networks, explicitly describing their logical interdependence.

Section 1.4 also describes a new parsing system, designed for use with systemic grammar in this program. The parser is an interpreter which accepts recognition grammars written in a procedural form. The formalism is a language called PROGRAMMAR, which has as its primitive operations those processes relevant to parsing natural language, such as building a syntactic structure tree, and creating and using feature lists describing its substructures.

Section 1.5 describes the basis for representing meaning in our system, and discusses the importance of a comprehensive representation of meaning for a model of language use. A formalism is developed for concepts within a language user's model of the world, representing objects, events, and relationships.

Section 1.6 presents that aspect which we have called "semantics", the detailed analysis of linguistic structures to extract an expression of their meaning. A system is developed to work in conjunction with the parser, a dictionary, and the problem-solving programs. It includes not only those aspects of meaning within a sentence, but also the effects of context. The system is organized around a set of specialized programs designed to analyze particular semantic structures, such as clauses and noun groups. Both the semantic knowledge and the definitions of individual words are in the form of programs. This section also describes the use of semantic markers to filter out possible interpretations, and discusses why they provide only a small part of a full semantic theory.

Section 2 compares the system with other work on semantics, inference, and syntactic parsing. It describes the differences in strategies, tactics, approaches, and achievements for a number of computer models of language understanding.

Section 3 presents an outline of a grammar of English. It is based on Halliday's theory of systemic grammar, but the details have been adapted to use within a recognition grammar as a part of an integrated intelligent system. It is unique in presenting a coherent outline of the way English is structured, rather than concentrating on describing particular linguistic phenomena in detail. It is not intended as a definitive grammar, but rather an example of the way that a systemic analysis can be used in various areas of syntax.

System networks are presented for all of the basic structures, and examples are given to illustrate the syntactic features they contain. These networks are distinct from the actual recognition grammar used in parsing. They serve as a framework within which the detailed programs are written.

Section 4 is an introduction to LISP, the computer language in which the system is written. It is designed for readers who have no previous knowledge of LISP, but who are interested in a full understanding of sections describing the model in detail. It does not attempt to explain LISP fully, but concentrates on those notations and conventions which are used heavily in the examples presented in this paper. No knowledge of LISP is called for in sections previous to Section 4.

Section 5 describes PROGRAMMAR, the language created for expressing the details of grammar within this system. It is contrasted with other representations of syntax for computers, and examples are given of simple grammars written as PROGRAMMAR programs. This section provides a manual of PROGRAMMAR instructions and operation, and gives examples of its use in particular parts of the grammar, such as conjunction.

Section 6 describes our use of the PLANNER language (Hewitt, 1971) in representing and manipulating complex meanings. PLANNER is a language for representing problem-solving procedures, which is more general than a specific problem-solving system, such as the General Problem Solver (Newell and Simon, 1963). It performs a variety of "bookkeeping" functions which allow the user to include his own heuristics and strategies for a particular subject domain.

Since no published basic introduction to PLANNER is available, we present a description of its operation and formalism. This is done in the context of simple examples illustrating its use within our system for answering questions and creating plans of action to carry out commands.

Section 7 gives the detailed model of the world used in our problem domain. It describes the basic concepts needed to represent the world of toy blocks, and shows how they are represented in our formalism. It illustrates the operation of the PLANNER programs which represent the system's knowledge of actions. It is included to provide a concrete example of the notion of "meaning" described in the more theoretical sections.

Section 8 presents the semantic analysis of English which we developed for this system. It is in the form of procedures which work with the parser to produce structures representing the meaning of sentences in our logical formalism. Its novelty lies in its approach to semantics as a practical problem of relating words and syntactic structures to a comprehensive logical formalism within a specific problem-solving system. As with the syntax, our emphasis is on outlining an overall system in which we can represent the range of semantic problems, rather than concentrating on one particular area. The section includes the basic analysis of the way meaning is conveyed by each syntactic unit, a discussion of the different types of context, an analysis of appropriate responses to different types of questions and commands, and consideration of illustrative specific problems, such as conjunction and time relationships.

1.2. Implementation of the System

The language-understanding problem is written in LISP to run under the PDP-10 ITS time-sharing system at the Artificial Intelligence Laboratory at MIT. The program is organized as indicated in Fig. 1. (Arrows indicate that one part of the program calls another directly.)

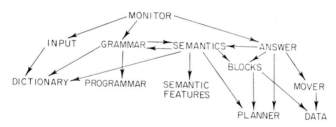

Fig. 1. Organization of the System.

1. MONITOR is a small LISP program which calls the basic parts of the system. The system is organized so that most of the communication between components is done directly, and the monitor is called only at the beginning and end of the understanding process.

2. INPUT is a LISP program which accepts typed input in normal English orthography and punctuation, looks up words in the dictionary, performs morphemic analysis (e.g., realizing that "running" is the "ing" form of the word "run", and modifying the dictionary definition accordingly), and returns a string of words, together with their definitions. This is the input with which the grammar works.

3. The GRAMMAR is the main coordinator of the language understanding process. It consists of a few large programs written in PRO-GRAMMAR to handle the basic units of the English language (such as clauses, noun groups, prepositional groups, etc.). There are two PRO-

GRAMMAR compilers, one which compiles into LISP, which is run interpretively for easy debugging, and another which makes use of the LISP compiler to produce assembly code for efficiency.

4. SEMANTICS is a collection of LISP programs which work in coordination with the GRAMMAR to interpret sentences. In general there are a few semantics programs corresponding to each basic unit in the grammar, each performing one phase of the analysis for that unit. These semantics programs call PLANNER to make use of deduction in interpreting sentences.

5. ANSWER is another collection of LISP programs which control the responses of the system, and take care of remembering the discourse for future reference. It contains a number of heuristic programs for producing answers which take the discourse into account, both in deciding on an answer and in figuring out how to express it in fluent English.

6. PROGRAMMAR is a parsing system which interprets grammars written in the form of programs. It has mechanisms for building a parsing tree, and a number of special functions for exploring and manipulating this tree in the GRAMMAR programs. It is written in LISP.

7. The DICTIONARY actually consists of two parts. The first is a set of syntactic features associated with each word used by the GRAMMAR. The second is a semantic definition for each word, written in a language which is interpreted by the SEMANTICS programs. There are special facilities for irregular forms (like "geese" or "slept"), and only the definitions of root words are kept, since INPUT can analyze a variety of endings. The definitions are actually kept on the LISP property list of the word, and dictionary lookup is handled automatically by LISP.

8. The system has a network of SEMANTIC FEATURES, kept on property lists and used for an initial phase of semantic analysis. The features subdivide the world of objects and actions into simple categories, and the semantic interpreter uses these categories to make some of its choices between alternative definitions for a word (for example "in" would mean "contained in" when applied to a hollow object like a box, but would mean "part of" when applied to a conglomerate like a stack, as in "the red block in the tall stack").

9. BLOCKS is a collection of PLANNER theorems which contain the system's knowledge about the properties of the particular physical world it deals with. Also included is knowledge about achieving goals in this world and making deductions about it. It is a very simple model, designed less as a realistic simulation of a robot than to give the system a world to talk about.

10. MOVER is a set of display routines which simulate the robot's world on the DEC 340 graphic display attached to the PDP-10 computer. It displays the scene indicated by the DATA currently in memory, and

any action called for is displayed in real time, so the human can get visual feedback from his commands to the robot. The input sentences and responses are also displayed.

11. PLANNER is the deductive system used by the program at all stages of the analysis, both to direct the parsing process and to deduce facts about the BLOCKS world. The system uses Micro-Planner, (Sussman *et al.*, 1970) an abbreviated version of Carl Hewitt's original PLANNER language (Hewitt, 1971). It is written in LISP.

12. The DATA component consists of facts about the current scene in the form of PLANNER assertions describing the objects, their sizes, shapes, colors, and locations. The system assumes it has some sort of robot "eye", and a system for analyzing visual data, so all of this information is initially known and does not have to be entered in English.

Implementation details. When operating with a 200 word vocabulary and a fairly complex scene, the program occupies approximately 80K of core. This includes the LISP interpreter, all of the programs, dictionary entries, and data, and enough free storage to remember a sequence of actions and to handle complex sentences and deductions. Figure 2 shows a detailed description of memory usage.

When running compiled, the system is fast enough to carry on a real-

	Parser	Semantics	Deduction	Other
Interpreters	PROGRAMMAR		PLANNER	LISP and Display
26.1	5.8		5.5	14.8
Knowledge of English 22.5	GRAMMAR 7.3	SEMANTICS 15.2		
Knowledge of Subject 16.5	DICTIONARY 1.7	DICTIONARY 6.0	BLOCKS 8.8	
Data for Scene 2.5			Assertions 1.3	Display 1.2
Total 67.6	14.8	21.2	15.6	16.0

Storage Allocation for Language Understanding Program
in Thousands of PDP-10 words

Note: Approximately 12 thousand additional words of free storage are necessary for a dialog like the one described in Section 1.3. As the length of dialog or complexity of the actions is increased, more free storage is needed.

FIG. 2. Memory requirements.

time discourse. Each sentence takes from 5 to 20 sec to analyze and respond to, and the display is designed to move at the speed of a real arm.

1.3. *Sample Dialog*

This section contains a sample of a dialog with the language-under-standing system. It carries out actions and answers questions about a simple scene containing a table, hand, and box, and several blocks and pyramids. The boldface lines in lower case were typed in by a person, and the upper case lines are the computer's response. Other lines are comments describing some of the features being exhibited.

The dialog was carried out in real time with the response of the "robot" displayed on a CRT screen. Figures are included to show the state of the scene at various points, beginning with Fig. 3.

1. **pick up a big red block.**

   OK.

The system answers "OK" when it carries out a command. In order to pick up the red block, it had to clear it off by finding a space for the green one and moving the green one away.

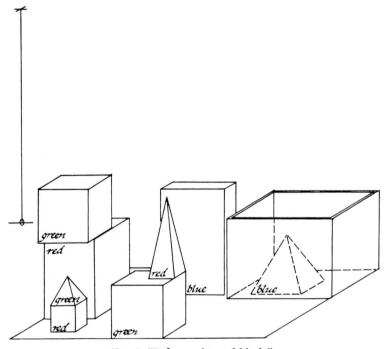

FIG. 3. "Pick up a big red block."

2. **grasp the pyramid.**

I DON'T UNDERSTAND WHICH PYRAMID YOU MEAN.

There are three pyramids in the scene, so the program does nothing.

3. **find a block which is taller than the one you are holding and put it into the box.**

The system has to figure out what is meant by "one" and "it," as well as using deduction to decide which block it is holding.

BY "IT", I ASSUME YOU MEAN THE BLOCK WHICH IS TALLER THAN THE ONE I AM HOLDING.

Printed out to keep us informed.

OK.

The hand has to set down the red block to pick up the taller blue one. Figure 4 shows the result of the system's manipulations so far.

4. **what does the box contain?**

THE BLUE PYRAMID AND THE BLUE BLOCK.

5. **what is the pyramid supported by?**

Earlier the system responded to "the pyramid" by saying "I don't

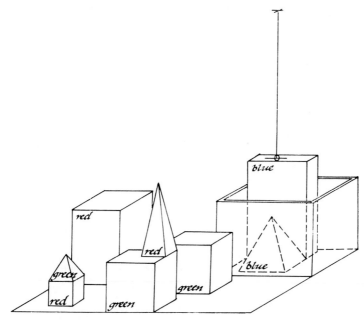

Fig. 4. "Find a block which is bigger than the one you are holding and put it into the box.

understand which pyramid you mean." Now, it assumes that we mean the one just mentioned.

    THE BOX.

  6. **how many blocks are not in the box?**

    Negatives such as "not" and "no" are handled whether they appear in clauses or noun groups (such as "no boxes").

    FOUR OF THEM.

  7. **is at least one of them narrower than the one which I told you to pick up?**

    The phrase "at least one of them" must be analyzed to refer back to the previous question, and "the one which . . ." must also refer to blocks. Noun groups can have complicated numbers such as "at least one", "more than three", exactly seven", etc. The memory of past events is used to deduce which block is "the one which I told you to pick up". Notice the complicated syntactic structure in which "the one" is actually the object of a clause embedded two levels deeper.

    YES, THE RED CUBE.

  8. **is it supported?**

    Passives can be used without a "by . . ." phrase.

    YES, BY THE TABLE.

  9. **can the table pick up blocks?**

    NO.

    The semantic rules make this a nonsensical question which therefore must be false.

 10. **can a pyramid be supported by a block?**

    YES.

    The deductive system finds an actual example, so it knows this is possible.

 11. **can a pyramid support a pyramid?**

    I DON'T KNOW.

    The question makes sense, but there is no example in the scene, so there is no easy way to tell without being able to examine the robot's programs.

 12. **stack up two pyramids.**

    I CAN'T.

    The robot tries and fails.

13. **the blue pyramid is mine.**

    I UNDERSTAND.

This data is added to the data base.

14. **I own blocks which are not red, but I don't own anything which supports a pyramid.**

    I UNDERSTAND.

Two new theorems are created for proving things about "owning".

15. **do I own the box?**

    NO.

The box supports whatever it contains, including a pyramid.

16. **do I own anything in the box?**

    YES, TWO THINGS: THE BLUE BLOCK AND THE BLUE PYRAMID.

17. **will you please stack up both of the red blocks and either a green cube or a pyramid?**

    OK.

Logical connectives such as "and" "or" "either" etc. are handled in both the grammar and semantics. A command is executed even if it looks like a question. The command is carried out by the following series of steps: It puts a green cube on the large red block (note that it chooses the green cube with nothing on it), then removes the small pyramid from the little red cube, so that it can use that cube to complete the stack as specified, resulting in the situation of Fig. 5.

18. **which cube is sitting on the table?**

    THE LARGE GREEN ONE WHICH SUPPORTS THE RED PYRAMID.

Ordinarily the system would be satisfied with calling this "a big green cube", but since we asked "which cube" it has to be more specific in naming it. The use of substitute nouns (such as "one") and pronouns in answers makes the discourse more natural.

19. **is there a large block behind a pyramid?**

    YES, THREE OF THEM: A LARGE RED ONE, A LARGE GREEN CUBE AND THE BLUE ONE.

20. **put a small one onto the green cube which supports a pyramid.**

"A small one" must contrast with the earlier phrase "a large block", so this means "a small block".

    OK.

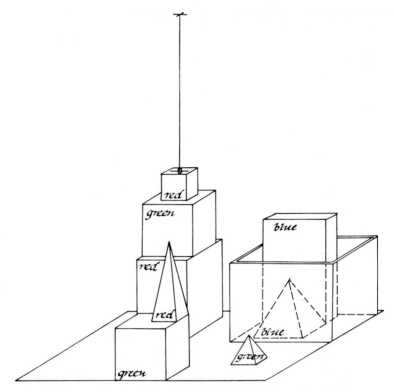

FIG. 5. "Will you please stack up both of the red blocks and either a green cube or a pyramid?"

21. put the littlest pyramid on top of it.

Words like "littlest" are not in the dictionary but are interpreted from the root forms like "little".

OK.

22. how many things are on top of green cubes?

I'M NOT SURE WHAT YOU MEAN BY "ON TOP OF" IN THE PHRASE "ON TOP OF GREEN CUBES".
DO YOU MEAN:
1—DIRECTLY ON THE SURFACE
2—ANYWHERE ON TOP OF?

When there are several interpretations and none is clearly better, the system has to ask the user for more information. The paraphrases were included with the dictionary definition of "on", and the request for more information occurs automatically when the heuristics for resolving ambiguities aren't sufficient. A request like this can also occur when the meaning of a pronoun such as "it" or "they" is unclear.

2

THREE OF THEM.

23. **had you touched any pyramid before you put the green one on the little cube?**

YES, THE GREEN ONE

The system deduces from its memory what event is being referred to, and can relate other events to it in time. The analysis includes complex tenses of verb groups, and there are special facilities for keeping track of the various forms of irregular verbs like "have".

24. **when did you pick it up?**

WHILE I WAS STACKING UP THE RED CUBE, A LARGE RED BLOCK AND A LARGE GREEN CUBE.

A time is described by naming the main goal which was being worked on.

25. **why?**

The system remembers immediately previous sentences to understand questions like this and the following ones.

TO GET RID OF IT.

By keeping track of selected parts of the original subgoal tree, the system has some understanding of its own motives.

26. **why did you do that?**

TO CLEAN OFF THE RED CUBE.

"That" refers to the action mentioned in the answer.

27. **why did you clear off that cube?**

Here, "that" means the one just referred to.

TO PUT IT ON A LARGE GREEN CUBE.

28. **why did you do that?**

TO STACK UP THE RED CUBE, A LARGE RED BLOCK AND A LARGE GREEN CUBE.

29. **why did you do that?**

BECAUSE YOU ASKED ME TO.

It remembers what it did, not how the request was worded.

30. **how did you do it?**

"It" refers to the action mentioned in the last question, rather than the answer.

BY PUTTING A LARGE RED BLOCK ON THE TABLE; THEN LETTING GO OF IT; THEN PUTTING A LARGE GREEN CUBE ON IT; THEN LETTING GO OF THAT CUBE; THEN PUTTING THE RED CUBE ON THAT CUBE; THEN LETTING GO OF THAT CUBE.

This is a description of the top-level subgoals used to achieve the goal.

31. how many objects did you touch while you were doing it?

Time references can refer to a time span, using words like "while".

FOUR OF THEM.

32. what did the red cube support before you started to clean it off?

THE GREEN PYRAMID.

By remembering what has been moved, it is possible to deduce things about earlier states of the scene. We can use complex nestings of clauses like "before you started to clean it off".

33. there were five blocks to the left of the box then.

"Then" must refer to the time mentioned in the last sentence.

NO, ONLY FOUR OF THEM: THE RED CUBE, TWO LARGE GREEN CUBES AND A LARGE RED BLOCK.

Earlier in the dialog, new information about "owning" was accepted at face value. But the system knows that it has complete information about the basic properties of objects, including location. It checks any statements about location or other such properties to see whether it agrees or disagrees.

34. put the blue pyramid on the block in the box.

This is syntactically ambiguous, but is understood without ambiguity since the parsing corresponding to "put the blue pyramid which is on the block in the box." does not make sense in the current scene, while "put the blue pyramid on the block which is in the box" does.

OK.

35. is there anything which is bigger than every pyramid but is not as wide as the thing that supports it?

The system understands quantifiers such as "every", "any", "some", etc., and structures such as "bigger than", "as wide as", etc. Here "it" refers to a noun group within the same sentence but two levels up in the parsing tree.

YES, THE BLUE BLOCK.

36. **does a steeple**

SORRY, I DON'T KNOW THE WORD "STEEPLE".

The system interrupts immediately when it sees a word it can't figure out.

37. **a "steeple" is a stack which contains two green cubes and a pyramid.**

The quote marks indicate that we are defining a new word.

I UNDERSTAND.

38. **are there any steeples now?**

NO.

The new definition is used as a description to recognize steeples.

39. **build one.**

OK.

The description given in the definition is enough to deduce a plan for building new objects as well as recognizing them. The word "one" means "a steeple", and the plan is carried out. First, one of the large green cubes is cleared off by removing the red cube and two pyramids. Then the two green cubes and the tall red pyramid are stacked up to fit the description.

40. **call the biggest block "superblock".**

OK.

We can also give objects names.

41. **have you picked up superblock since we began?**

YES.

42. **why did you drop it?**

BY "IT", I ASSUME YOU MEAN THE SUPERBLOCK.
I CAN'T EXPLAIN A NONEXISTENT EVENT.

There is no record in memory of any block being dropped.

43. **is there anything to the right of the red pyramid?**

YES, FOUR THINGS: THE BOX, THE RED CUBE, THE BLUE PYRAMID AND THE BLOCK NAMED SUPERBLOCK.

Once an object has a name, the name is used to help identify it in responses.

44. **thank you.**

YOU'RE WELCOME!

Idioms can be defined without modifying the grammar.

1.4 *Syntax*

1.4.1 *Syntax and Meaning*

The decision to consider syntax as a proper study devoid of semantics is a basic tenet of many recent linguistic theories. Language is viewed as a way of organizing strings of abstract symbols, and competence is explained in terms of symbol-manipulating rules. At one level this has been remarkably successful. Rules have been formulated which describe in great detail how most sentences are put together. But with the possible exception of current work in generative semantics, such theories have been unable to provide any but the most rudimentary and unsatisfactory accounts of semantics.

The problem is not that current theories are finding wrong answers to the questions they ask; it is that they are asking the wrong questions. What is needed is an approach which can deal meaningfully with the question "How is language organized to convey meaning?" rather than "How are syntactic structures organized when viewed in isolation?".

Syntax helps the speaker to convey meaning beyond the meanings of individual words. The structure of a sentence can be viewed as the result of a series of syntactic choices made in generating it. The speaker encodes meaning by choosing to build the sentence with certain syntactic features, chosen from a limited set. The problem of the hearer is to recognize the presence of those features and use them in interpreting the meaning of the utterance.

Our system is based on a theory called *Systemic Grammar* (Halliday, 1967, 1970) in which these choices of features are primary. This theory recognizes that meaning is of prime importance to the way language is structured. Instead of placing emphasis on a "deep structure" tree, it deals with "system networks" describing the way different features interact and depend on each other. The primary emphasis is on analyzing the limited and highly structured sets of choices which are made in producing a sentence or constituent. The exact way in which these choices are "realized" in the final form is a necessary but secondary part of the theory.

We will begin by describing some of the basic concepts of systemic grammar, and then compare it to better known analyses. The first is the notion of syntactic *units* in analyzing the constituent structure of a sentence (the way it is built up out of smaller parts). If we look at other forms of grammar, we see that syntactic structure is usually represented as a binary tree, with many levels of branching and few branches at any node. The tree is not organized into "groupings" of phrases which are used for conveying different parts of the meaning. For example, the sentence "The three big red dogs ate a raw steak." would be parsed with something like the first tree in Fig. 6.

Systemic grammar pays more attention to the way language is organized into units, each of which has a special role in conveying meaning. In English we can distinguish three basic *ranks* of units, the CLAUSE, the GROUP, and the WORD. There are several types of groups: NOUN GROUP (NG), VERB GROUP (VG), PREPOSITION GROUP (PREPG), and ADJECTIVE GROUP (ADJG). In a systemic grammar, the same sentence might be viewed as having the second structure in Fig. 6.

In this analysis, the WORD is the basic building block. There are word classes like "adjective", "noun", "verb", and each word is an integral unit—it is not chopped into hypothetical bits (like analyzing "dogs" as being composed of "dog" and "-s" or "dog" and "plural"). Instead we view each word as exhibiting *features*. The word "dogs" is the same basic vocabulary item as "dog", but has the feature "plural" instead of "singular". The words "took", "take", "taken", "taking", etc., are all the same basic word, but with differing features such as "past participle" (EN), "infinitive" (INF), "-ing" (ING), etc. When discussing features, we will use several notational conventions. Any word appearing in upper-

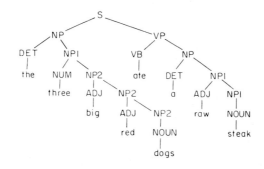

Tree 1

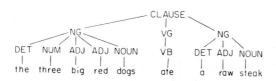

Tree 2

FIG. 6. Parsing Trees.

case letters is the actual symbol used to represent a feature in our grammar and semantic programs. A feature name enclosed in quotes is an English version which is more informative.

The next unit above the WORD is the GROUP, of which there are four types mentioned above. Each one has a particular function in conveying meaning. Noun groups (NG) describe objects, verb groups (VG) carry complex messages about the time and modal (logical) status of an event or relationship, preposition groups (PREPG) describe simple relationships, while adjective groups (ADJG) convey other kinds of relationships and descriptions of objects. These semantic functions are described in more detail in Section 8.

Each GROUP can have "slots" for the words of which it is composed. For example, a NG has slots for "determiner" (DET), "numbers" (NUM), "adjectives" (ADJ), "classifiers" (CLASF), and a NOUN. Each group can also exhibit features, just as a word can. A NG can be "singular" (NS) or "plural" (NPL), "definite" (DEF) as in "the three dogs" or "indefinite" (INDEF) as in "a steak", and so forth. A VG can be "negative" (NEG) or not, can be MODAL (as in "could have seen"), and can have a complex tense.

Finally, the top rank is the CLAUSE. We speak of clauses rather than sentences since the sentence is more a unit of discourse and semantics than a separate syntactic structure. It is either a single clause or a series of clauses joined together in a simple structure such as "A and B and . . . ". We study these conjoining structures separately since they occur at all ranks, and there is no real need to have a separate syntactic unit for sentence.

The clause is the most complex and diverse unit of the language, and is used to express relationships and events, involving time, place, manner and many other aspects of meaning. It can be a QUESTION, a DECLARATIVE, or an IMPERATIVE; it can be "passive" (PASV) or "active" (ACTV); it can be a YES-NO question or a WH- question (like "Why . . .?" or "Which . . .?").

Looking at our sample parsing tree, Tree 2 in Fig. 6, we see that the clauses are made up of groups, which are in turn made up of words. However few sentences have this simple three-layer structure. Groups often contain other groups (for example, "the call of the wild" is a NG, which contains the PREPG "of the wild" which in turn contains the NG "the wild"). Clauses can be parts of other clauses (as in "Join the Navy *to see the world*."), and can be used as parts of groups in many different ways (for example, in the NG "the man *who came to dinner*" or the PREPG "by *leaving the country*".) This phenomenon is called *rankshift*, and is one of the basic principles of systemic grammar.

If the units can appear anywhere in the tree, what is the advantage of grouping constituents into "units" instead of having a detailed structure like the one shown in our first parsing tree? The answer is in the systems of syntactic features each type of unit can exhibit. For example, we might note that all sentences must be either IMPERATIVE, DECLARATIVE, or a QUESTION, and that in the last case they must choose as well between being a YES-NO question or a WH- question containing a word such as "why" or "which". Each unit has associated with it a set of such features, which are of primary significance in conveying meaning. These are not unrelated observations we can make about a unit. They are related by a definite logical structure. The choice between YES-NO and WH- is meaningless unless the clause is a QUESTION, but if it is a QUESTION, the choice must be made. Similarly, the choice between QUESTION, IMPERATIVE, and DECLARATIVE is mandatory for a MAJOR clause (one which could stand alone as a sentence), but is not possible for a "secondary" (SEC) clause, such as "the country *which possesses the bomb.*" The choice between PASV (as in "the ball was attended by John",) and ACTV (as in "John attended the ball.") is on a totally different dimension, since it can be made regardless of which of these other features are present.

We can represent these logical relationships graphically using a few simple conventions. A set of mutually exclusive features (such as QUESTION, DECLARATIVE, and IMPERATIVE) is called a *system,* and is represented by connecting the features with a vertical bar:

$$
\left|
\begin{array}{l}
\text{QUESTION} \\
\text{DECLARATIVE} \\
\text{IMPERATIVE}
\end{array}
\right.
$$

The vertical order is not important, since a system is a set of unordered features among which we will choose one. Each system has an *entry condition* which must be satisfied in order for the choice to be meaningful. This entry condition can be an arbitrary boolean condition on the presence of other features. The simplest case (and most common) is the presence of a single other feature. For example, the system just depicted has the feature MAJOR as its entry condition, since only MAJOR clauses make the choice between DECLARATIVE, IMPERATIVE, and QUESTION.

This simple entry condition is represented by a horizontal line, with the condition on the left of the system being entered. We can diagram some of our CLAUSE features as:

```
                          | DECLARATIVE
              | MAJOR———| IMPERATIVE
                                                    | YES-NO
CLAUSE——|                 | QUESTION———|
              | SEC                                 | WH-
```

Often there are independent systems of choices sharing the same entry condition. For example, the choice between SEC and MAJOR and the choice between PASV and ACTV both depend directly on the presence of CLAUSE. This type of relationship will be indicated by a bracket in place of a vertical bar.

```
                      | MAJOR——...
                  ———|
                      | SEC
CLAUSE
                      | PASV
                  ———|
                      | ACTV
```

If we want to assign a name to a system (to talk about it), we can put the name above the line leading into it:

```
VOICE | PASV
——————|
      | ACTV
```

We can look at these notations as representing the logical operations of "or" and "and", and we can use them to represent more complex entry conditions. If the choice between the features C and D depends on the presence of either A or B, we draw:

```
A———          | D
         ——|
B———          | C
```

and if the entry condition for the "C–D" system is the presence of both A and B, we write:

```
A———          | C
        ——|
B———          | D
```

Finally, we can allow "unmarked" features, in cases where the choice is between the presence or absence of something of interest. We might have a system like:

```
NEGATIVITY      | NEGATIVE
————————————————|
                | - - -
```

in which the feature "nonnegative" is not given a name, but is assumed unless the feature NEGATIVE is present.

In addition we can study the different functions a syntactic "unit" can have as a part of a larger unit. In "Nobody wants to be alone.", the clause "to be alone" has the function of OBJECT in the sentence, while the noun group "nobody" is the SUBJECT. We can note that a transitive clause must have units to fill the functions of SUBJECT and OBJECT, or that a WH- question has to have some constituent which has the role of "question element" (like "why" in "Why did he go?" or "which dog" in "Which dog stole the show?").

In most current theories, these features and functions are implicit in the syntactic rules. There is no explicit mention of them, but the rules are designed in such a way that every sentence will in fact be one of the three types listed above, and every WH- question will in fact have a question element. The difficulty is that there is no attempt in the grammar to distinguish significant features such as these from the many other features we could note about a sentence, and which are also implied by the rules.

If we look at the "deep structure" of a sentence, again the features and functions are implicit. The fact that it is a YES–NO question is indicated by a question marker hanging from a particular place in the tree, and the fact that a component is the object or subject is determined from its exact relation to the branches around it. The problem isn't that there is no way to find these features in a parsing, but that most theories don't bother to ask "Which features of a syntactic structure are important to conveying meaning, and which are just a by-product of the symbol manipulations needed to produce the right word order."

The work of relating the set of features to the actual surface structure in Systemic Grammar is done by realization rules. These carry out much of the work which would be done by transformations in transformational grammar (TG). In TG, the sentences "Sally saw the squirrel.", "The squirrel was seen by Sally.", and "Did Sally see the squirrel?" would be derived from almost identical deep structures, and the difference in final form is produced by transformations. In systemic grammar, these would be analyzed as having most of their features in common, but differing in one particular choice, such as PASSIVE *vs.* ACTIVE, or DECLAR-ATIVE *vs.* QUESTION. The realization rules would then describe the exact word order used to signal these features.

1.4.2 *Parsing*

In implementing a systemic grammar for a computer program for understanding language, we are concerned with the process of recognition rather than that of generation. We do not begin with choices of features and try to produce a sentence. Instead we are faced with a string of letters, and the job is to recognize the patterns and features in it. We need the inverse of realization rules—interpretation rules which

look at a pattern, identify its structure, and recognize its relevant
features.

The parsing system for our program is an interpreter for PROGRAM-
MAR, a language for writing grammars. It is basically a top-down left-
to-right parser, but it modifies these properties when it is advantageous
to do so. By writing in a language designed for specifying grammars,
we can express the regularities of language in a straightforward way,
as simply as with traditional syntax rule forms. The primitives of the
language are those operations which have particular relevance to natural
language and its parsing.

A program for parsing language is as much a "generative" description
of the language as is a set of rules for producing sentences. The meaning
of "generative" in Chomsky's original sense (Chomsky, 1957, 1965) is
that the grammar should associate a structural description to each permis-
sible sentence in the language. A parsing program does just that.

By making the formalism for specifying grammars a programming
language, we enable the grammar to use special tools to handle complex
constructions and irregular forms. For example, we can set up programs
to define certain words, like "and", and "or", as "demons", which cause
an interrupt in the parsing process whenever they are encountered in
the normal left-to-right order, in order to run a special program for conjoined structures. Idioms can also be handled using this "interrupt"
concept. In fact, the process can be interrupted at any point in the
sentence, and any other computations (either semantic or syntactic)
can be performed before going on. These may themselves do bits of
parsing, or they may change the course the basic program will take after
they are done. When we see the sentence "He gave the boy plants to
water." we don't get tangled up in an interpretation which would be
parallel to "He gave the house plants to charity." The phrase "boy
plants" doesn't make sense like "house plants" or "boy scouts", so we
reject any parsing which would use it. This ability to integrate semantics
with syntax is particularly important in handling discourse, where the
interpretation of a sentence containing such things as pronouns may
depend in complex ways on the preceding discourse and knowledge
of the subject matter.

1.4.3 Ambiguity and Understanding

Readers familiar with parsing systems may by now have wondered
about the problem of ambiguity. A PROGRAMMAR program tries to
find a possible parsing for a sentence, and as soon as it succeeds, it
returns its answer. This is not a defect of the system, but an active part
of the concept of language for which it was designed. The language
process is not segmented into the operation of a parser, followed by the

operation of a semantic interpreter. Rather, the process is unified, with the results of semantic interpretation being used to guide the parsing. The last statement in a program for parsing a noun group may be a call to a noun-group semantic interpreter. If it is impossible to interpret the phrase semantically at the time it is found, the parsing is immediately redirected.

The way of treating ambiguity is not through listing all possible interpretations of a sentence, but in being intelligent in looking for the first one, and being even more intelligent in looking for the next one if that fails. There is no automatic backup mechanism in PROGRAMMAR, because blind automatic backup is tremendously inefficient. A good PROGRAMMAR program will check itself when a failure occurs, and based on the structures it has seen and the reasons for the failure, it will decide specifically what should be tried next. PROGRAMMAR contains primitives for passing along reasons for failure and for performing the specific backup steps necessary.

As a concrete example, we might have the sentence "I rode down the street in a car." At a certain point in the parsing, the NG program may come up with the constituent "the street in a car." Before going on, the semantic analyzer will reject the phrase "in a car" as a possible modifier of "street", and the program will attach it instead as a modifier of the action represented by the sentence. Since the semantic programs are part of a general deductive system with a definite world-model, the semantic evaluation which guides parsing can include both general knowledge (cars don't contain streets) and specific knowledge (for example, Melvin owns a red car). Humans take advantage of this sort of knowledge in their understanding of language, and it has been pointed out by a number of linguists and computer scientists that good computer handling of language will not be possible unless computers can do so as well.

Few sentences seem ambiguous to humans when first read. They are guided by an understanding of what is said to pick a single parsing and a very few different meanings. By using this same knowledge to guide its parsing, a computer understanding system can take advantage of the same technique to parse meaningful sentences quickly and efficiently.

1.5. Basic Approach to Meaning

1.5.1 Representing Knowledge

We can describe the process of understanding language as a conversion from a string of sounds or letters to an internal representation of "meaning". In order to do this, a language-understanding system must have some formal way to express its knowledge of a subject, and must be able to represent the "meaning" of a sentence in this formalism. The formalism must be structured so the system can use its knowledge in conjunction with a problem-solving system to make deductions, accept new information, answer questions, and interpret commands.

In our system, the PLANNER language is used as a basis for problem solving, and meaning is represented in PLANNER expressions. This section describes the basis for representing meaning, while Section 1.6 shows how more complex information can be represented and used by PLANNER.

First we must decide what kinds of things are to be represented in the formalism. As a beginning, we would like to be able to represent "objects", "properties," and "relations." Using a simple prefix notation, we can represent such facts as "Boise is a city." and "Noah was the father of Jafeth." as:

(CITY BOISE)   (FATHER-OF NOAH JAFETH)

Here, BOISE, NOAH, and JAFETH are specific objects, CITY is a property which objects can have, and FATHER-OF is a relation. It is a practical convenience to list properties and relations first, even though this may not follow the natural English order. Notice that properties are in fact special types of relations which deal with only one object. Properties and relations will be dealt with in identical ways throughout the system. In fact, it is not at all obvious which concepts should be considered properties and which relations. For example, "DeGaulle is old." might be expressed as (OLD DEGAULLE) where OLD is a property of objects or as (AGE DEGAULLE OLD), where AGE is a relation between an object and its age. In the second expression, OLD appears in the position of an object, even though it can hardly be construed as a particular object like BOISE or DEGAULLE. This suggests that we might like to let properties or relations themselves have properties and enter into other relations. This has a deep logical consequence which will be discussed in later sections.

In order to avoid confusion, we will need some conventions about notation. Most objects and relationships do *not* have simple English names, and those that do often share their names with a range of other meanings. The house on the corner by the market doesn't have a proper name like Jafeth, even though it is just as much a unique object. For the internal use of the system, we will give it a unique name by stringing together a descriptive word and an arbitrary number, then prefixing the result with a colon to remind us it is an object. The house mentioned above might be called :HOUSE374. Properties and relations must also go under an assumed name, since (FLAT X) might mean very different things depending on whether X is a tire or a musical note. We can do the same thing (using a different punctuation mark, #) to represent these two meanings as #FLAT1 and #FLAT2. When the meaning intended is clear, we will omit the numbers, but leave the punctuation marks to remind us that it is a property or relation rather than a specific object. Thus, our facts listed above should be written:

(#CITY :BOISE) (#FATHER-OF :NOAH :JAFETH),
(#OLD :DEGAULLE) or (#AGE :DEGAULLE #OLD).

We are letting properties serve in a dual function. We can use them to say things about objects [as in "The sky is blue."—(#BLUE :SKY)] or we can say things about them as if they were objects [as in "Blue is a color."—(#COLOR #BLUE)]. We want to extend this even further, and allow entire relationships to enter into other relationships. (We distinguish between "relation", the abstract symbol such as #FATHER-OF, and "relationship", a particular instance such as (#FATHER-OF :NOAH :JAFETH)). In accord with our earlier convention about naming things, we can give the relationship a name, so that we can treat it like an object and say (#KNOW :I :REL76) where :REL76 is a name for a particular relationship like (#FATHER-OF :NOAH :JAFETH). We can keep straight which name goes with which relationship by putting the name directly into the relationship. Our example then becomes (#FATHER-OF :NOAH :JAFETH :REL76). There is no special reason to put the name last, except that it makes indexing and reading the statements easier. We can tell that :REL76 is the name of this relation, and not a participant since FATHER-OF relates only two objects. Similarly, it has to be a participant in the relationship (#KNOW :I :REL76) since #KNOW needs two arguments.

We now have a system which can be used to describe more complicated facts. "Harry slept on the porch after he gave Alice the jewels." would become a set of assertions:

(#SLEEP :HARRY :REL1) (#LOCATION :REL1 :PORCH)
(#GIVE :HARRY :ALICE :JEWELS :REL2)
(#AFTER :REL1 :REL2)

This example points out several facts about the notation. The number of participants in a relationship depends on the particular relation, and can vary from 0 to any number. It is fixed for any particular relationship. We do not need to give every relationship a name—it is present only if we want to be able to refer to that relationship elsewhere. This will often be done for events, which are a type of relationship with special properties (such as time and place of occurrence).

1.5.2 General Considerations

Before going on, let us stop and ask what we are doing. In the preceding paragraphs, we have developed a notation for representing certain kinds of meaning. In doing so we have glibly passed over such issues as

what it means to be an "object" or a "property", and what logical status
a symbol such as #BLUE or #CITY should have. We will not attempt
to give a philosophical answer to these questions, but instead take a more
pragmatic approach to meaning.

Language is a process of communication between people, and is
inextricably enmeshed in the knowledge that those people have about
the world. That knowledge is not a neat collection of definitions and
axioms, complete, concise and consistent. Rather it is a collection of
concepts designed to manipulate ideas. It is in fact incomplete, highly
redundant, and often inconsistent. There is no self-contained set of
"primitives" from which everything else can be defined. Definitions are
circular, with the meaning of each concept depending on the other
concepts.

This might seem like a meaningless change—saying that the meaning
of words is represented by the equally mysterious meanings of "concepts"
which exist in the speaker's and hearer's minds, but which are open to
neither immediate introspection nor experiment. However, there is a
major difference. The structure of concepts which is postulated can be
manipulated by inference processes within the computer. The "internal
representation" of a sentence is something which the system can obey,
answer, or add to its knowledge. It can relate a sentence to other concepts, draw conclusions from it, or store it in a way which makes it useable in further deductions and analysis.

This can be compared to the use of "forces" in physics. We have no
way of directly observing a force like gravity, but by postulating its
existence, we can write equations describing it, and relate these
equations to the physical events involved. Similarly, the "concept" representation of meaning is not intended as a direct picture of something
which exists in a person's mind. It is a fiction that gives us a way to make
sense of data, and to predict actual behavior.

The justification for our particular use of concepts in this system is
that it is thereby enabled to engage in dialogs that simulate in many ways
the behavior of a human language user. For a wider field of discourse,
the conceptual structure would have to be expanded in its details, and
perhaps in some aspects of its overall organization. The main point is
that we can in fact gain a better understanding of language use by
postulating these fictitious concepts and structures, and analyzing the
ways in which they interact with language.

We would like to consider some concepts as "atomic". These are taken
to have their own meaning rather than being just combinations of other
more basic concepts. A property or relation is atomic not because of
some special logical status, but because it serves a useful purpose in

relation to the other concepts in the speaker's model of the world. For example, the concept #OLD is surely not primitive, since it can be defined in terms of #AGE and number. However, as an atomic property it will often appear in knowledge about people, the way they look, the way they act, etc. Indeed, we could omit it and always express something like "having an age greater than 30", but our model of the world will be simpler and more useful if we have the concept #OLD available instead.

There is no sharp line dividing atomic concepts from nonatomic ones. In general, such distinctions will depend on the needs of the particular language community. For most purposes it would be absurd to have separate atomic concepts for such things as #CITY-OF-POPULATION-23,485 or #PERSON-WEIGHING-BETWEEN-178-AND-181. But it might in fact be useful to distinguish between #BIG-CITY, #TOWN, and #VILLAGE, or between #FAT, and #THIN, since our model may often use these distinctions.

If our "atomic" concepts are not logically primitive, what status do they have? What is their "meaning"? How are they defined? The answer is again relative to the world-model of the speaker. Facts cannot be classified as "those which define a concept" and "those which describe it." Ask someone to define #PERSON or #JUSTICE, and he will come up with a formula or slogan. #JUSTICE is defined in his world-model by a series of examples, experiences, and specific cases. The model is circular, with the meaning of any concept depending on the entire knowledge of the speaker, not just the kind which would be included in a dictionary. There must be a close similarity between the models held by the speaker and listener, or there could be no communication. If my concept of #DEMOCRACY and yours do not coincide, we may have great difficulty understanding each other's political viewpoints. Fortunately, on simpler things such as #BLUE, #DOG, and #AFTER, there is a pretty good chance that the models will be practically identical. In fact, for simple concepts, we can choose a few primary facts about the concept and use them as a "definition", which corresponds to the traditional dictionary.

Returning to our notation, we see that it is intentionally general, so that our system can deal with concepts as people do. In English we can treat events and relationships as objects, as in "The war destroyed Johnson's rapport with the people." Within our representation of meaning we can similarly treat an event such as #WAR or a relationship of #RAPPORT in the same way we treat objects. We do not draw a sharp philosophical distinction between "specific objects", "properties", "relationships", "events", etc.

1.6 Semantics

1.6.1 What is Semantics?

There has never been a clear definition of what the field of "semantics" should cover, but attempts to program computers to understand natural language have clarified what a semantic theory has to do, and how it must connect with the syntactic and logical aspects of language. In practical terms, we need a transducer that can work with a syntactic analyzer, and produce data which is acceptable to a logical deductive system. Given a syntactic parser with a grammar of English, and a deductive system with a base of knowledge about particular subjects, the role of semantics is to fill the gap between them.

The semantic theory must describe relationships at three different levels. First, it must define the meanings of words. We pointed out in Section 1.5 that the full meaning of a word or concept cannot be defined in a simple dictionary entry, but involves its relationship to an entire vocabulary and structure of concepts. However, we can talk about the formal description attached to a word which allows it to be integrated into the system. In what follows, we use the word "meaning" in this more limited sense, describing those aspects attached to a word as its dictionary definition.

The formalism for definitions should not depend on the details of the semantic programs, but should allow users to add to the vocabulary in a simple and natural way. It should also handle the quirks and idiosyncracies of meaning, not just well-behaved standard words.

The next level relates the meanings of groups of words in syntactic structures. We need an analysis of the ways in which English structures convey meaning, and the roles the words and syntactic features play.

Finally, a sentence in natural language is never interpreted in isolation. A semantic theory must describe how the meaning of a sentence depends on its context. It must deal both with the linguistic setting (the context within the discourse) and the real-world setting (the interaction with knowledge of nonlinguistic facts.)

1.6.2 The Semantic System

With these goals in mind, let us consider how to implement such a semantic system. Section 1.5 discussed the person's "model of the world" which is organized around "objects" having "properties" and entering into "relationships." In later sections, we will show how these are combined to form more complicated logical expressions, using PLANNER. Looking at the properties of English syntax, we see that these basic elements of the "world model" are just what English is good at conveying.

For describing objects, there is the NOUN GROUP. It contains a noun, which indicates the kind of object; adjectives and classifiers, which describe further properties of the object; and a complex system of quantifiers and determiners describing its logical status—whether it is a particular object, ("the sun"), a class of objects ("people"), a particular set of objects ("John's lizards"), an unspecified set containing a specified number of objects ("three bananas"), etc.

For describing relationships and events, there are the CLAUSE, PREPOSITION GROUP, and ADJECTIVE GROUP. The CLAUSE is especially suited for dealing with relationships having a particular time reference, working in coordination with the VERB GROUP, which functions to convey information about time and modality. Clauses can also be used to represent an event or relationship as an object (as in "*His going* pleased me."), or to modify a particular object within a NOUN GROUP (in "the man *who broke the bank*"). The PREPG is a way of expressing relationships which do not need as much flexibility in including modifiers such as time, place, and manner (such as "the man *in the blue vest*"). The ADJG is used in some constructions to describe properties and some special kinds of relationships of objects (such as "Her gift was *bigger than a breadbox*.")

The semantic system is built around a group of about a dozen programs which are experts at looking at these particular syntactic structures. They look at both the structures and the meanings of the words to build up PLANNER expressions which will be used in answering questions and making deductions. Since the parser uses systemic grammar, the semantic programs can look directly for syntactic features such as PASSIVE, PLURAL, or QUESTION to make decisions about the meaning of the sentence or phrase.

Since each of these semantic specialists can work separately, there is no need to wait for a complete parsing before beginning semantic analysis. The NOUN GROUP specialist can be called as soon as a NOUN GROUP has been parsed, to see whether it makes sense before the parser goes on. In fact, the task can be broken up, and a preliminary NOUN GROUP specialist can be called in the middle of parsing (for example, after finding the noun and adjectives, but before looking for modifying clauses or prepositional phrases) to see whether it is worth continuing, or whether the supposed combination of adjectives and noun is nonsensical. Any semantic program has full power to use the deductive system, and can even call the grammar to do a special bit of parsing before going on with the semantic analysis. For this reason it is very hard to classify the semantic analysis as "top-down" or "bottom-up". In general each structure is analyzed as it is parsed, which is a bottom-up approach.

However whenever there is a reason to delay analysis until some of the larger structure has been analyzed, the semantic specialist programs can work in this top-down manner.

1.6.3 Words

A semantic system needs to deal with two different kinds of words. Some words, like "that" or "than", in "He knew *that* they were madder *than* hornets," would be difficult to define except in terms of their function in the sentence structure. They signal certain syntactic structures and features, and have no other meaning. The distinction between these "function words" and the "content words" which make up the bulk of our vocabulary is not sharp, since many words serve a combination of purposes (for example, numbers are basically "function words", but each one has its unique meaning). Nonetheless, it is reasonable to require that the definitions of content words like "snake" or "walk" should not presume detailed knowledge of the syntax of the language. In defining the word "mighty", we should not have to worry about whether it appears in "The sword is mighty," or "the mightiest warrior", or "a man mightier than a locomotive." We should be able to say "mighty" means having the property represented conceptually as #MIGHT, and let the semantic system do the rest. The definition of each word is a LISP program to be run at an appropriate time in the semantic analysis. For simple cases, there are standard functions with a special format for usual types of definitions. Complex cases may involve special operations on the semantic structure being built, which may depend on the context. This flexibility is important in many places. For example, the word "one" when used as a noun (as in "the green one") refers back to previously mentioned nouns. It could not be defined by a simple format, as could "block" or "dog", since access to the previous discourse is needed to determine what is really being referred to. In our system, the definitions of such words are compatible with the definitions of all other nouns—the semantic specialists don't have to distinguish among them. When the NG specialist is ready to use the definition of the noun, it calls it as a program. In the usual case, this program sets up a standard data structure. In the case of "one", it calls a heuristic program for understanding back-references, and its effect on the meaning will depend on the discourse. Similarly, the verb "be" is called like any other verb by the semantic specialist, but its definition is a complex program describing its different uses.

The use of procedures to represent meanings of words gives a flexibility which allows these exceptional words to be handled as well as the more ordinary forms. At the same time, it provides a strict test for the representation of the meaning of a word, since the procedures can actually be run in an integrated language-understanding system.

1.6.4 Ambiguity

A semantic theory must account for multiple meanings of words, phrases, and sentences, explaining not only how multiple interpretations can occur, but also how the hearer picks a single meaning. Words may have several "senses", producing multiple possible interpretations of phrases and sentences involving them. Sometimes a sentence may also be described with several different syntactic structures, leading to semantic ambiguities. Finally, some ambiguities result from the semantic analysis. The sentence "A man sitting in this room fired the fatal shot." will be ambiguous even if we agree on a single meaning for each word, and a surface structure for the sentence. It could mean "a man who *is* sitting in this room", or "who *was* sitting in this room". This could be treated as a syntactic ambiguity in the deep structure, but in our analysis it is instead treated as a semantic ambiguity involving the time reference.

In describing the parser it was pointed out that we do not carry forward simultaneous parsings of a sentence. We try to find the "best" parsing, and try other paths only if we run into trouble. In semantics we take the other approach. If a word has two meanings, then two semantic descriptions are built simultaneously, and used to form two separate phrase interpretations.

We can immediately see a problem here. There is dire danger of a combinatorial explosion. If words A, B, C, and D each have three meanings, then a sentence containing all of them may have $3 \times 3 \times 3 \times 3$, or 81 interpretations. The possibilities for a long sentence are astronomical.

Of course a person does not build up such a tremendous list. As he hears a sentence, he filters out all but the most reasonable interpretations. We know that a "ball" can be either a spherical toy or a dancing party, and that "green" can mean either the color green, or unripe, or inexperienced. But when we see "the green ball", we do not get befuddled with six interpretations, we know that only one makes sense. The use of "green" for "unripe" applies only to fruit, the use as "inexperienced" applies only to people, and the color only to physical objects. The meaning of "ball" as a party fits none of these categories, and the meaning as a "spherical toy" fits only the last one. We can subdivide the world into rough classes such as "animate", "inanimate", "physical", "abstract", "event", "human", etc. and can use this classification scheme to filter out meaningless combinations of interpretations.

Some semantic theories (Katz & Fodor, 1964) are based almost completely on this idea. We would like to use it for what it is—not a complete representation of meaning, but a rough classification which eliminates fruitless semantic interpretations. Our system has the ability to use these "semantic markers" to cut down the number of semantic interpretations of any phrase or sentence.

A second method used to reduce the number of different semantic interpretations is to do the interpretation continuously. We do not pile up all possible interpretations of each piece of the sentence, then try to make logical sense of them together at the end. As each phrase is completed, it is understood. If we come across a phrase like "the colorful ball" in context, we do not keep the two different possible interpretations in mind until the utterance is finished. We immediately look in our memory to see which interpretation is meaningful in the current context of discourse, and use only that meaning in the larger semantic analysis of the sentence. Since our system allows the grammar, semantics and deduction to be easily intermixed, it is possible to do this kind of continuous interpretation.

Finally we must deal with cases where we cannot eliminate all but one meaning as "senseless". There will be sentences where more than one meaning makes sense, and there must be some way to choose the correct one in a given context. In Section 1.6.5, we discuss the use of the overall discourse context in determining the plausibility of a particular interpretation.

1.6.5 Discourse

We have discussed why a semantic system should deal with the effect of "setting" on the meaning of a sentence. A semantic theory can account for three different types of context.

First, there is the *local discourse* context, which covers the discourse immediately preceding the sentence, and is important to semantic mechanisms like pronoun reference. If we ask the question "Did you put *it* on a green *one?*" or "*Why?*" or "How many of *them* were *there then?*", we assume that it will be possible to fill in the missing information from the immediate discourse. There are a number of special mechanisms for using this kind of information, and they form part of a semantic theory.

Second, there is an *overall discourse* context. A hearer will interpret the sentence "The group didn't have an identity." differently depending on whether he is discussing mathematics or sociology. There must be a systematic way to account for this effect of general subject matter on understanding. In addition to the effects of general subject on choosing between meanings of a word, there is an effect of the context of particular things being discussed. If we are talking about Argentina, and say "The government is corrupt.", then it is clear that we mean "the government of Argentina". If we say "Pick up the pyramid.", and there are three pyramids on the table, it will not be clear which one is meant. But if this immediately follows the statement "There is a block and a pyramid in the box.", then the reference is to the pyramid in the box. This would have been clear even if there had been several sentences between these two. Therefore this is a different problem than the local discourse of pronoun reference. A semantic theory must deal with all of these different forms of overall discourse context.

Finally, there is a context of knowledge about the world, and the way that knowledge affects our understanding of language. If we say "The city councilmen refused the demonstrators a permit because they feared violence.", the pronoun "they" will have a different interpretation than if we said "The city councilmen refused the demonstrators a permit because they advocated revolution." We understand this because of our sophisticated knowledge of councilmen, demonstrators, and politics—no set of syntactic or semantic rules could interpret this pronoun reference without using knowledge of the world. Of course a semantic theory does not include a theory of political power groups, but it must explain the ways in which this kind of knowledge can interact with linguistic knowledge in interpreting a sentence.

Knowledge of the world may affect not only such things as the interpretation of pronouns, but may alter the parsing of the syntactic structures as well. If we see the sentence "He hit the car with a rock." the structure will be parsed differently from "He hit the car with a dented fender.", since we know that cars have fenders, but not rocks.

In our system, most of this discourse knowledge is called on by the semantic specialists, and by particular words such as "one", "it", "then", "there", etc. We have concentrated particularly on local discourse context, and the ways in which English carries information from one sentence to the next. A number of special pieces of information are kept, such as the time, place, and objects mentioned in the previous sentence. This information is referenced by special structures and words like pronouns, "then", and "there". The meaning of the entire previous sentence can be referred to in order to answer a question like "Why did you do *that?*" or just "Why?".

1.6.6 Goals of a Semantic Theory

For Katz and Fodor (1964), the goals of a semantic theory are mainly to account for "the number and content of the readings of a sentence, detecting semantic anomalies, and deciding upon paraphrase relations between sentences." For us, these are not primary goals, but by-products of the analysis made possible by a more complete semantic theory. A phrase is a semantic anomaly if the system produces no possible interpretations for it. Two sentences are paraphrases if they produce the same representation in the internal formalism for meaning, and the "number and content" of the readings of a sentence are the immediate result of its semantic analysis. Which of these will happen depends on the entire range of ways in which language communicates meaning, not on a restricted subset such as the logical relations of markers. Once we have a conceptual representation for meaning, solutions to problems such as these are secondary by-products of the basic analysis which relates a sentence to the representation of its meaning. In addition, we are not restricted to dealing with those aspects of meaning which are "independent of setting." We can talk about sentences being anomalies or paraphrases in a given context, as well as without regard to context, since the theory can include a systematic analysis of the interaction of context with understanding.

2. COMPARISON WITH PREVIOUS PROGRAMS

2.1 Language Understanding Systems

In Section 1 we discussed ways of representing information and meaning within a language-comprehending system. In order to compare our ideas with those in previous systems, we will establish a broad classification of the field. Of course, no set of pigeon-holes can completely characterize the differences between programs, but they can give us some viewpoints from which to analyze different people's work, and can help us see past the superficial differences. In Section 2.1 we will deal only with the ways that programs represent and use their knowledge of the subject matter they discuss. We will distinguish four basic types of systems called "special format", "text based", "limited logic", and "general deductive".

2.1.1 Special Format Systems

Most of the early language-understanding programs were of the special format type. Such systems usually use two special formats designed for their particular subject matter—one for representing the knowledge they keep stored away, and the other for the meaning of the English input. Some examples are: BASEBALL (Green et al., 1963), which stored tables of baseball results and interpreted questions as "specification lists" requesting data from those tables; SAD SAM (Lindsay, 1963), which interpreted sentences as simple relationship facts about people, and stored these in a network structure; STUDENT (Bobrow, 1968), which interpreted sentences as linear equations and could store other linear equations and manipulate them to solve algebra problems; and ELIZA (Weizenbaum, 1966), whose internal knowledge is a set of sentence rearrangements and key words, and which sees input as a simple string of words.

These programs all make the assumption that the only relevant information in a sentence is that which fits their particular format. Although they may have very sophisticated mechanisms for using this information (as in CARPS (Charniak, 1969), which can solve word problems in calculus), they are each built for a special purpose, and do not handle information with the flexibility which would allow them to be adapted to other uses. Nevertheless, their restricted domain often allows them to use special purpose heuristics which achieve impressive results with a minimum of concern for the complexities of language.

2.1.2 *Text Based Systems*

Some researchers were not satisfied with the limitations inherent in the special-format approach. They wanted systems which were not limited by their construction to a particular specialized field. Instead they used English text, with all of its generality and diversity, as a basis for storing information. In these "text based" systems, a body of text is stored directly, under some sort of indexing scheme. An English sentence input to the understander is interpreted as a request to retrieve a relevant sentence or group of sentences from the text. Various ingenious methods were used to find possibly relevant sentences and decide which were most likely to satisfy the request.

PROTOSYNTHEX I (Simmons *et al.*, 1966) had an index specifying all the places where each "content word" was found in the text. It tried to find the sentences which had the most words in common with the request (using a special weighting formula), then did some syntactic analysis to see whether the words in common were in the right syntactic relationship to each other. Semantic Memory (Quillian, 1968) stored a slightly processed version of English dictionary definitions in which multiple-meaning words were eliminated by having humans indicate the correct interpretation. It then used an associative indexing scheme which enabled the system to follow a chain of index references. An input request was in the form of two words instead of a sentence. The response was the shortest chain which connected them through the associative index (e.g., if there is a definition containing the words A and B and one containing B and C, a request to relate A and C will return both sentences).

Even with complex indexing schemes, the text based approach has a basic problem. It can only spout back specific sentences which have been stored away, and can not answer any question which demands that something be deduced from more than one piece of information. In addition, its responses often depend on the exact way the text and questions are stated in English, rather than dealing with the underlying meaning.

2.1.3 Limited Logic Systems

The "limited logic" approach attempted to correct these faults of text based systems, and has been used for most of the more recent language-understanding programs. First, some sort of more formal notation is substituted for the actual English sentences in the base of stored knowledge. This notation may take many different forms, such as "description lists" (Raphael, 1968), "kernels" (Simmons, 1966), "concept-relation-concept triples" (Simmons et al., 1966), "data nodes" (Quillian, 1969), "rings" (Thompson, 1968), "relational operators" (Tharp, 1969), etc. Each of these forms is designated for efficient use in a particular system, but at heart they are all doing the same thing—providing a notation for simple assertions of the sort described in Section 1.5. It is relatively unimportant which special form is chosen. All of the different methods can provide a uniform formalism which frees simple information from being tied down to a specific way of expressing it in English. Once this is done, a system must have a way of translating from the English input sentences into this internal assertion format, and the greatest bulk of the effort in language-understanding systems has been this "semantic analysis", which was discussed at length in Section 1.6. For now we are more interested in what can be done with the assertions once they have been put into the desired form.

Some systems (Quillian, 1969; Tharp, 1969), remain close to text based systems, only partially breaking down the initial text input. The text is processed by some sort of dependency analysis and left in a network form, either emphasizing semantic relationships or remaining closer to the syntactic dependency analysis. What is common to these systems is that they do not attempt to answer questions from the stored information. As with text based systems, they try to answer by giving back bits of information directly from the data base. They may have ways to decide what parts of the data are relevant to a request, but they do not try to break the question down and answer it by logical inference. Because of this, they suffer the same deficiencies as text based systems. They have a mass of information stored away, but little way to use it except to print it back out.

Most of the systems which have been developed recently fit more comfortably under the classification "limited logic". In addition to their data base of assertions (whatever they are called), they have some mechanism for accepting more complex information, and using it to deduce the answers to more complex questions. By "complex information" we mean the type of knowledge containing logical quantifiers and relationships (such as "Every canary is either yellow or purple," or "If A is a part of B and B is a part of C, then A is a part of C."), as well as knowledge of heuristics and procedures relevant to the subject matter. By "complex questions", we mean questions which are not answerable by giving out one of the data base assertions, but demand some logical inference to produce an answer.

One of the earliest limited logic programs was SIR (Raphael, 1968), which could answer questions using simple logical relations (like the "part" example in the previous paragraph). The complex information was not expressed as data, but was built directly into the SIR operating program. This meant that the types of complex information it could use were highly limited, and could not be easily changed or expanded. The complex questions it could answer were similar to those in many later limited logic systems, consisting of four basic types. The simplest is a question which translates into a single assertion to be verified or falsified (e.g., "Is John a bagel?"). The second is an assertion in which one part is left undetermined (e.g., "Who is a bagel?") and the system responds by "filling in the blank". The third type is an extension of this, which asks for all possible blank-fillers (e.g., "Name all bagels."), and the fourth adds counting to this listing facility to answer count questions (e.g., "How many bagels are there?"). SIR had special logic for answering "how many" questions, using information like "A hand has five fingers.", and in a similar way each limited logic system had special built-in mechanisms to answer certain types of questions.

The DEACON system (Thompson, 1968), had special "verb tables" to handle time questions, and a bottom-up analysis method which allowed questions to be nested. For example, the question "Who is the commander of the batallion at Fort Fubar?" was handled by first internally answering the question "What batallion is at Fort Fubar?" The answer was then substituted directly into the original question to make it "Who is the commander of the 69th batallion?", which the system then answered. PROTOSYNTHEX II (Simmons, 1966) had special logic for taking advantage of the transitivity of "is" (e.g., "A boy is a person.", "A person is an animal.", therefore "A . . ."). PROTOSYNTHEX III (Simmons et al., 1968) and SAMENLAQ II (Shapiro, 1969) bootstrapped their way out of first-order logic by allowing simple assertions about relationships (e.g., "North-of is the converse of South-of."). CONVERSE (Kellogg, 1968) converted questions into a "query language" which allowed the form of the question to be more complex but used simple table lookup for finding the answers. Weizenbaum (1967) used the ELIZA system as a basis for limited logic programs and used them as a framework for discussing the relevance of context.

All of the limited logic systems are basically similar, in that complex information is not part of the data, but is built into the system programs. Those systems which could add to their initial data base by accepting English sentences could accept only simple assertions as input. The questions could not involve complex quantified relationships (e.g., "Is there a country which is smaller than every U. S. State?").

2.1.4 *General Deductive Systems*

The problems of limited logic systems were recognized very early (see Raphael (1968) p. 90), and people looked for a more general approach to storing and using complex information. If the knowledge could be expressed in some standard mathematical notation (such as the predicate calculus), then all of the work logicians have done on theorem proving could be utilized to make a theoretically efficient deductive system. By expressing a question as a theorem to be proved, the theorem prover could actually deduce the information needed to answer any question which could be expressed in the formalism. Complex information not easily useable in limited logic systems could be neatly expressed in the predicate calculus, and a body of work already existed on computer theorem proving. This led to the "general deductive" approach to language-understanding programs.

The early programs used logical systems less powerful than the full predicate calculus (Bar-Hillel, 1964; Coles, 1968; Darlington, 1964), but the big boost to theorem proving research was the development of the Robinson resolution algorithm (Robinson, 1965), a very simple "complete uniform proof procedure" for the first-order predicate calculus. This meant that it became easy to write an automatic theorem proving program with two important characteristics. First, the procedure is "uniform"—we need not (and in fact, cannot) tell it how to go about proving things in a way suited to particular subject matter. It has its own fixed procedure for building proofs, and we can only change the sets of logical statements (or "axioms") for it to work on. Second, it guarantees that if any proof is possible using the rules of predicate calculus, the procedure will eventually find it (even though it may take a very long time). These are very pretty properties for an abstract deductive system, but the price is a low level of practicality. We would like to argue that in fact they have led to the worst deficiencies of the theorem-proving question-answerers, and that a very different approach is called for.

The "uniform procedure" approach was adopted by a number of systems (see discussion in Green, 1968, 1969) as an alternative to the kind of specialized limited logic discussed in the previous section. It was felt that there must be a way to present complex information as data rather than embedding it into the inner workings of the language-understanding system. There are many benefits in having a uniform notation for representing problems and knowledge in a way which does not depend on the quirks of the particular program which will interpret them. It enables a user to describe a body of knowledge to the computer in a "neutral" way without knowing the details of the question-answering system, and guarantees that the system will be applicable to any subject, rather than being specialized to handle only one.

Predicate calculus seemed to be a good uniform notation, but in fact it has a serious deficiency. By putting complex information into a "neutral" logical formula, these systems ignored the fact that an important part of a person's knowledge concerns how to go about figuring things out. Our heads don't contain neat sets of logical axioms from which we can deduce everything through a "proof procedure". Instead we have a large set of heuristics and procedures for solving problems at different levels of generality. In ignoring this type of knowledge, programs run into tremendous problems of efficiency. As soon as a "uniform procedure" theorem prover gets a large set of axioms (even well below the number needed for really understanding language), it becomes bogged down in searching for a proof, since there is no easy way to guide its search according to the subject matter. In addition, a proof which takes many steps (even if they are in a sequence which can be easily predicted by the nature of the theorem) may take impossibly long since it is very difficult to describe the correct proving procedure to the system.

It is possible to write theorems in clever ways to implicitly guide the deduction process, and a recent paper (Green, 1969) describes some of the problems and techniques for "programming" in first-order logic. Since first-order logic is a declarative rather than imperative language, specifying how to do something takes a good deal of work.

It might be possible to add strategy information to a predicate calculus theorem prover, but with current systems such as QA3 (Green, 1968), to change strategies "the user must know about set-of-support and other program parameters such as level bound and term-depth bound. To radically change the strategy, the user presently has to know the LISP language and must be able to modify certain strategy sections of the program" (Green, 1969, p. 236). In newer programs such as QA4, there will be a special strategy language to go along with the theorem proving mechanisms. It will be interesting to see how close these new strategy languages are to PLANNER, and whether there is any advantage to be gained by putting them in a hybrid with a resolution-based system.

2.1.5 *Procedural Deductive Systems*

The problem with the limited logic systems wasn't that they expressed their complex information in the form of programs or procedures. The problem was that in these systems, new subject matter required new subprograms, and

> ". . . each change in a subprogram may affect more of the other subprograms. The structure grows more awkward and difficult to generalize . . . Finally the system may become too unwieldy for further experimentation."

(Raphael, 1968, p. 91).

What was needed were new programming techniques capable of using procedural information, but at the same time expressing this information in ways which did not depend on the peculiarities and special structure of a particular program or subject of discussion.

A system which partially fits this description is Woods' (1968). It uses a quantificational query language for expressing questions, then assumes that there are "semantic primitives" in the form of LISP subroutines which decide such predicates as (CONNECT FLIGHT-23 BOSTON CHICAGO) and which evaluate functions such as "number of stops", "owner", etc. It differs from limited logic systems in that the entire system is designed without reference to the way the particular "primitive" functions operate on the data base. Note, however, that the information which the system was designed to handle (the Official Airline Guide) is particularly amenable to simple table-lookup routines. Were less structured information involved, these primitive routines might run into the same problems of interconnectedness described by Raphael.

PLANNER (Hewitt, 1969, 1971) is a goal-oriented procedural language designed to deal with these problems. It handles simple assertions efficiently, and it can include any complex information that can be expressed in the predicate calculus. More important, complex information is expressed as procedures, and these may include knowledge of how best to go about attempting a proof. The language is "goal-oriented", in that we need not be concerned about the details of interaction among procedures. For example, theorems which may at some point ask whether an object is sturdy need not specify the program that assesses sturdiness. Instead they may say something like "Try to find an assertion that X is sturdy, or prove it using anything you can." If we know of special procedures likely to give a quick answer, we can specify that these be tried first. If at some point we add a new procedure for evaluating sturdiness, we do not need to find out which theorems use it. We need only add it to the data base, and the system will automatically try it, along with any others, whenever any theorem calls for such a test.

The ability to add new theorems without relating them to other theorems is the advantage of a "uniform" notation. In fact PLANNER is a uniform notation for expressing procedural knowledge just as predicate calculus is a notation for a more limited range of information. The added advantage is its flexible control structure. If we know that a particular proof will fail unless one of a specified set of theorems succeeds, we can write PLANNER procedures in such a way that only theorems from that set will be used in attempting a proof. Furthermore, if we wish to try theorems in a particular order, that order may be specified, either directly, or depending upon arbitrarily complex calculations which take place when the subgoal is set up.

Notice that this control structure makes it very difficult to specify the abstract logical properties of PLANNER, such as consistency and completeness. It is not easy to fit it into traditional ways of proving things about logical systems. It is worth pointing out here that completeness may in fact be a bad property. It means that if the theorem-prover is given something to prove which is in fact false, it will exhaust every possible way of trying to prove it. By forsaking completeness, we allow ourselves to use good sense in deciding when to give up.

In a truly uniform system, the theorem prover is forced to "rediscover the world" every time it answers a question. Every goal forces it to start from scratch, looking at all of the theorems in the data base. At best it may use nonspecific heuristics to limit its selections. PLANNER can operate in this "blindman" mode, but it should have to do this only rarely—when discovering something that was not known or understood when the basic theorems were written. The rest of the time it can go about proving things it knows how to do, without having to piece together a proof from scratch each time.

2.2 Comparison with Other Parsers

2.2.1 Older Parsers

When work first began on analyzing natural language with computers, no theories of syntax existed which were explicit enough to be used. The early machine-translator designers were forced to develop their own linguistics as they worked, and they produced rough and ready versions. The parsers were collections of "packaging routines", "inserted structure passes", "labeling subroutines", etc. (Garvin, 1965) which evolved gradually as the grammars were expanded to handle more and more complex sentences. They had the same difficulties as any program designed in this way—as they became more complex it became harder and harder to understand the interactions within them.

When the machine-translation effort failed, it seemed clear that it had been premature to try handling all of English without a better background of linguistic theory and an understanding of the mathematical properties of grammars. Computer programs for natural language took two separate paths. The first was to ignore traditional syntax entirely, and to use some sort of more general pattern matching process to get information out of sentences. Systems such as STUDENT (Bobrow, 1968), SIR (Raphael, 1968), ELIZA (Weizenbaum, 1966), and Semantic Memory (Quillian, 1968) made no attempt to do a complete syntactic analysis of the inputs. They either limited the user to a small set of fixed input forms or limited their understanding to those things they could get while ignoring syntax.

The other approach was to take a simplified subset of English which could be handled by a well-understood form of grammar, such as one of the variations of context-free grammars. There has been much interesting research on the properties of abstract languages and the algorithms needed to parse them. Using this theory, a series of parsing algorithms and representations were developed. For a summary of the computer parsers designed before 1966, see Bobrow (1967). A more recent development is Earley's context-free parser (1966), which operates in a time proportional to the cube of the length of a sentence.

The problem faced by all context-free parsers (including the mammoth Harvard Syntactic Analyzer (Kuno, 1965)) is that they cannot handle the full complexity of natural language. The intrinsic theoretical deficiencies of such parsers are discussed by Chomsky (1957). In addition, many aspects of language which in principle can be handled by such systems, in fact can be dealt with only at the cost of introducing gross inefficiencies and unnecessary complexities.

In an effort to go beyond the limitations of context-free parsers, some parsers (Petrick, 1965; Zwicky, 1965) have attempted to make use of Chomsky's transformational grammar. These parsers try to "unwind" the transformations to reproduce the deep structure of a sentence, which can then be parsed by a context-free "base component". It soon became apparent that this was a very difficult task. Although transformational grammar is theoretically a "neutral" description of language, it is in fact highly biased toward the process of generating sentences rather than interpreting them. Adapting generation rules to use in interpretation is relatively easy for a context-free grammar, but extremely difficult for transformational grammars. Woods (1969) discusses the problems of "combinatorial explosion" inherent in the inverse transformational process. Present transformational parsers can only handle small subsets of English in an inefficient way.

2.2.2 Augmented Transition Networks

In the past few years, three related parsing systems have been developed to deal with the full complexity of natural language. The first was by Thorne, Bratley, and Dewar (Thorne, 1968 and 1969), and the more recent ones are by Bobrow and Fraser (1969) and Woods (1969). The three programs operate in very similar ways, and since Woods' is the most advanced and best documented, we will use it for comparison. In his paper Woods compares his system with the other two.

The basic idea of these parsers is the "augmented transition network". The parser is seen as a transition network much like a finite-state recognizer used for regular languages in automata theory.

The first extension is in allowing the networks to make recursive calls to other networks (or to themselves). The condition for following a particular state transition is not limited to examining a single input symbol. The condition on the arc can be something like "NP" where NP is the name of an initial state of another network. This recursively called NP network then examines the input and operates as a recognizer. If it ever reaches an accepting state, it stops, and parsing continues from the end of the NP arc in the original network. These "recursive transition networks" have the power of a context-free grammar, and the correspondence between a network and its equivalent grammar is quite simple and direct.

To parse the full range of natural language, we need a critical addition. Instead of using "recursive transition networks" these parsers use "augmented transition networks", which can "make changes in the contents of a set of registers associated with the network, and whose transitions can be conditional on the contents of those registers" (Woods, 1969). This is done by "adding to each arc of the transition network an arbitrary condition which must be satisfied in order for the arc to be followed, and a set of structure building actions to be executed if the arc is followed."

Augmented transition networks have the power of Turing machines, since they have changeable registers and can transfer control depending on the state of those registers. Clearly they can handle any type of grammar which could possibly be parsed by any machine. The advantage of augmented transition networks is that their operation appears to be closer to the actual operations humans use in understanding language. Thus they give a natural and understandable representation for grammars.

2.2.3 *Networks and Programs*

How do such parsers compare with PROGRAMMAR? In fact, grammars described as networks and grammars described as programs are just two different ways of talking about doing exactly the same thing. Picture a flowchart for a PROGRAMMAR grammar (see Section 5), in which calls to the function PARSE are drawn on the arcs rather than at the nodes. Every arc then is either a request to accept the next word in the input (when the argument of PARSE is a word class), or a recursive call to one of the grammar programs. At each node (i.e., segment of program between conditionals and PARSE calls) we have "a set of arbitrary structure building actions." Our flowchart is just like an augmented transition network.

Now picture how Woods' networks are fed to the computer. He uses a notation (Woods, 1969, p. 17) which looks very much like a LISP-embedded computer language, such as PROGRAMMAR or PLANNER. In fact, the networks could be translated almost directly into PLANNER programs (PLANNER rather than LISP or PROGRAMMAR because of the automatic backup features—see the discussion in Section 6).

It is an interesting lesson in computer science to look at Woods' discussion of the advantages of networks, and "translate" them into the advantages of programs. For example, he talks about efficiency of representation. "A major advantage of the transition network model is . . . the ability to merge the common parts of many context free rules." Looking at grammars as programs, we can call this "sharing subroutines". He says (p. 42)

> "The augmented transition network, through its use of flags, allows for the merging of similar parts of the network by recording information in registers and interrogating it . . . and to merge states whose transitions are similar except for conditions on the contents of the registers."

This is the use of subroutines with arguments. In addition, the networks can (p. 44)

> capture the regularities of the language . . . whenever there are two essentially identical parts of the grammar which differ only in that the finite control part of the machine is remembering some piece of information . . . it is sufficient to explicitly store the distinguishing piece of information in a register and use only a single copy of the subgraph.

This is clearly the use of subroutines with a parameter.

Similarly we can go through the arguments about efficiency, the ease of mixing semantics with syntax, the ability to include operations which are "natural" to the task of natural language analysis, etc. All of them apply identically whether we are looking at "transition networks" or "programs".

What about Woods' claims that augmented transition networks retain the perspicuity (ease of reading and understanding by humans) of simpler grammar forms. He says (p. 38) that transformational grammars have the problem that

> the effect of a given rule is intimately bound up with its interrelation to other rules . . . it may require an extremely complex analysis to determine the effect and purpose.

This is true, but it would also be true for any grammar complex enough to handle all of natural language. The simple examples of transition networks are indeed easy to read (as are simple examples of most grammars), but in a network for a complete language, the purpose of a given state would be intimately bound up with its interrelation to other states, and the same problems of complexity arise. The network representation would be no more or less perspicuous than the flow chart for a program.

Though the basic principles are much the same in Woods' system and the present one, the systems do differ. The difference is not in the theoretical power of the parser, but in the types of analysis being carried out.

The most important difference is the theory of grammar being used. All of the network systems are based on transformational grammar. They try to reproduce the "deep structure" of a sentence while doing surface structure recognition. This is done by using special commands to explicity build and rearrange the deep structures as the parsing proceeds. PROGRAMMAR is oriented towards systemic grammar, with its identification of significant features in the constituents being parsed. It therefore emphasizes the ability to examine the features of constituents anywhere on the parsing tree, and to manipulate the feature descriptions of nodes.

A second difference is in the implementation of special additions to the basic parser. For example in section 1.4 we noted how words like "and" could be defined to act as "demons" which interrupt the parsing whenever they are encountered, and start a special program for interpreting conjoined structures. This has many uses, both in the standard parts of the grammar (such as "and") and in handling idioms and unusual structures. If we think in network terms, this is like having a separate arc marked "and" leading from every node in the network. Such a feature could probably be added to the network formulation, but it seems much more natural to think in terms of programs and interrupts.

A third difference is the backup mechanism. The network approach assumes some form of nondeterminism. If there are several arcs leaving a node, there must be some way to try following all of them. Either we have to carry forward simultaneous interpretations, or keep track of our choices in such a way that the network can automatically revise its choice if the original choice does not lead to an accepting state. This could be done in the program approach by using a language such as PLANNER with its automatic backup mechanisms. But as we indicated in section 1.4, it is not obvious that automatic backup is desirable in handling natural language. There are advantages instead in an intelligent parser which can understand the reasons for its failure at a certain point, and can guide itself accordingly instead of backing up blindly. This is important both theoretically and also as a matter of practical efficiency. Woods is also concerned with ways to modify networks to avoid unnecessary and wasteful backup by "making the network more deterministic." (p. 45). It might be interesting to explore a compromise solution in which automatic backup facilities existed, but could be turned on and off. We could give PROGRAMMAR special commands that would cause it to remember the state of the parsing so that later the grammar could ask to back up to that state and try something else. This is an interesting area for further work on PROGRAMMAR.

It is difficult to compare the performance of different parsers since there is no standard grammar or set of test sentences. Bobrow and Woods have not published the results of any experiments with a larger grammar, but Thorne has published two papers (1968, 1969) with a number of sample parsings. Our parsing system, with its current grammar of English, and a specially prepared vocabulary, has successfully parsed all of these examples. They take from 1 to 5 sec. apiece, and some samples of more complicated parsings achieved by the system are included in Appendix B. For this use of the parser without semantic knowledge, it is necessary to artificially avoid those false paths which should normally be eliminated by semantic criteria. This is done by listing only those syntactic classes of a word whch are relevant to its use in the particular sentence being parsed.

3. A GRAMMAR FOR ENGLISH

This section presents an outline of the detailed syntax of English used by the system. This description has no pretense of being a full grammar of English, or of being accurate in every detail.[2] It is presented to il-

---

[2] The grammar as described here is a rough version, guided by the desire to get an entire system in operation, rather than a need for exact detail. It evolved through the course of the research, and has not gone through the polishing phase which would remove the irregularities of its development. Many of the specific details are insufficient, and possibly wrong. It is intended foremost as a demonstration of an approach to syntax.

lustrate the type of grammar which can be designed within the framework of the syntactic theories described in Section 1.4. In writing a grammar, we felt it important not to produce ad hoc rules suited only to a tiny domain. The grammar presented is in fact substantially more general than required for the world of toy blocks. Many aspects of English are included in the parsing programs, but are not handled in the semantic parts of the system, including various aspects of tense, modality, quantifiers, and conjunction. There are still whole areas of syntax which we have not dealt with, particularly those which are used to convey the reaction, mood. and emphasis of a speaker.

The system networks and examples presented here are not a complete specification of the grammar, but are the basis for the detailed recognition program. The actual PROGRAMMAR programs are available on request.

There is no available comprehensive presentation of English syntax based on systemic grammar. The analysis here may disagree in many ways with fragments of English systemic grammar presented elsewhere, or with existing unpublished versions. Some differences are simply notational, others are intentional simplifications, and some represent theoretical differences (for example, our analysis of the transitivity system puts much of the structure into the semantic rather than the syntactic rules, while Halliday's (1967) is more purely syntactic).

3.1 *The CLAUSE*

The structure exhibiting the greatest variety in English is the CLAUSE. It can express relationships and events involving time, place, manner, and other modifiers. Its structure indicates what parts of the sentence the speaker wants to emphasize, and can express various kinds of focus of attention and emotion. It determines the purpose of an utterance—whether it is a question, command, or statement—and is the basic unit which can stand alone. Other units can occur by themselves when their purpose is understood, as in answer to a question, but the clause is the primary unit of discourse.

The CLAUSE has several main ingredients and a number of optional ones. Except for special types of incomplete clauses, there is always a verb group, containing the verb, which indicates the basic event or relationship being expressed by the CLAUSE. Almost every CLAUSE contains a subject, except for IMPERATIVE (in which the semantic subject is understood to be the person being addressed), and embedded clauses in which the subject lies somewhere else in the syntactic structure. In addition to the subject, a CLAUSE may have various kinds of objects, which will be explained in detail later. It can take many types of modifiers (CLAUSES, GROUPS, and WORDS) which indicate time, place, manner, causality, and a variety of other aspects of meaning. One part of the CLAUSE system network is shown in Fig. 7.

Beginning at the top of the network, we see a choice between MAJOR (a clause which could stand alone as a sentence) and "secondary" (SEC). A MAJOR clause is either an IMPERATIVE (a command), a DECLARATIVE, or a QUESTION. Questions are either YES–NO— answerable by "yes" or "no", as in:

(s1) Did you like the show?

or WH- (involving a question element like "when," "where," "which," "how," etc.).

The choice of the WH- feature leads into a whole network of further choices, which are shared by QUESTION and two kinds of secondary clauses we will discuss later. In order to share the network, we have used a simple notational trick—Certain symbols contain a "*"; when

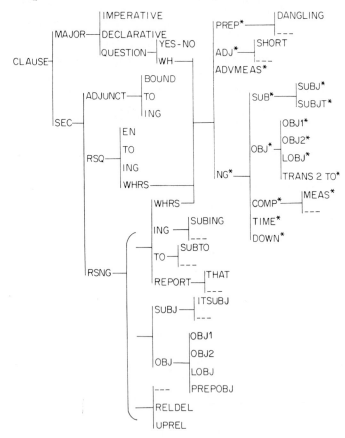

Fig. 7. Network 1—CLAUSE.

they are being applied to a question, we replace the "*" with "Q", while when they are applied to relative clauses, we use "REL." For example, the feature "PREP*" in the network will be referred to as PREPQ when we find it in a question, but PREPREL when it is in a relative clause. This complex of features is basically the choice of what element of the sentence is being questioned. English allows us to use almost any part of a clause as a request for information. For example, in a PREPQ, a prepositional group in the clause is used, as in:

(s2) *With what* did you erase it?

We more commonly find the preposition in a DANGLING position, as in:

(s3) *What* did you erase it *with?*

We can tell by tracing back through Network 1 that sentence s3 has the features PREPQ, DANGLING, WH- , QUESTION, and MAJOR.

We can use a special question adverb to ask questions of time, place, and manner, as in:

(s4) *Why* did the chicken cross the road?
(s5) *When* were you born?
(s6) *How* will you tell her the news?
(s7) *Where* has my little dog gone?

These are all marked by the feature ADJQ (adjunct question). In discourse they can also appear in a short form (SHORT) in which the entire utterance is a single word, as in:

(s8) *Why?*

We can use the word "how" in connection with a measure adverb (like "fast") to ask an ADVMEASQ, like:

(s9) *How fast* can he run the mile?

The most flexible type of WH- question uses an entire noun group as the question element, using a special pronoun (like "what" or "who") or a determiner (like "which," or "how many") to indicate that it is the question element. These clauses have the feature NGQ, and they can be further divided according to the function of the NG in the clause, It can have any of the possible NG functions (these will be described more formally with regard to the next network). For example, it can be the subject, giving a SUBJQ, like:

(s10) *Which hand* holds the M and M's?

It can be the subject of a THERE clause (see below), giving us a SUBJTQ:

(s11) *How many Puerto Ricans* are there in Boston?

A complement is the second half of an "is" clause, like:

(s12) Her hair is *red.*

and it can be used to form a COMPQ:

(s13) *What color* was her hair?

or with a "measure" in a MEASQ:

(s14) *How deep* is the ocean?

The noun group can be an object, leading to the feature OBJQ, as in:

(s15) *What* do you want? or

(s16) *Who* did you give the book?

These are both OBJ1Q, since the first has only one object ("what"), and the second questions the first, rather than the second object ("who", instead of "the book"). We use the ordering of the DECLARATIVE form "You gave *me the book*". If this were reversed, we would have an OBJ2Q, like:

(s17) *What* did you give him?

If we use the word "to" to express the first object with a two object verb like "give," we can get a TRANS2TOQ, like:

(s18) To *whom* did you give the book? or

(s19) *Who* did you give the book to?

Sometimes a NG can be used to indicate the time in a clause, giving us a TIMEQ:

(s20) *What* day will the iceman come?

In a more complex style, we can embed the question element within an embedded clause, such as:

(s21) *Which car* did your brother say that he was expecting us to tell Jane to buy?

The NG "which car" is the question element, but is in fact the object of the clause "Jane to buy . . .," which is embedded several layers deep. This kind of NGQ is called DOWNQ. The role of the question element in the embedded clause can include any of those which we have been describing. For example it could be the object of a preposition, as in:

(s22) *What state* did you say Lincoln was born *in*?

Looking at the network for the features of secondary clauses, we see three main types—ADJUNCT, "Rank-Shifted Qualifier" (RSQ), and "Rank-Shifted to act as a Noun Group" (RSNG). ADJUNCT clauses are used as modifiers to other clauses, giving time references, causal relationships, and other similar information. We can use a BOUND clause containing a "binder" such as "before," "while," "because," "if," "so," "unless," etc., as in:

(s23) *While Nero fiddled,* Rome burned.

(s24) *If it rains,* stay home.

(s25) Is the sky blue *because it is cold?*

To express manner and purpose, we use a TO clause or an ING clause:

(s26) He died *to save us from our sins.*

(s27) The bridge was built *using primitive tools.*

The RSQ clause is a constituent of a NG, following the noun in the "qualifier" position (see Section 3.3 for a description of the positions in a NG). It is one of the most commonly used secondary clauses, and can be of four different types. Three of them are classified by the form of the verb group within the clause—TO, ING, and EN (where we use "EN" to represent a past participle, such as "broken"):

(s28) the man *to see about a job*

(s29) the piece *holding the door on*

(s30) a face *weathered by sun and wind*

Notice that the noun being modified can have various roles in the clause. In examples 28 and 29, "piece" is the subject of "hold", while "man" is the object of "see". We could have said:

(s31) the man *to do the job*

in which "man" is the subject of "do". Our semantic analysis sorts out these possibilities in determining the meaning of a secondary clause.

The fourth type of RSQ clause is related to WH- questions, and is called a WHRS. It uses a wh- element like "which" or "what", or a word like "that" to relate the clause to the noun it is modifying. The different ways it can use this "relating" element are very similar to the different possibilities for a question element in a WH- question, and in fact the two share part of the network. Here we use the letters REL to indicate we are talking about a relative clause, so the feature PREP* in Network 1 becomes PREPREL. In sentences (s2) through (s22), we illustrated the different types of WH- questions. We can show parallel sentences for WHRS RSQ clauses. The following list shows some examples and the relevant feature names:

(s32) the thing *with which you erased it*   PREPREL

(s33) the thing *that you erased it with*   PREPREL DANGLING

(s34) the reason *why the chicken crossed the road*   ADJREL

(s35) the day *when you were born*   ADJREL

(s36) the way *we will tell her the news*   ADJREL

(s37) the place *my little dog has gone*   ADJREL

(s38) the reason *why*   ADJREL SHORTREL

(s39) the hand *which rocks the cradle*   SUBJREL

(s40) the number of Puerto Ricans *there are in Boston*   SUBJTREL

(s41) the color *her hair was last week*   COMPREL

(s42) the depth *the ocean will be*   MEASREL

(s43) the information *that you want*   OBJ1REL

(s44) the man *you gave the book*   OBJ1REL

(s45) the book *which you gave him*   OBJ2REL

(s46) the man to *whom you gave the book*   TRANS2TOREL

(s47) the man *you gave the book to*   TRANS2TOREL
(s48) the day *the iceman came*   TIMEREL
(s49) the car *your brother said he was expecting us to tell Jane to buy*
                                                          DOWNREL
(s50) the state *you said Lincoln was born in*   DOWNREL

Notice that in sentences 36, 37, 40, 41, 42, 44, 47, 48, 49, and 50, there is no relative word like "which" or "that." These could just as well all have been put in, but English gives us the option of omitting them. When they are absent, the CLAUSE is marked with the feature RELDEL.

Returning to our network, we see that there is one other type of basic clause, the RSNG. This is a clause which is rank-shifted to serve as a NG. It can function as a part of another clause, a preposition group, or an adjective group. There are four basic types. The first two are TO and ING, as in:

(s51) I like *to fly*.   TO
(s52) *Building houses* is hard work.   ING
(s53) He got it by *saving coupons*.   ING

Notice that in s51, the RSNG clause is the object (OBJ1), in s52 it is the subject (SUBJ), and in s53 it is the object of a preposition (PREPOBJ). We can have a separate subject within the TO and ING clauses, giving us the features SUBTO and SUBING:

(s54) I wanted *Ruth to lead the revolution*.   SUBTO
(s55) They liked *John's leading it*.   SUBING

The SUBING form takes its subject in the possessive.

In addition to ING and TO, we have the REPORT CLAUSE, which has the structure of an entire sentence, and is used as a participant in a relation about things like hearing, knowing, and saying:

(s56) She heard *that the other team had won*.
(s57) *That she wasn't there* surprised us.
(s58) I knew *he could do it*.

The word "that" is used in s56 and s57 to mark the beginning of the REPORT CLAUSE, so they are assigned the feature THAT. The absence of "that" is left unmarked.

If the subject of clause is in turn a RSNG clause, we may have trouble understanding it:

(s59) *That anyone who knew the combination could have opened the lock* was obvious.

There is a special mechanism for rearranging the sentence by using the word "it", so that the complicated subject comes last:

(s60) It was obvious *that anyone who knew the combination could have opened the lock*.

In this case, we say that the RSNG clause is serving as an ITSUBJ. TO and ING clauses can do the same:

(s61) It will be fun *to see them again.*

(s62) It was dangerous *going up without a parachute.*

The final type of RSNG is the WHRS, which is almost identical to the WHRS RSQ described above. Rather than go through the details again, we will indicate how a few of our RSQ examples (sentences 32 to 50) can be converted, and will leave the reader to do the rest.

(s63) I don't know *what he did it with.*   PREPREL DANGLING

(s64) Ask him *when he was born.*   ADJREL

(s65) He told me *why.*   ADJREL SHORTREL

(s66) It is amazing *how many Puerto*   SUBJTREL
Ricans there are in Boston.

(s67) Only her hairdresser knows *what*   COMPREL
color her hair was.

etc.

Let us examine one case more carefully:

(s68) I knew *which car your brother said that he was expecting us to to tell Jane to buy.*

Here we have a DOWNREL clause, "which car . . . . buy", serving as the object of the CLAUSE "I knew . . .". However, this means that somewhere below, there must be another clause with a slot into which the relative element can fit. In this case, it is the RSNG TO clause "Jane to buy", which is missing its object. This clause then has the feature UPREL, which indicates that its missing constituent is somewhere above in the structure. More specifically it is OBJ1UPREL.

Once this connection is found, the program might change the pointers in the structure to place the relative as the actual OBJ1 of the embedded clause structure. In the current grammar, the pointers are left untouched, and special commands to the moving function "*" are used when the object is referenced by the semantic program.

3.2 *Transitivity in the Clause*

In addition to the systems we have already described, there is a TRANSITIVITY system for the CLAUSE, which describes the number and nature of its basic constituents. We mentioned earlier that a CLAUSE had such components as a subject and various objects. The transitivity system specifies these exactly. We have adopted a very surface-oriented notion of transitivity, in which we note the number and basic nature of the objects, but do not deal with their semantic roles, such as "range" or "beneficiary". Halliday's analysis (1967) is somewhat different, as it includes aspects which we prefer to handle as part of the semantic analysis. Our simplified network is shown in Fig. 8.

The first basic division is into clauses with the main verb "be", and those with other verbs. This is done since BE clauses have very different possibilities for conveying meaning, and they do not have the full range of syntactic choices open to other clauses. BE clauses are divided into two types—THERE clauses, like:

(s69) *There was* an old woman who lived in a shoe.

and intensive (INT) BE clauses:

(s70) War *is* hell.

A THERE CLAUSE has only a subject, marked SUBJT, while an INT CLAUSE has a subject (SUBJ) and a complement (COMP). The complement can be either a NG, as in s70 or:

(s71) He was *an agent of the FBI.*

or a PREPG:

(s72) The king was *in the counting house.*

or an ADJG:

(s73) Her strength was *fantastic.*

(s74) My daddy is *stronger than yours.*

Other clauses are divided according to the number and type of objects they have. A CLAUSE with no objects is intransitive (ITRNS):

(s75) He is running.

With one object it is transitive (TRANS):

(s76) He runs *a milling machine.*

With two objects TRANS2:

(s77) I gave *my love a cherry.*

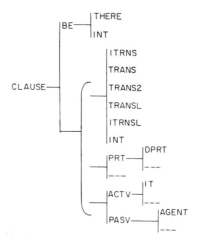

FIG. 8. Network 2—CLAUSE TRANSITIVITY

Some verbs are of a special type which use a location as a second object. One example is "put", as in:

(s78) Put the block *on the table.*

Note that this cannot be considered a TRANS with a modifier, as in:

(s79) He runs a milling machine *in Chicago.*

since the verb "put" demands that the location be given. We cannot say "Put the block." This type of CLAUSE is called TRANSL, and the location object is the LOBJ. The LOBJ can be a PREPG as in s78, or a special adverb, such as "there" or "somewhere", as in:

(s80) *Where* did you put it? or

(s81) Put it *there.*

Some intransitive verbs also need a locational object for certain meanings, such as:

(s82) The block is sitting *on the table.*

This is called ITRNSL.

Finally, there are intensive clauses which are not BE clauses, but which have a complement, as in:

(s83) He felt *sick.*

(s84) He made me *sick.*

We have not run into these with our simple subject matter, and a further analysis will be needed to handle them properly.

Any of the constituents we have been mentioning can be modified or deleted when these features interact with the features described in Network 1. For example in:

(s85) the block which I told *you to put on the table*

the italicized CLAUSE is TRANSL, but its OBJ1 is missing since it is an UPREL.

English has a way of making up new words by combining a verb and a "particle" (PRT), producing a combination like "pick up", "turn on", "set off", or "drop out". There is a special meaning attached to the pair, which may be very different from either word in isolation. Our dictionary contains a table of such pairs, and the grammar programs use them. A CLAUSE whose verb is a part of PRT pair has the feature PRT. The particle can appear either immediately after the word:

(s86) He *threw away* the plan.

or in a displaced position (marked by the feature DPRT):

(s87) He *threw* the plans *away.*

Regardless of whether there is a PRT or not, we have the choice between the features passive (PASV) and active (ACTV). ACTV places the semantic subject first:

(s88) *The President* started the war.

while PASV puts the semantic object first:

(s89) *The war* was started by the President.

If there is a PREPG beginning with "by", it is interpreted as the semantic subject (as in s89), and the CLAUSE has the feature AGENT.

If the CLAUSE is active and its subject is a RSNG CLAUSE, we can use the IT form described earlier. This is marked by the feature IT, and its subject is marked ITSUBJ, as in sentences 60, 61, and 62.

3.3 *Noun Groups*

The best way to explain the syntax of the NOUN GROUP is to look at the "slot and filler" analysis, which describes the different components it can have. Some types of NG, such as those with pronouns and proper nouns, will not have this same construction, and they will be explained separately later.

We will diagram the typical NG structure, using a "*" to indicate that the same element can occur more than once. Most of these "slots" are optional, and may or may not be filled in any particular NG. The meanings of the different symbols are explained below.

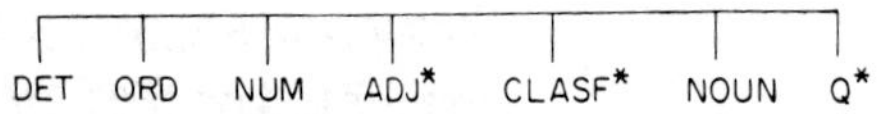

$$\text{DET} \quad \text{ORD} \quad \text{NUM} \quad \text{ADJ}^* \quad \text{CLASF}^* \quad \text{NOUN} \quad \text{Q}^*$$

FIG. 9. Noun Group Structure.

The most important ingredient is the NOUN, which is almost always present (if it isn't, the NG is incomplete (INCOM)). It gives the basic information about the object or objects being referred to by the NG. Immediately preceding the NOUN, there are an arbitrary number of "classifiers" (CLASF). Examples of CLASF are:

(s90) *plant* life

(s91) *water meter cover adjustment* screw

Notice that the same class of words can serve as CLASF and NOUN— in fact Halliday uses one word class (called NOUN), and distinguishes between the functions of "head" and "classifier". We have separated the two because our dictionary gives the meaning of words according to their word class, and nouns often have a special meaning when used as a CLASF.

Preceding the classifiers we have adjectives (ADJ), such as "big beautiful soft red. . ." We can distinguish adjectives from classifiers by the fact that adjectives can be used as the complement of a BE CLAUSE, but classifiers cannot. We can say "red hair", or "horse hair", or "That hair is red.", but we cannot say "That hair is horse.", since "horse" is a CLASF, not an ADJ. Adjectives can also take on the comparative

(COMPAR) and superlative (SUP) forms ("red, redder, and reddest"), while classifiers cannot ("horse, horser, and horsest"?).

Immediately following the NOUN we can have various qualifiers (Q), which can be a PREPG:

(s92) the man *in the moon*

or an ADJG:

(s93) a night *darker than doom*

or a CLAUSE RSQ:

(s94) the woman *who conducts the orchestra*

We have already discussed the many types of RSQ clauses. In later sections we will discuss the PREPG and ADJG types which can occur as qualifiers.

Finally, the first few elements in the NG work together to give its logical description—whether it refers to a single object, a class of objects, a group of objects, etc. The determiner (DET) is the normal start for a NG, and can be a word such as "a", or "that", or a possessive. It is followed by an "ordinal" (ORD). There is an infinite sequence of number ordinals ("first, second, third . . .") and a few others such as "last" and "next". These can be recognized since they are the only words that can appear between a DET like "the" and a number, as in:

(s95) the *next* three days

Finally there is a number (NUM). It can either be a simple integer like "one", "two", etc. or a more complex construction such as "at least three", or "more than a thousand". It is possible for a NG to have all of its slots filled, as in:

DET	ORD	NUM	ADJ	ADJ	CLASF	CLASF	NOUN
the	first	three	old	red	city	fire	hydrants

Q(PREPG)   Q(CLAUSE)

without covers   you can find

It is also possible to have combinations of almost any subset. With these basic components in mind, let us look at the system network for NG in Fig. 10.

First we can look at the major types of NG. A NG made up of a pronoun is called a PRONG. It can be either a question, like "who" or "what", or a nonquestion (the unmarked case) like "I", "them", "it", etc. The feature TPRONG marks a NG whose head is a special TPRON, like "something", "everything", "anything", etc. These enter into a peculiar construction containing only the head and qualifiers, and in which an adjective can follow the head, as in:

(s96) anything *green* which is bigger than the moon

The feature PROPNG marks an NG made up of proper nouns, such as "Oklahoma", or "The Union of Soviet Socialist Republics."

These three special classes of NG do not have the structure described

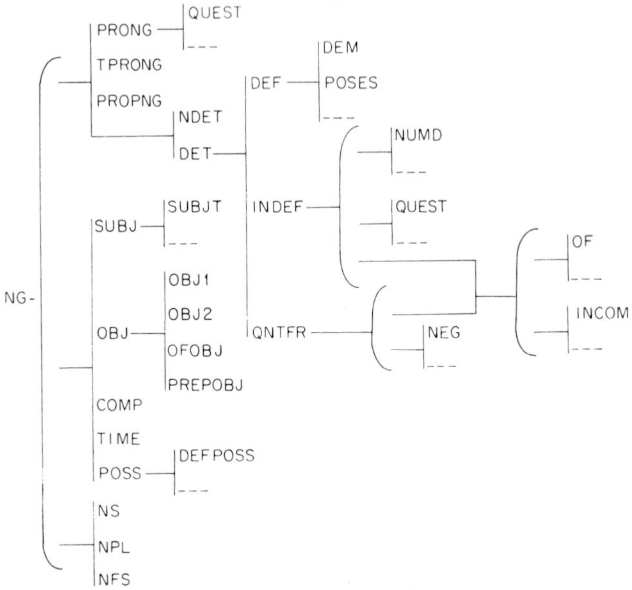

FIG. 10. Network 3—NG.

above. The PRONG is a single pronoun. the PROPNG is a string of proper nouns, and the TPRONG has its own special syntax. The rest of the noun groups are the unmarked (normal) type. They could be classified according to exactly which constituents are present, but in doing so we must be aware of our basic goals in systemic grammar. We could note whether or not a NG contained a CLASF or not, but this would be of minor significance. On the other hand, we do note, for example, whether it has a DET, and what type of DET it has, since this is of key importance in the meaning of the NG and the way it relates to other units. We distinguish between those with a determiner (marked DET) and those without one (NDET), as in:

(s97) *Cats* adore *fish.*   NDET
(s98) *The cat* adored *a fish.*   DET

The DET can be definite (like "the" or "that"), indefinite (like "a" or "an"), or a quantifier (QNTFR) (like "some", "every", or "no"). The definite determiners can be either demonstrative ("this", "that", etc.) or the word "the" (the unmarked case), or a possessive NG. The NG "the farmer's son" has the NG "the farmer" as its determiner, and has the feature POSES to indicate this.

An INDEF NG can have a number as a determiner, such as:

(s99) *five* gold rings
(s100) *at least a dozen* eggs

in which case it has the feature NUMD, or it can use an INDEF determiner, such as "a". In either case it has the choice of being a question. The question form of a NUMD is "how many", while for other cases it is "which" or "what".

Finally, an NG can be determined by a quantifier (QNTFR). Although quantifiers could be subclassified along various lines, we do so in the semantics rather than the syntax. The only classifications used syntactically are between singular and plural (see below), and between negative and nonnegative.

If a NG is either NUMD or QNTFR, it can be of a special type marked OF, like:

(s101) three *of* the offices

(s102) all *of* your dreams

An OF NG has a determiner, followed by "of", followed by a definite NG.

A determined NG can also choose to be incomplete, leaving out the NOUN, as in

(s103) Give me *three.*

(s104) I want *none.*

Notice that there is a correspondence between the cases which can take the feature OF, and those which can be INCOM. We cannot say either "the of them" or "Give me the." Possessives are an exception (we can say "Give me Juan's." but not "Juan's of them"), and are handled separately (see below).

The middle part of Fig. 10 describes the different possible functions a NG can serve. In describing the CLAUSE, we described the use of an NG as a SUBJ, COMP, and objects (OBJ) of various types. In addition, it can serve as the object of a PREPG (PREPOBJ), in:

(s105) the rape of *the lock*

If it is the object of "of" in an OF NG, it is called an OFOBJ:

(s106) none of *your tricks*

A NG can also be used to indicate TIME, as in:

(s107) *Yesterday* the world ended.

(s108) *The day she left*, all work stopped.

Finally, a NG can be the possessive determiner for another NG. In:

(s109) *the cook's* kettle

the NG "the cook" has the feature POSS, indicating that it is the determiner for the NG "the cook's kettle", which has the feature POSES.

When a PRONG is used as a POSS, it must use a special possessive pronoun, like "my", "your", etc. We can use a POSS in an incomplete NG, like

(s110) Show me *yours.*

(s111) *John's* is covered with mud.

There is a special class of pronouns used in these noun groups (labelled DEFPOSS), such as "yours", "mine", etc.

Continuing to the last part of Fig. 10, we see features of person and number. These are used to match the noun to the verb (if the NG is the subject) and the determiner, to avoid combinations like "these kangaroo" or "the women wins". In the case of a PRONG, there are special pronouns for first, second, and third person, singular and plural. The feature NFS occurs only with the first-person singular pronouns ("I", "me", "my", "mine"), and no distinction is made between other persons, since they have no effect on the parsing. A singular pronoun or other singular NG is marked with the feature NS. The pronoun "you" is always treated as if it were plural and no distinction is made between "we", "you", "they", or any plural (NPL) NG as far as the grammar is concerned. Of course there is a semantic difference, which will be considered in later sections.

3.4 *Preposition Groups*

The PREPG is a comparatively simple structure used to express a relationship. It consists of a preposition followed by an object (PREPOBJ), which is either a NG or a RSNG CLAUSE. In some cases, the preposition consists of a two or three word combination instead of a single word, as in:

(s112) *next to* the table

(s113) *on top of* the house

The grammar includes provision for this, and the dictionary lists the possible combinations and their meanings. The words in such a combination are marked as PREP2. The network for the PREPG is in Fig. 11.

The PREPG can serve as a constituent of a CLAUSE in several ways. It can be a complement:

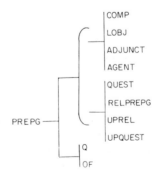

Fɪɢ. 11. Network 4—PREPG.

(s114) Is it *in the kitchen?*
a locational object (LOBJ):
(s115) Put it *on the table.*
an ADJUNCT:
(s116) He got it *by selling his soul.*
or an AGENT:
(s117) It was bought *by the devil.*
If the PREPG is a constituent of a QUESTION CLAUSE, it can be the question element by having a QUEST NG as its object:
(s118) in *what city*
(s119) for *how many days*
(s120) by *whom*
in which case the PREPG is also marked QUEST. A PREPREL CLAUSE contains a RELPREPG:
(s121) the place *in which* she works
If the CLAUSE is an UPQUEST or an UPREL, the PREPG can be the constituent which is "missing," the piece which provides the upward reference. In this case it is also marked UPREL:
(s122) the lady I saw you *with*
or UPQUEST:
(s123) Who did you knit it *for?*
In these cases, it is also marked SHORT to indicate that the object is not explicitly in the PREPG. It can also be short if it is a PREPG in a DANGLING PREPQ or PREPREL CLAUSE:
(s124) what do you keep it *in?*
Within a NG, a PREPG serves as a qualifier (Q):
(s125) the man *in the iron mask*
or as the body of an OF NG:
(s126) some *of the people*

3.5 *Adjective Groups*

The ADJG is a specialized unit serving as a complement of an intensive clause, as a qualifier (Q) to an NG, or as a CLAUSE ADJUNCT. The network is shown in Fig. 12.

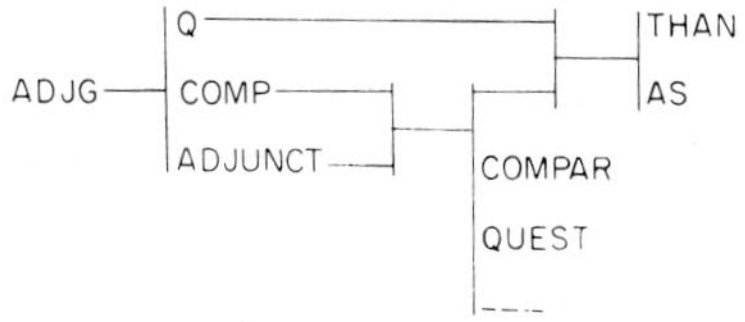

FIG. 12. Network 5—ADJG.

An ADJG which serves as an ADJUNCT contains an adverb, like "fast" in:

(s127) He could run *faster than an arrow.*

in place of an adjective. The other two types of ADJG use an adjective, as in a qualifier:

(s128) a hotel *as bad as the other one*

or a complement:

(s129) They were *blissful.*

The basic forms for an ADJG include THAN:

(s130) holier *than* thou

AS:

(s131) *as* quick *as* a flash

comparative:

(s132) This one is *bigger.*

or question:

(s133) *How well* can he take dictation?

The network is arranged to show that a qualifier ADJG can be only of the first two forms—we cannot say "a man bigger" without using "than", or say "a man big". In the special case of a TPRON such as "anything" as in:

(s134) anything *strange*

the word "strange" is considered an ADJ which is a direct constituent of the NG, rather than an ADJG.

The grammar does not yet account for more complex uses of the word "than".

3.6 *Verb Groups*

The English verb group is designed to convey a complex combination of tenses so that an event can relate several time references. For example, we might have:

(s135) By next week you *will have been living* here for a month.

This is said to have the tense "present in past in future". Its basic reference is to the future—"next week", but it refers back to the past from that time, and also indicates that the event is still going on. This type of recursive tense structure has been analyzed by Halliday (1966) and our grammar adopts a variant of his scheme.

Essentially the choice is among four tenses, PAST, PRESENT, FUTURE, and MODAL. Once a choice between these has been made, a second, third, fourth, and even fifth choice can be made recursively. The combination of tenses is realized in the syntax by a sequence of the auxiliary verbs "be", "have", and "going to", along with the ING, EN, and infinitive (INF) forms of the verbs. The restrictions on the recursion are:

1. PRESENT can occur only at the outer ends of the series (at first and/or final choice).
2. Except in the final two positions, the same tense cannot be selected twice consecutively.
3. Future can occur only once other than in last position.
4. Modal can be only in final position.

It is important to distinguish between the position of a word in the VG and the position of its tense in the recursive tense feature—the direction is reversed. In s135, "will" is the first word, and "living" the last, while the tense is PRESENT in PAST in FUTURE. Some sample verb groups and their tenses are shown in Fig. 13.

The structure of a finite VG (one taking part in this tense system—see below for other types) is a sequence of verbs and auxiliaries in which the last is the "main verb" (marked MVB and remembered by the parser), and the first is either a MODAL, the word "will", or a "finite" verb (one carrying tense and number agreement with the subject). Interspersed in the sequence there may be adverbs, or the word "not" (or its reduced form "n't"). The best way to describe the relationship between the sequence of verbs and the tense is by giving a flow chart for parsing a VG. This is a good example of the usefulness of representing syntax in the form of procedures, as it describes a relatively complex system in a clear and succinct way.

In the flow chart (Fig. 14) the variable T represents the tense, and the symbol "·" indicates the addition of a member to the front of a list. The "=" indicates replacement in the FORTRAN sense, and the function "REMOVE" removes words from the input string. The features used are

ACTIVE

took – past
takes – present
will take – future
can take – modal
has taken – past in present
was taking – present in past
was going to have taken – past in future in past
was going to have been taking – present in past in future in past

PASSIVE

is taken – present
could have been taken – past in modal
has been going to have been taken – past in future in past in present

Figure 13—Verb Group Tenses

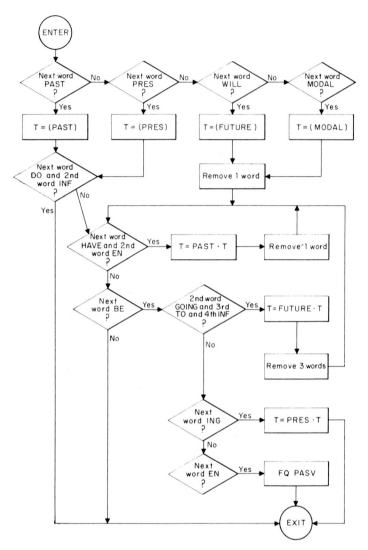

Fig. 14. Syntax of VG Tense Structure.

those described for verbs in Section 3.7. The command (FQ PASV) indicates that the entire VG is to be marked with the feature PASV (passive voice). The flow chart does not indicate the entire parsing, but only that part relevant to determining the tense.

This system of tenses is operative only for FINITE verb groups. The network for the VG in general is shown in Fig. 15.

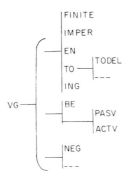

Fig. 15. Network 6—VG.

There are several types of VG which do not enter the normal tense system, but which have a specialized form. The IMPER VG is used in imperatives:

(s136) *Fire* when ready.

(s137) *Don't drop* the baby.

It consists of a verb in the infinitive form, possibly preceded by the auxiliary "do" or its negative form "don't". The EN VG is used in EN RSQ CLAUSES, like:

(s138) a man *forsaken* by his friends

and consists of a past participle verb. The ING VG is made up of an ING verb or the verb "being" followed by an EN verb. It is used in various types of ING clauses:

(s139) *Being married* is great.

(s140) the girl *sitting* near the wall

Similarly, the TO VG is used in TO clauses. In the case of conjoined structures, the "to" may be omitted from the second clause, as in:

(s141) We wanted to stop the war and *end* repression.

Such a VG is marked TODEL.

We separate those verb groups whose main verb is "be" from the others, as they do not undergo the further choice between PASV and ACTV. These correspond to the same features for clauses, and are seen in the structure by the fact that a PASV VG contains a form of the auxiliary "be" followed by the main verb in the EN form, as in:

(s142) The paper *was finished* by the deadline.

(s143) He wanted *to be kissed* by the bride.

Finally, any VG can be negative, either by using a negative form of an auxiliary like "don't", "hasn't", or "won't", or by including the word "not".

3.7 Words

Our grammar uses a number of separate word classes, each of which can be divided into subclasses by the features assigned to individual words. It was necessary to make arbitrary decisions as to whether a distinction between groups of words should be represented by different classes or different features within the same class. Actually we could have a much more tree-like structure of word classes, in which the ideas of classes and features were combined. Since this has not been done, we will present a list of the different classes in alphabetical order, and for each of them give descriptions of the relevant features. Many words can be used in more than one class, and some classes overlap to a large degree (such as NOUN and CLASF). In our dictionary, we simply list all of the syntactic features the word has for all of the classes to which it can belong. When the parser parses a word as a member of a certain class, it sorts out those features which are applicable. Figure 16 is a list of the word classes and their features.

ADJ—Adjective is one of the constituents of a NG as well as being the main part of an ADJG. This class includes words like "big", "ready", and "strange". The only features are superlative (as in "biggest") and comparative (as in "bigger").

ADV—We use the name "adverb" to refer to a whole group of words used to modify other words or clauses, words which don't really fit anywhere else. The basic classification depends on what is being modified, and has the terms (ADVADV VBAD PREPADV CLAUSEADV). An ADVADV is a word like "very" which modifies other adverbs and adjectives. A VBAD modifies verbs, and includes the class of words ending in "-ly" like "quickly" and "easily". A PREPADV modifies prepositions, as "directly" in "directly above the stove". A CLAUSE-ADV is a constituent of a clause, and can be either TIMW or PLACE. A TIMW like "usually", "never", "then", or "often" appears as a CLAUSE constituent specifying the time. The PLACE ADV "there" can either be an adjunct, as in:

(s144) *There* I saw a miracle.

or an LOBJ, as in:

(s145) Put it *there*.

BINDER—Binders are used to "bind" a secondary clause to a major clause, as in:

(s146) *Before* you got there, we left.

(s147) I'll go *if* you do.

We do not assign any other features to binders.

CLASF—In Section 3.3 we discussed the use of CLASF as a constituent

CLASS	FEATURES
ADJ	ADJ COMPAR SUP
ADV	ADV ADVADV LOBJ PLACE PREPADV TIMW TIM2 VBAD
BINDER	BINDER
CLASF	CLASF
DET	DEF DEM DET INCOM INDEF NEG NONUM NPL NS OFD PART QDET QNTFR
NOUN	MASS NOUN NPL NS POSS TIME TIM1
NUM	NPL NS NUM
NUMD	NUMD NUMDALONE NUMDAN NUMDAT NUMDAS
ORD	ORD TIMORD
PREP	PLACE PREP NEED2
PREP2	PREP2
PRON	POSSDEF NEG NFS NPL NS OBJ POSS PRON PRONREL SUBJ QUEST
PRONREL	NPL NS PRONREL
PROPN	NPL NS POSS PROPN
PRT	PRT
QADJ	PLACE QADJ
TPRON	NEG NPL NS TPRON
VB	AUX BE DO EN HAVE IMPERF INF ING INGOB INGOB2 INT ITRNS ITRNSL MODAL MVB NEG PAST PRES QUAX REPOB REPOB2 SUBTOB SUBTOB2 TOOB2 TO2 TRANS TRANSL TRANSL2 TRANS2 VB VFS VPL VPRT V3PS WILL

Fig. 16—Word Classes and Applicable Features

of a NG. The CLASF is often another NOUN, but it appears in a position like an adjective, as in "*boy* scout".

DET—Determiners are used as constituents of NGs, as described in 3.3. They can have a number of different features, as described in the network of Fig. 17.

A DET can be indefinite, like "a" or "an" or the question determiners (QDET) "which", "what", and "how many". It can be definite, like "the" or the demonstrative determiners "this", "that", "those", and "these". Or it can be a quantifier (QNTFR) like "any", "every", "some",

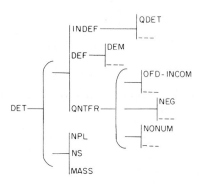

FIG. 17. Network 7—DET.

etc. Quantifiers can have the feature OFD, indicating that they can be used in an OF NG like:

(s148) *some* of my best friends

We originally had a separate feature named INCOM indicating whether they could be used in an incomplete NG like:

(s149) Buy *some*.

but later analysis showed these features were the same. Not all quantifiers are OFD—we cannot say "every of the cats" or "Buy every." Quantifiers can also be negative, like "none" or "no", or can be NONUM, indicating that they cannot be used with a number, such as "many" or "none" (we can say "any three cats" or "no three cats", but not "none three" or "many three"). The NG program takes these features into account in deciding what NG constituents to look for. It also has to find agreement in number between the DET and the NOUN. A DET can have the features "singular" (NS), "plural" (NPL), or MASS (like "some" or "no", which can go with MASS nouns like "water"). A DET can have more than one of these—"the" has all three, while "all" is MASS and NPL, and "a" is just NS.

NOUN—The main constituent of a NG is its NOUN. It has a feature of number, identical to that of the determiners it must match. The word "parsnip" is NS, "parsnips" is NPL, and "wheat" is MASS. Some nouns may have more than one of these, such as "fish", which is all three since it can be used in "a fish", "three fish", or "Fish is my favorite food." In addition, a NOUN can be possessive (POSS), like "parsnip's".

In order to tell whether a NG is functioning as a time element in a CLAUSE, we need to know whether its NOUN can refer to time. We therefore have two features—TIME words like "day", and "month", as in:

(s150) The next *day* it started to snow.

and TIM1 words like "yesterday" and "tomorrow". This illustrates the interaction between syntax and semantics. A phrase like "the next visit" can be used to indicate a time, since a "visit" is an event. The actual distinction should be the semantic difference between "event" and "nonevent".

The grammar could be changed to look at the semantic features rather than syntactic features of the NOUN in deciding whether it could be the head of a TIME NG.

NUM—The class of numbers is large (uncountably infinite) but not very interesting syntactically. For our purposes we only note the features NS (for "one") and NPL (for all the rest). In fact, our system does not accept numbers in numeric form, and has only been taught to count to ten.

NUMD—In complex number specifications, like "at least three" or "more than a million", there is a NUMD. The features they can have are (NUMDAN NUMDAS NUMDAT NUMDALONE). NUMDAN words such as "more" and "fewer" are used with "than", while NUMDAS words such as "few" fit into the frame "as . . . as", and NUMDAT words are preceded by "at", as in "at least", and "at most". NUMDALONE indicates that the NUMD can stand alone with the number, and includes "exactly" and "approximately".

ORD—The class of ordinals includes the ordinal numbers "first", "second", etc., and a few other words which can fit into the position between a determiner and a number, like "next", "last", and "only". Notice that superlative adjectives can also fill this slot in the NG.

PREP—Every PREPG begins with a preposition, either alone, or as part of a combination such as "on top of". In the combination case, the words following the initial PREP have the feature PREP2. A PREP which cannot appear without a PREP 2 (such as "next" which appears in "next to") is marked NEED2.

PRON—Pronouns can be classified along a number of dimensions, and we can think of a large multi-dimensional table with most of its positions filled. They have number features (NS NPL NFS) (note that instead of the more usual division into first, second, and third person, singular and plural, we have used a reduced one in which classes with the same syntactic behavior are lumped together). They can be possessive, such as "your" or "my", or DEFPOSS, like "yours" or "mine". Some of the personal pronouns distinguish between a subject form like "I" and an object form like "me". There are also special classes like demonstrative ("this" and "that") and PRONREL—the pronouns used in relative clauses, such as "who", "which", and "that". Those which can be used as a question element, such as "which" and "who" are marked QUEST.

PROPN—Proper nouns include single words like "Carol", or phrases such as "The American Legion" which could be parsed, but are interpreted as representing a particular object (physical or abstract). A PROPN can be NPL or NS, and is assumed to be NS unless defined otherwise.

PRT—In Section 3.2, we discussed clauses which use a combination of a "particle" and a verb, like "pick up" or "knock out". The second word of these is a PRT.

QADJ—One class of QUESTION CLAUSE uses a QADJ such as "where", "when", or "how" as its question element. They can also be used in various kinds of relative clauses, as explained in Section 3.1.

TPRON—There is a small class of words made up of a quantifier and the suffix "-thing" which enter into a special type of NG construction like "anything green". This is not an abbreviation for a quantifier followed by a noun, since the hypothetical NG "any block green" would have the same structure.

VB—The verb has the most complex network of features of any word in our grammar. They describe its tense, transitivity, number, and use, as well as marking special verbs like "be". The network is in Fig. 18. Verbs are divided into auxiliaries and others (unmarked). Auxiliaries are the "helping verbs" which combine with others in complex

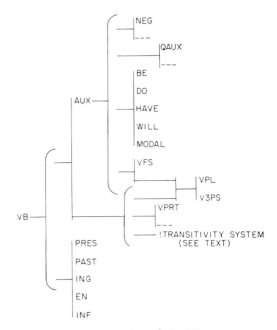

Fig. 18. Network 8—VB.

VG structures. They can have special negative forms, like "can't", or can appear standing alone at the beginning of a QUESTION, in which case they have the function QAUX, as in:

(s151) *Will* I ever finish?

The auxiliaries include "be", "do", "have", "will", and the modals like "could", "can", and "must". Separate features are used for these, as they are critical in determining the structure of a VG. An AUX can choose from the system of person and number, distinguishing "third-person singular" (V3PS) as in "is"; "plural", as in "have"; or "first singular" (VFS), used only for "am".

Nonauxiliary verbs can be VPRT, which combine with a PRT, and they have a whole cluster of transitivity features. In Section 3.2 we described the different transitivity features of the CLAUSE, and these are controlled by the verb. We therefore have the features (TRANS ITRNS TRANS2 TRANSL ITRANSL INT). In addition, the verb can control what types of RSNG CLAUSE can serve as its various objects. The feature names combine the type of CLAUSE (ING TO REPORT SUBTO SUBING) with either -OB or -OB2, to get a product set of features like SUBTOB and INGOB2.

For example, the verb "want" has the features TOOB and SUBTOB, but not INGOB, REPOB, etc., since "I want to go." and "I want you to go." are possible, but "I want going.", "I want that you go.", etc. are not.

Finally, all of these kinds of verbs can be in various forms such as ING ("breaking"), EN ("broken"), infinitive ("break"), PAST ("broke"), and present ("breaks"). The network does not illustrate all of the relations, as some types (like MODAL) do not make all of these choices.

3.8 *Conjunction*

One of the most complex parts of English is the system of conjunction. This section presents a simplified version which has been implemented using the special interrupt feature of PROGRAMMAR (see Section 5.2.2 for details).

The basic concept is that *any unit* in a sentence can be replaced by a COMPOUND unit of the same type. In the sentence:

(s152) I baked *a chocolate cake, three pies, and some hashish brownies.*

the object is a COMPOUND NG with three components. There can be a compound ADJ, as in:

(s153) a *red or yellow* flag

or a phrase can be ambiguous, as in:

(s154) *black cats and horses*

This can be interpreted as having either a COMPOUND NG, composed of the noun groups "black cats" and "horses", or a single NG with a COMPOUND NOUN, "cats and horses".

The features of a COMPOUND unit are determined by its components and by the type of conjunction. The conjunction features are from the network in Fig. 19.

The first choice is the actual conjunction used. The feature BOTH indicates a word at the beginning of a COMPOUND structure, as in:

(s155) *both* you and your family

the specific word depends on the conjunction—"both" with "and", "either" with "or," and "neither" with "nor". The features BOTH and NOR combine in:

(s156) neither you nor I

A conjoined structure can be made up of two elements with a conjunction (as in the previous three examples), or a LIST connected with commas and a conjunction before the last element (as in s152), or it can be a list connected with conjunctions (a LISTA), as in:

(s157) cabbages *and* kings *and* sealing wax *and* things

Every constituent but the first is marked with the feature COMPONENT. The COMPOUND unit also takes on features from its constituents. It may have features such as number and tense, relevant to its syntactic function. For example, a COMPOUND NG with the feature AND must be plural (NPL), while one with the feature OR will have the number feature of its initial constituent.

Finally, there can be "forked" structures like:

(s158) We dropped the watermelon and ran.

Notice that this cannot be viewed in the same way, since "dropped the watermelon" is not a single constituent of any unit. This sentence is viewed as a conjunction of two clauses, sharing the subject "we". The

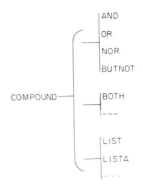

FIG. 19. Network 9—Conjunction.

second clause is marked with the feature SUBJFORK to indicate this. Similarly, the subject and verb can be shared, as in:

(s159) He gave Greg the apple and Gloria the pear.

The clause "Gloria the pear" is marked as VBFORK and SUBJFORK. The only constituents relative to a fork are those necessary for the clause structure. In:

(s160) They easily saw the trouble and cheerfully fixed it.

the parser does not determine whether the "easily" applies to both constituents, but leaves this decision to semantics. This is in keeping with our orientation of syntax to surface structure and the belief that much of "deep structure" is more the province of the semantic analyzer.

3.9 Analysis of Word Endings

This section describes the "spelling rules" used by the program in recognizing inflectional endings of words. For spoken language, these would be called the "morphophonemic" rules, but since we deal with written language, they are "morphographemic."

These rules enable a reader to recognize that, for example, "pleasing" is a form of "please", while "beating" is a form of "beat". There is a structure of conventions for doubling consonants, dropping "e", changing "i" to "y", etc. when adding endings, and a corresponding set for removing them.

A word like "running" need not have a separate entry in the dictionary, since it is a regular inflected form of "run". The program can use an interpretive procedure to discover the underlying form and attach the appropriate syntactic features for the inflection.

In designing a formalism for these rules, it seems most natural to express them as a program for interpretation. The flow chart in Fig. 20 is designed to handle a number of inflectional endings—"-n't" for negative, "-'s" and "-'" for possessive, "-s" and its various forms for plural nouns and singular third-person verbs, "-ing", "-ed", and "-en" verb forms, the superlative "-est" and comparative "-er", and the adverbial "-ly".

As the flowchart shows, these endings share many aspects of morphographemic structure, and the program representation is able to capture these generalities as well as detailing those aspects peculiar to each ending. It is not a complete description, but covers a wide variety of words, and could easily be expanded to treat more special cases.

The function "cutoff" indicates what is to be cut from the end of the word. The ordinals "1st", "2nd", etc. count letters from the end of the word backwards, ignoring those which have been cut off. Several classes of letters are relevant to endings—VOWEL includes (A E I O U Y),

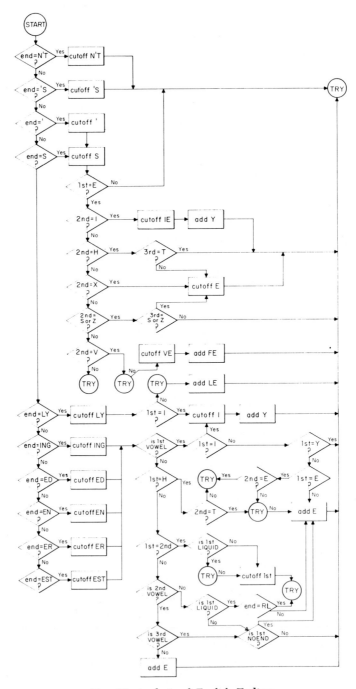

Fig. 20. Analysis of English Endings.

LIQUID is (L R S V Z), and NOEND is (C G S V Z). The label "TRY" represents the part of the program which tries looking up the supposed root in the dictionary. It uses whatever letters have not been "cut off". At some places, the program tries an interpretation, then if that fails, carries out a different analysis and tries again.

The program can correctly analyze such roots as: bashes–bash, bathes–bathe, leaning–lean, leaving–leave, dented–dent, danced–dance, dogs–dog, kisses–kiss, curved–curve, curled–curl, rotting–rot, rolling–roll, played–play, plied–ply, realest–real, palest–pale, knives–knife, prettily–pretty, nobly–noble, etc.

It is important to note that exceptions do not need to be explicitly included in the analysis program. The word "was" is directly in the dictionary, and the rules will therefore never be applied in trying to analyze it. The distinction between lexical idiosyncrasies and generalities is empirical. A productive rule like the one relating "sang" and "sing", or "rang" and "ring" might well be included in a more complete program, while less productive ones (such as relating "will" to "won't") will be left as separate dictionary entries.

It is tempting to see this program as a simple finite state machine, but this is not the best formalism for several reasons. First, the tests which can be done to a word in deciding on a transition are not, in general, simple checks of the next input letter. Whether a certain analysis is possible may depend, for example, on how many syllables there are in the word, or on some complex phonological calculation involving vowel shifts. Semantic and syntactic information should be applied as well in many cases.

The morphographemic analysis alone is sufficient to do a great deal of the interpretation of English endings. In fact, some systems (Thorne, 1969) use it to avoid having a dictionary of open class words. The inflection of the words in the input determines their syntactic class possibilities. Of course, without a dictionary, they cannot attempt to deal with the meanings of words, beyond trying to match them with other occurrences of the same root.

People rarely operate at this level of ignorance. They use their lexical knowledge to realize that "under" is not a comparative form of some adjective "und", and that "bely" is not an adverbial form of "be". This knowledge can readily be integrated into the interpretive program. Once a possible morphographemic analysis is found, the hypothetical root can be checked in the dictionary. If it is not there, the program can try another analysis. Notice that in the flow chart, words ending in a double LIQUID, followed by an inflection, are first tried in the form with the doubled consonant (as in "rolling"–"roll"), then if that fails, another try is made with the single consonant ("patrolled"–"patrol").

If the root is found in the dictionary, its syntactic class is checked to see if the ending is appropriate (e.g. a "-est" ending can apply only to an ADJ). The list of syntactic features is changed to take the ending into account. For example, the ending "-s" changes the feature NS (singular noun) to NPL (plural noun) and the feature INF (infinitive verb) to V3PS (third-person singular verb). A word which fits into more than one category may have more than one set of features changed.

4. AN INTRODUCTION TO LISP

4.1 List Structures

LISP is a computer language for handling complex symbolic data structures. The basic building blocks of LISP are *atoms* and *lists*. An atom is either a number or a string of alphanumeric characters containing no delimiters.[3]

For example, some atoms are:

    105   0.99482   SPIRO   A3*5B   THISISAVERYLONGATOM

In the language program, atoms are used for such things as English words, syntactic features, semantic markers, names of relations, actions, and properties, specific objects and events, and the names of variables.

The basic data structure is the *list*, an ordered set of elements (either atoms or other lists). The list is enclosed in a pair of parentheses. (1 3 ABCE 1) is a list of four elements, all of which are atoms.

    (PUT (THE BLOCK) (IN (THE BOX)))

is a list of three elements. The first is the atom PUT, the second is a two element list (THE BLOCK), and the third is a two element list, whose second element is another list. This ability to nest lists within lists gives LISP its characteristic parenthesized appearance, and enables it to build and manipulate tree-like data structures. The list containing no items can be written as ( ), and is called NIL. It is used to represent the logical value "false." The atom T is often used to represent "true." List structures (or *expressions*) are often printed with the depth of parenthesis nesting indicated by indentation. Elements of the same list appear directly below each other. This is not part of LISP syntax, but a

---

[3] LISP is used primarily in research centers, where the development of the language proceeds hand in hand with its use. Therefore, there is no standard LISP, and many of the details presented here (such as which characters are permitted in an atom name) may vary from version to version. Weissman (1967), and McCarthy *et al.* (1962) introduce the original LISP, but anyone using a particular version should be sure to read the documentation for it. The details used here are in accord with MACLISP, as implemented on the PDP-10 at the Artificial Intelligence Laboratory. See White (1970) for details.

typographical convenience. The extent of a list is determined solely by the matching of associated pairs of parentheses.

The significance of a list is up to the programmer. It may be a list of separate entities, like meanings of a word, or the words in a sentence, or instead particular positions within the list may be assigned special significance. For example, we use three element lists like (#SUPPORT A B) to represent a two-place relation, putting the relation name in the first position. A node of the parsing tree produced by PROGRAMMAR is a five element list whose members are: a list of syntactic features; a pointer to the beginning of the phrase in the sentence; a pointer to the end of the phrase; a list of its daughter nodes; and an expression representing the semantic content of the phrase.

4.2 *Evaluation*

LISP programs operate by interpreting lists in a special way called *evaluation*. The first element in the list is interpreted as the name of a *function*, to be applied to the set of *arguments*, given by the rest of the list. For example, the list (PLUS 3 4) when evaluated returns a *value* of 7, while (TIMES 2 2 2) evaluates to 8. In the normal operation of LISP, expressions are typed in at an interactive console, and their value is typed back by the system. In using the members of the list as arguments, they are in turn evaluated. The list (PLUS (TIMES 3 5) (PLUS 1 8) 6) tells LISP to apply the function PLUS to three arguments, the first of which is produced by applying TIMES to 3 and 5, the second by applying PLUS to 1 and 8, and the third is 6. LISP always uses this prefix notation for operations rather ·than the more usual infix notation like $3*5 + (1 + 8) + 6$.

4.3 *Functions*

The idea of function is used more widely in LISP than in other programming languages. In addition to built-in functions (like those for arithmetic), the user writes programs by creating his own functions. As a simple example, we might define a function F which accepts two arguments, X and Y, and has as its value $X^2 + 7XY + 5$. We would type at the console:

(DEFUN F (X Y)
    (PLUS (SQUARE X)(TIMES 7 X Y) 5))

The function DEFUN is used to define functions,[4] and when this expression is evaluated, a definition for a function named F is entered in the

---

[4] DEFUN is an example of a function which is not found in many LISP implementations—the exact syntax for defining a function may appear in a number of forms.

system. Evaluating the expression (F 3 5) will cause the system to first assign the values 3 and 5 to the variables X and Y, respectively. It then will evaluate the expression which begins with PLUS. It will call the function SQUARE with the argument 3, TIMES with arguments 7, 3, and 5, and add the results along with 5. It prints out the final value 119 on the console. In fact, SQUARE is not a predefined LISP function. Before evaluating an expression using F, we would have to define it in the same way by typing:

(DEFUN SQUARE (X) (TIMES X X))

As it runs, LISP accumulates the user's function definitions, then uses them in evaluating his programs. Large programs are built up of a collection of functions which perform the various subroutines. Our language understanding system contains over 500 separate function definitions.

4.4 Variables

In the functions defined above, we have used the letters X and Y to represent variables. Any nonnumeric atom can be used as a variable name. A value is assigned to a variable in two ways. Above, the values 3 and 5 were assigned to X and Y when the function definition was applied to particular arguments. This *variable binding* occurs whenever functions are called. In addition, there is a replacement function named SETQ which acts like the "=" of FORTRAN. Evaluating the expression (SETQ BREAD (PLUS 2 2)) would cause the variable BREAD to have the value 4. If we now evaluated (TIMES BREAD BREAD) the result would be 16.

4.5 Nonevaluating Functions

The details presented so far are not consistent as they stand. The expression (DEFUN SQUARE (X) (TIMES X X)) is evaluated to define the function SQUARE. If DEFUN acted like PLUS, it would try to evaluate its arguments. Instead, functions have the option of taking their arguments directly without evaluation. DEFUN takes the atom SQUARE as a name, the list (X) as a list of variables, and the expression (TIMES X X) as a list to be stored away and evaluated whenever the function is applied.

Many of the functions used in our program are of the nonevaluating type (called FEXPR). For example, (PARSE CLAUSE MAJOR) causes the function PARSE to be called with the atoms CLAUSE and MAJOR as arguments—it does not interpret them as variable names. Many PLANNER functions are nonevaluating. The expression (THGOAL (#ON A B)) does not evaluate its argument by applying the function #ON to arguments which are the values of A and B. Rather the list (#ON A B) is taken as a pattern to be matched in looking for relevant data. The simplest nonevaluating function is QUOTE, which simply returns its argument without evaluating it. So, for example, if we use the function LIST (which evaluates its arguments), the result of:

(LIST (PLUS 2 2) (TIMES 3 3))

will be the list (4 9), while the result of

(LIST (QUOTE(PLUS 2 2)) (TIMES 3 3))

will be ((PLUS 2 2) 9).

4.6 *Program Control Functions*

Functions can decide which arguments to evaluate, and in what order. For example, SETQ accepts the first argument directly as a variable name (without evaluating to find its current value), but evaluates its second argument to find the value to be assigned. Program control is often handled by the functions AND, OR, COND, and PROG, which interpret their arguments as lists of expressions to be evaluated in a particular sequence. AND evaluates its arguments in order, but if any one of them returns NIL as its value, the rest are not evaluated, and AND returns NIL. Thus AND returns non-NIL (i.e., a logical value of "true") only if every argument evaluates to a non-NIL expression. OR keeps evaluating its arguments in order until it finds one which is non-NIL, then immediately returns that value as the value of OR without evaluating the rest. COND is the conditional, used like an "if–then" statement. Each argument is a pair of expressions. The first member of the first pair is evaluated, and if it is non-NIL the value of the second member of that pair is returned as the value of COND. If the first member evaluated to NIL, COND repeats the process with the next pair, etc. Thus (COND (A B) (C D). . .) is like IF A THEN B, ELSE: IF C THEN D, ELSE . . .

PROG is used to write programs in a style more like other programming languages, giving a sequence of expressions to be evaluated, and naming places in that sequence so that control can be transferred with a GO command. Its first argument is a list of variables to be used in the program, and the rest are location *tags* (any atom), and expressions to be evaluated. The values produced by the expressions are ignored, but they can have *side effects* such as inputting, printing, changing the values of variables, and modifying existing list structures. The function RETURN causes an exit from the PROG. To illustrate these, we can write a simple function which finds the smallest divisor of a number, returning NIL if the number is prime. It guesses divisors, beginning with 2, and increasing by 1 on every loop around. If the guess reaches the original number, it returns NIL, and if it ever divides the original number with no remainder, the guess is returned as the smallest divisor.

```
(DEFUN SMALLESTDIV (X)
  (PROG (GUESS)
    (SETQ GUESS 2)
    FIRSTPLACE
    (COND ((EQUAL GUESS X) (RETURN NIL))
          ((EQUAL (REMAINDER X GUESS) 0)
           (RETURN GUESS)))
    (SETQ GUESS (PLUS GUESS 1))
    (GO FIRSTPLACE)))
```

4.8 Property Lists

Every atom is given a *property list,* on which the programmer can put arbitrary pairs of *indicators* and *values.* An indicator can be any atom, and the value any LISP expression. There are functions PUTPROP and GET which put properties onto atoms, and get their values. In our system, much of the information is kept on property lists. The syntactic features of a word are kept as the property WORD, its definition as the property SMNTC, its past-tense form (if irregular) as PASTT, etc.

5. A DESCRIPTION OF PROGRAMMAR

5.1 Basic Operation of the Parser

5.1.1 Grammar and Computers

Section 5 describes the language PROGRAMMAR, which is used as the formalism for expressing a recognition grammar of English in our system. Before giving its details, we summarize some of the principles of grammar used in computer language processing.

The basic form of most grammars used by computers is a list (ordered or unordered) of "replacement rules," which represent a process of sentence generation. Each rule states that a certain string of symbols (its left side) can be replaced by a different string of symbols (its right side). These symbols include both the actual symbols of the language (called terminal symbols) and additional "nonterminal" symbols. One nonterminal symbol is designed as a starting symbol, and a string of terminal symbols is a sentence if and only if it can be derived from the starting symbol through successive application of the rules. For example we can write Grammar 1 as in Fig. 21.

By starting with S and applying the list of rules (1.1 1.2 1.5 1.6 1.4 1.2 1.7 1.5 1.9) in that order, we get the sentence "The giraffe eats the apple." Several things about this set of rules are noteworthy here. Each rule can be applied any number of times at any point in the derivation where the

1.1 S → NP VP
1.2 NP → DETERMINER NOUN
1.3 VP → VERB/INTRANSITIVE
1.4 VP → VERB/TRANSITIVE NP
1.5 DETERMINER → the
1.6 NOUN → giraffe
1.7 NOUN → apple
1.8 VERB/INTRANSITIVE → dreams
1.9 VERB/TRANSITIVE → eats

FIG. 21—GRAMMAR 1.

symbol appears. In addition, each rule is optional. We could just as well
have reversed the applications of 1.6 and 1.7 to get "The apple eats the
giraffe.", or have used 1.3 and 1.8 to get "The giraffe dreams." This type
of derivation can be represented graphically as in Fig. 22.

We will call this the parsing tree for the sentence, and use the usual
terminology for trees (node, subtree, daughter, parent, etc.). In addition
we will use the linguistic terms "phrase" and "constituent" interchange-
ably to refer to a subtree. This tree represents the "immediate constituent"
structure of the sentence. The PROGRAMMAR language is a general
parsing system which, although oriented toward systemic grammar, can
be used to parse grammars based on other theories. In describing
PROGRAMMAR we use a .conventional analysis of English in order to
make the description independent of the analysis presented in Section 3.

5.1.2 Context-free and Context-sensitive Grammars

Grammar 1 is an example of what is called a context-free grammar. The
left side of each rule consists of a single symbol, and the indicated replacement can occur whenever that symbol is encountered. There are a
great number of different forms of grammar which can be shown to be
equivalent to this one, in that they can characterize the same languages.
It has been pointed out that they are not theoretically capable of expressing all of the rules of English. More important, even though they could
theoretically handle the bulk of the English language, they cannot do
this at all efficiently. Consider the simple problem of subject–verb agreement. We would like a grammar which generates "The giraffe dreams."

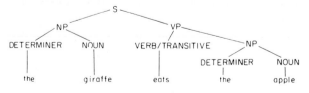

FIG. 22. Parsing Tree.

and "The giraffes dream.", but not "The giraffe dream." or "The giraffes dreams.". In a context-free grammar, this is done by introducing two starting symbols, S/PL and S/SG for plural and singular, respectively, then duplicating each rule to match. For example, we would have:

1.1.1 S/PL → NP/PL VP/PL
1.1.2 S/SG → NP/SG VP/SG
1.2.1 NP/PL → DETERMINER NOUN/PL
1.2.2 NP/SG → DETERMINER NOUN/SG
   . . .
1.6.1 NOUN/PL → giraffes
1.6.2 NOUN/SG → giraffe
etc.

If we then wish to handle the difference between "I am", "he is", etc. we must introduce an entire new set of symbols for first person. This sort of duplication propagates multiplicatively through the grammar, and arises in all sorts of cases. For example, a question and the corresponding statement will have much in common concerning their subjects, objects, verbs, etc., but in a context-free grammar, they will in general be expanded through two entirely different sets of symbols.

One way to avoid this problem is to use context-sensitive rules. In these, the left side may include several symbols, and the replacement occurs when that combination of symbols occurs in the string being generated. Systemic grammar introduces context dependence by introducing features associated with constituents at every level of the parsing tree. A rule of the grammar may depend, for example, on whether a particular clause is transitive or intransitive. In the examples "Fred found a frog.", "A frog was found by Fred.", and "What did Fred find?", all are transitive, but the outward forms are quite different. A context-sensitive rule which checked for this feature directly in the string being generated would have to be quite complex. Instead, we can allow each symbol to have additional subscripts, or features which control its expansion. In a way, this is like the separation of the symbol NP into NP/PL and NP/SG in our augmented context-free grammar. But it is not necessary to develop whole new sets of symbols with a set of expansions for each. A symbol such as CLAUSE may be associated with a whole set of features (such as TRANSITIVE, QUESTION, SUBJUNCTIVE, OBJECT-QUESTION, etc.) but there is a single set of rules for expanding CLAUSE. These rules may at various points depend on the set of features present.

5.1.3 *Grammars as Programs*

In Section 1.4 we pointed out that a complete generative description of a language can be in the form of a program for parsing it. We can think of a grammar as a set of instructions for parsing a sentence in the language. A rule like: NP → DETERMINER NOUN can be interpreted as the instruction "If you want to find a NP, look for a DETERMINER followed by a NOUN." Grammar 1 could be diagrammed as shown in Fig. 23.

As the procedure is followed, a parsing tree is built to keep track of the

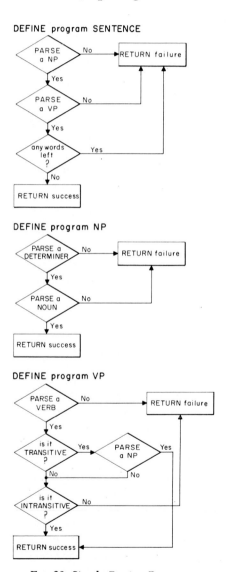

FIG. 23. Simple Parsing Program.

results. The basic function used in writing a grammar is PARSE, which builds the structure of this parsing tree. Its arguments are syntactic features (including the name of a syntactic unit) specifying the type of node being searched for at that point in the parsing. It tries to add a constituent of the specified type to the parsing tree, using the words yet unparsed in the sentence, in left-to-right order. The different syntactic units, such as CLAUSE and NOUN GROUP each correspond to a PROGRAMMAR program for parsing them. If asked to parse one of these, PARSE activates the program for that unit, giving it as input the part of the sentence yet to be parsed and the list of initial features. If the command is to parse something other than a unit, PARSE interprets its arguments as a list of features which must be found in the dictionary definition of the next word in the sentence. If so, it attaches a node for that word to the parsing tree, and removes the word from the remainder of the sentence. If not, it fails. If a PROGRAMMAR program has been called and succeeds, the new node is attached to the parsing tree as a daughter of the node for the unit whose program initiated the PARSE instruction. If it fails, the tree is left unchanged.

5.1.4 The Form of PROGRAMMAR Grammars

Written in PROGRAMMAR, the programs would appear as in Fig. 24.

This example illustrates some of the basic features of PROGRAMMAR. First it is embedded in LISP, and much of its syntax is LISP syntax. Units such as SENTENCE are defined as PROGRAMMAR programs of no arguments. Each tries to parse the string of words left to be parsed in the sentence. The exact form of this input string is described in Section 5.2.7. The value of (PARSE SENTENCE) will be a list structure corresponding to the parsing tree for the complete sentence.

Each time a call is made to the function PARSE, the system begins to build a new node on the tree. Since PROGRAMMAR programs can call each other recursively, it is necessary to keep a pushdown list of nodes which are not yet completed (i.e., the entire rightmost branch of the tree). These are all called "active" nodes, and the one formed by the most recent call to PARSE is called the "currently active node".

We can examine our sample program to see the basic operation of the language. Whenever a PROGRAMMAR program is called directly by the user, a node of the tree structure is set up, and a set of special variables are bound (see Section 5.2.8). The lines of the program are then executed in sequence, as in a LISP PROG, except when they have the special form of a BRANCH statement (a list whose first member (the CONDITION) is nonatomic, and which has either 2 or 3 other members, called DIRECTIONS). Line 2.3 of GRAMMAR 2 is a three-direction

```
2.1   (PDEFINE SENTENCE
2.2   (((PARSE NP) NIL FAIL)
2.3   ((PARSE VP) FAIL FAIL RETURN)))

2.4   (PDEFINE NP
2.5   (((PARSE DETERMINER) NIL FAIL)
2.6    ((PARSE NOUN) RETURN FAIL)))

2.7   (PDEFINE VP
2.8   (((PARSE VERB) NIL FAIL)
2.9    ((ISQ H TRANSITIVE) NIL INTRANS )
2.10   ((PARSE NP) RETURN NIL)
2.11 INTRANS
2.12   ((ISQ H INTRANSITIVE) RETURN FAIL)))
```

Rules 1.6 to 1.9 would have the form:

```
2.13  (DEFPROP GIRAFFE (NOUN) WORD)
2.14  (DEFPROP DREAM (VERB INTRANSITIVE) WORD)
      etc.
```

FIG. 24—Grammar 2

branch, and all the other executable lines of the program are two-direction branches.

When a branch statement is encountered, the condition is evaluated, and branching depends on its value. In a two-direction branch, the first direction is taken if it evaluates to non-NIL, the second direction if it is NIL. In a three-direction branch, the first direction is taken only if the condition is non-NIL, and there is more of the sentence to be parsed. If no more of the sentence remains, and the condition evaluates non-NIL, the third direction is taken.

The directions can be of three types. First, there are three reserved words, NIL, RETURN, and FAIL. A direction of NIL sends evaluation to the next statement in the program. FAIL causes the program to return NIL after restoring the sentence and the parsing tree to their state before that program was called. RETURN causes the program to attach the currently active node to the completed parsing tree and return the subtree below that node as its value.

If the direction is any other atom, it acts as a GO statement, transferring evaluation to the statement immediately following the occurrence of that atom as a tag. For example, if a failure occurs in line 2.9, evaluation continues with line 2.12. If the direction is nonatomic, the result is the same as a FAIL, but the direction is put on a special failure message list, so the calling program can see the reason for failure. The statement (GOCOND TAG1 TAG2) causes the program to go to TAG1 if there are words left to be parsed, and to TAG2 otherwise.

Looking at the programs, we see that SENTENCE will succeed only if it first finds a NP, then finds a VP which uses up the rest of the sentence. If no NP is found, the second direction in line 2.2 will cause a failure. If no VP is found, the second direction in 2.3 will fail, while if a VP is found, but some of the sentence remains, the first direction in 2.3 fails.

In the program VP, we see that the first branch statement checks to see whether the next word is a verb. If so, it removes it from the remaining sentence, and goes on. If not, VP fails. The second statement uses the PROGRAMMAR function ISQ, one of the functions used for checking features. (ISQ A B) checks to see whether the node or word pointed to by A has the feature B. H is one of a number of special variables used to hold information associated with a node of the parsing tree (see Section 5.2.8). It points to the last word or constituent parsed by that program. Thus the condition (ISQ H TRANSITIVE) succeeds only if the verb just found by PARSE has the feature TRANSITIVE. If so, the direction NIL sends it on to the next statement to look for a NP, and if it finds one it returns success. If either no such NP is found or the verb is not TRANSITIVE, control goes to the tag INTRANS, and if the verb is INTRANSITIVE, the program VP succeeds. Note that a verb can have both the features INTRANSITIVE and TRANSITIVE, and the parsing will then depend on whether or not an object NP is found.

5.1.5 Context-Sensitive Aspects

So far, we have done little to go beyond a context-free grammar. How, for example, can we handle agreement? One way to do this would be for the VP program to look back in the sentence for the subject, and check its agreement with the verb before going on. We need a way to climb around on the parsing tree, looking at its structure. In PROGRAMMAR, this is done with the pointer PT and the moving function named "*".

Whenever the function * is called, its arguments form a list of instructions for moving PT from its present position. These instructions can be quite general, saying things like "Move left until you find a unit with feature X, then up until you find a CLAUSE, then down to its last constituent, and left until you find a unit meeting the arbitrary condition Y." The instruction list contains nonatomic CONDITIONS and atomic INSTRUCTIONS. The instructions are taken in order, and when a condition is encountered, the preceding instruction is carried out repeatedly until the condition is satisfied. If the condition is of the form (ATOM), it is satisfied only if the node pointed to by PT has the feature ATOM. Any other condition is evaluated by LISP, and is satisfied if it returns a non-NIL value. Section 5.2.9 lists the instructions for *.

For example, evaluating (* C U) will set the pointer to the parent of the currently active node. (The mnemonics are: Current, Up) The call (* C DLC PV (NP)) will start at the current node, move down to the rightmost completed node (i.e., not currently active) then move left until it finds a node with the feature NP (Down-Last-Completed, Previous). If * succeeds, it returns the new value of PT and leaves PT set to that value. If it fails at any point in the list, because the existing tree structure makes a command impossible, or because a condition cannot be satisfied, PT is left at its original position, and * returns NIL.

In order to check for subject–verb agreement, we can now add another branch statement to the VP program in Figure 24 between lines 2.8 and 2.9 as follows:

2.8.1 ((OR(AND(ISQ(* C PV DLC)SINGULAR)

(ISQ H SINGULAR))

2.8.2   (AND(ISQ PT PLURAL)(ISQ H PLURAL)))

2.8.3 NIL (AGREEMENT))

This is an example of a branch statement with an error message. It moves the pointer from the currently active node (the VP) to the previous node (the NP) and down to its last constituent (the noun). It then checks to see whether this shares the feature SINGULAR with the last constituent parsed by VP (the verb). If not it checks to see whether they share the feature PLURAL. Notice that once PT has been set by *, it remains at that position. If agreement is found, evaluation continues as before with line 2.9. If not, the program VP fails with the message (AGREEMENT).

So far in these examples we have not made much use of features, except on words. As the grammar gets more complex, they become much more important. As a simple example, we may wish to augment our grammar to accept the noun groups "these fish," "this fish," "the giraffes," and "the giraffe," but not "these giraffe," or "this giraffes." We can no longer check a single word for agreement, since "fish" gives no clue to number in the first two, while "the" gives no clue in the third and fourth. Number is a feature of the entire noun group, and we must interpret it in some cases from the form of the noun, and in others from the form of the determiner.

We can rewrite our programs to handle this complexity as shown in Grammar 3 (Fig. 25).

We have used the PROGRAMMAR functions FQ and TRNSF, which attach features to constituents. The effect of evaluating (FQ A) is to add the feature A to the list of features for the currently active node of the parsing tree. TRNSF is used to transfer features from some other

```
3.1   (PDEFINE SENTENCE
3.2   (((PARSE NP)NIL FAIL)
3.3   ((PARSE VP) FAIL FAIL RETURN)))

3.4   (PDEFINE NP
3.5   (((AND(PARSE DETERMINER)(FQ DETERMINED))NIL NIL FAIL)
3.6   ((PARSE NOUN)NIL FAIL)
3.7   ((CQ DETERMINED)DET NIL)
3.8   ((AND(° H)(TRNSF (QUOTE(SINGULAR PLURAL))))RETURN
                                                        FAIL)
3.9   DET
3.10  ((AND (° H)(TRNSF (MEET(FE(° H PV (DETERMINER)))
3.11                          (QUOTE(SINGULAR PLURAL)))))
3.12  RETURN
3.13  FAIL)))

3.14  (PDEFINE VP
3.15  (((PARSE VERB)NIL FAIL)
3.16  ((MEET(FE H)(FE(° C PV (NP)))(QUOTE(SINGULAR PLURAL)))
3.17  NIL
3.18  (AGREEMENT))
3.19  ((ISQ H TRANSITIVE)NIL INTRANS)
3.20  ((PARSE NP)RETURN NIL)
3.21 INTRANS
3.22 ((ISQ H INTRANSITIVE)RETURN FAIL)))
```

FIG. 25—Grammar 3

node to the currently active one. Its argument is a list of features to be looked for, and any of them present in the node being pointed to by the pointer are taken. For example, line 3.8 looks for the features SINGULAR and PLURAL in the last constituent parsed (the NOUN), and adds whichever ones it finds to the currently active node (the NP).

The branch statement beginning with line 3.10 is more complex. The function ° finds the determiner of the NP being parsed. The function FE finds the list of features of this node, and the function MEET intersects this with the list of features (SINGULAR PLURAL). This intersection is then the set of allowable features to be transferred to the NP node from the noun. Therefore if there is no agreement between the NOUN and the determiner, TRNSF fails to find any features to transfer, and the resulting failure causes the rejection of such phrases as "these giraffe."

In line 3.7 we use the function CQ which checks for features on the current node. (CQ DETERMINED) will be non-NIL only if the current node has the feature DETERMINED (i.e., it was put there in line 3.5). Therefore, a noun group with a determiner is marked with the feature DETERMINED, and is also given features corresponding to the intersection of the number features associated with the determiner, if there is one, and the noun. Notice that this grammar can accept noun groups without determiners, as in "Giraffes eat apples." since line 3.5 fails only if a determiner is found and there are no more words in the sentence.

In conjunction with the change to the NP program, the VP program must be modified to check with the NP for agreement. The branch statement beginning on line 3.16 does this by making sure there is a number feature common to both the subject and the verb.

This brief description explains some of the basic features of PROGRAMMAR. In a simple grammar, their importance is not obvious, and indeed there seem to be easier ways to achieve the same effect. As grammars become more complex, the special aspects of PROGRAMMAR become more and more important. The flexibility of writing a grammar as a program is needed both to handle the complexities of English syntax, and to combine the semantic analysis of language with the syntactic analysis in an intimate way.

5.2 Programming Details

5.2.1 Operation of the System

Since the grammar is itself a program, the overhead mechanism needed for the basic operation of the parser consists mostly of special functions to be used by the grammar. The system maintains a number of global variables, and keeps track of the parsing tree as it is built by the main function, PARSE. When the function PARSE is called for a unit which has been defined as a PROGRAMMAR program, the system collects information about the currently active node, and saves it on a pushdown list (PDL). It then sets up the necessary variables to establish a new active node, and passes control to the PROGRAMMAR program for the appropriate unit. If this program succeeds, the system attaches the new node to the tree, and returns control to the node on the top of the PDL. If it fails, it restores the tree to its state before the program was called, then returns control.

When the function PARSE is called with a first argument which has not been defined as a PROGRAMMAR program, it checks to see whether the next word has all of the features listed in the arguments. If so, it forms a new node pointing to that word, with a list of features which is the intersection of the list of features for that word with the allowable features for the word class indicated by the first argument of the call. For example, the word "blocks" will have the possibility of being either a plural noun or a third-person-singular present-tense verb. Therefore, before any parsing it will have the features (NOUN VERB N-PL VB-3PS TRANSITIVE PRESENT). If the expression (PARSE VERB TRANSITIVE) is evaluated when "blocks" is the next word in the sentence to be parsed, the feature list of the resulting node will be the intersection of this combined list with the list of allowable features for the word-class VERB. If we have defined:

(DEFPROP VERB (VERB INTRANSITIVE TRANSITIVE
PRESENT PAST VB-3PS VB-PL) ELIM),

The new feature list will be (VERB TRANSITIVE PRESENT VB-3PS). (ELIM is simply a property indicator chosen to indicate this list which eliminates features). Thus, even though words may have more than one part of speech, when they appear in the parsing tree, they will exhibit only those features relevant to their actual use in the sentence, as determined up to that point.

5.2.2 *Special Words*

Some words, such as the conjunctions "and" and "or," are handled in special ways in the grammar. When one of these is encountered, the normal process is interrupted and a special program is called to decide what steps should be taken in the parsing. This is done by giving these words the syntactic features SPEC or SPECL. Whenever the function PARSE is evaluated, before returning, it checks the next word in the sentence to see if it has the feature SPEC. If so, the SPEC property on the property list of that word indicates a function to be evaluated before parsing continues. This program can in turn call PROGRAMMAR programs and make an arbitrary number of changes to the parsing tree before returning control to the normal parsing procedure. SPECL has the same effect, but is checked for when the function PARSE is called, rather than just before it returns. Various other special variables and functions allow these programs to control the course of the parsing process after they have been evaluated. By using these special words, it is possible to write simple and efficient programs for some of the aspects of grammar which cause the greatest difficulty.

For example, "and" can be defined as a program which is diagrammed in Fig. 26.

For example, given the sentence "The giraffe ate the apples and peaches." the program would first encounter "and" after parsing the NOUN apples. It would then try to parse a second NOUN, and would succeed, resulting in the structure of Fig. 27.

If we had the sentence "The giraffe ate the apples and drank the vodka." the parser would first try the same thing. However, "drank" is not a NOUN, so the AND program would fail and the NOUN "apples" would be returned unchanged. This would cause the NP "the apples" to succeed, so the AND program would be called again, since the check for a SPEC word occurs every time a unit succeeds. It would fail to find a NP begin-

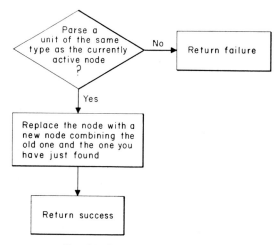

FIG. 26. Conjunction Program.

ning with "drank", so the NP "the apples" would be returned, causing the VP to succeed. This time, AND would try to parse a VP and would find "drank the vodka". It would therefore make up a combined VP and cause the entire SENTENCE to be completed as in Fig. 28.

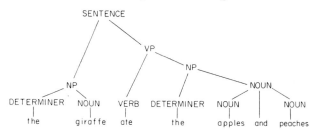

FIG. 27. Conjoined Noun Structure.

A program to do nothing more than this would take only three or four lines in a PROGRAMMAR grammar. The present system is more complex as it handles lists (like "A, B, and C") other conjunctions (such as "but") and special constructions (such as "both A and B"). The conjunction

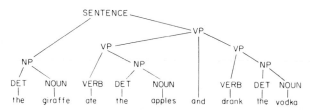

FIG. 28. Conjoined Clauses.

program is called by all of the conjunctions, the words "either", "neither", and "both", and the mark "," which appears as a separate word in the input.

The function ** is used to look ahead for a repetition of the special word, as in ". . . and . . . and . . .". If one is found, a unit of the type most recently parsed is parsed again, trying to extend all the way to the repeated conjunction or comma. This is iterated as long as there are repetitions, with special checks made for structures like "A, B, *and* C" or "A and B *but* not C". As each new mode is parsed, its structure is saved, and when the last is found, a new node is created for the compound. Its features combine those for the type of conjunction with those appropriate for the type of unit (e.g., a compound NG connected with "and" is given the feature "plural" (NPL).) The list of constituent structures is put on the tree as a list of subnodes of the conjoined structure, which then replaces the original unit on the parsing tree.

Compounds with a preceding word like "both" are parsed differently, since the word is encountered before any unit has been parsed. In this case it is possible to adopt the more general strategy of attempting the longest possible unit first. These words have a SPECL definition, so the program is called as the next unit is about to be parsed. The conjunction program looks for the matching conjunction ("and" with "both", "or" with "either", and "nor" with "neither") and tries to parse the unit extending only to the conjunction. If this succeeds, the normal conjunction procedure is followed. If not, some shorter subcomponent is the conjoined one, and nothing happens until the parser attempts a sub-unit, when the process is repeated.

A SPECL program can modify the parsing in several ways. For example it can call the function FLUSHME, which simply removes the word from the input sentence (i.e., it is ignored). It can take arbitrary actions on the current parsing tree, can indicate to PROGRAMMAR that it should SKIP parsing the unit and use instead results provided by the SPECL program, or it can indicate an action to be taken after the normal parsing is DONE. Finally, a SPEC or SPECL program can abort the entire parsing, indicating a response to the user. For example, the word "thank" calls a SPECL program which checks to see if the next word is "you". If so, the parsing is given up, and the system replies "you're welcome". Currently there is no backup procedure to modify the interpretation of an ambiguous structure like "A and B or C". This will in fact be parsed as (A and (B or C)). Notice that "either A and B or C" will be parsed correctly as ((A and B) or C).

The exact format for a SPEC or SPECL definition is a LISP list to which will be appended two items—the initial feature list of the unit being parsed and an indicator of whether it is a word or a unit which called the program. The resultant form is then evaluated.

5.2.3 *Possessives*

One of the best examples of the advantages of procedural grammars is the ability to handle left-branching structures like possessives. In a normal top-down parser, these present difficulties, since any NG can begin with a possessive NG, which can in turn begin with a possessive NG, etc., as in "my mother's sister's student's cat's fur". Special care must be taken to avoid infinite loops.

In our grammar this is handled by a check after the NOUN or PRO-NOUN is found in a NG. If it has the feature "possessive" (POSS) (e.g., "my" or "block's") a node is created for the NG thus far parsed, and this is placed on the tree as a constituent (the determiner) of a NG to be continued. The program then returns to the point where it was after finding a determiner, and continues looking. This can happen any number of times, but in each case is triggered by the presence of another possessive word. It therefore loops only as much as necessary. This departure from top-down parsing involves no changes to the parser, and only a simple loop in the program. Any other left-branching structure can be handled similarly.

5.2.4 *The Dictionary*

Since PROGRAMMAR is embedded in LISP, the facilities of LISP for handling atom names are used directly. To define a word, a list of syntactic features is put on its property list under the indicator WORD, and a semantic definition under the indicator SMNTC. Two facilities are included to avoid having to repeat information for different forms of the same word. First, there is an alternate way of defining words, by using the property indicator WORD1. This indicates that the word given is an inflected form, and its properties are a modified form of the properties of its root. A WORD1 definition has three elements, the root word, the list of features to be added, and the list of features to be removed. For example, we might define the word "go" by: (DEFPROP GO (VERB INTRANSITIVE INFINITIVE) WORD) We could then define "went" as: (DEFPROP WENT (GO (PAST)(INFINITIVE)) WORD1) This indicates that the feature INFINITIVE is to be replaced by the feature PAST, but the rest (including the semantic definition) is to remain the same as for "go".

The other facility is the system described in Section 3.9 which checks for inflectional endings. If a definition for a reduced root word is found, appropriate changes are made for the ending (such as changing the feature SINGULAR to PLURAL). The program which does this is not a part of the PROGRAMMAR system, but is specifically designed for English. For any other language, this input function would have to be rewritten according to that language's rules of morphographemic structure. In terms of interacting with the rest of the system, the only requirement for such a program is that its output be a list, each member of which corresponds to a word in the original sentence, and is in the form described in Section 5.2.7. This list is bound to the variable SENT, and is the way in which PROGRAMMAR sees its input.

The other data in the dictionary consists of tables of verb–particle and preposition–preposition combinations like "pick up" and "on top of". The tables are stored on the property list of the initial word of the combination, under the indicator PRTT or PREPP, respectively. It is a list of pairs, each member of which has the second word of the combination as its first element, and a syntactic structure for the combined form (see Section 5.2.7) as its second element. There may be more than one combination for the same initial word (e.g., "pick up", "pick out"), and three-word combinations can be defined by making the second element of a pair an association list of the same form for a third word (as for "on top of").

5.2.5 Backup Facilities

As explained in Section 1.4.3, there is no automatic backup, but there are a number of special functions which can be used in writing grammars. The simplest, (POPTO X), simply removes nodes from the tree. The argument is a list of features, and the effect is to remove daughters of the currently active node, beginning with the rightmost and working leftward until one is reached with all of those features (POP X) is the same, except that it also removes the node with the indicated features. If no such node exists, neither function takes any action. (POP) is the same as (POP NIL), and a non-nil value is returned by both functions if any action has been taken.

A useful feature is the CUT variable. One way to simplify the bookkeeping needed for backup is to follow a simple strategy when going forward, first trying to find the longest possible constituent at any point. If for any reason an impasse is reached, the system can return and try again, limiting the constituent from going as far along in the sentence. For example, in the sentence "Was the typewriter sitting on the cake?", the parser will first find the auxiliary verb "was", then try to parse the subject. It will find the noun group "the typewriter sitting on the cake", which in another context might well be the subject ("the typewriter sitting on the cake is broken."). It then tries to find the verb, and discovers none of the sentence is left. To back up, it must change the subject. A very clever program would look at the structure of the noun group and would realize that the modifying clause "sitting on the cake" must be dropped. A more simple-minded but still effective approach would use the following instructions:

$$(** \text{ N PW})$$
$$(\text{POP})$$
$$((\text{CUT PTW})\text{SUBJECT (ERROR)})$$

The first command sets the pointer PTW to the last word in the constituent (in this case, "cake"). The next removes that constituent. The third sets a special pointer, CUT to that location, then sends the program back to the point where it was looking for a subject. It would now try to find a subject again, but would not be allowed to go as far as the word "cake". It might now find "the typewriter sitting," an analog to "The man sitting is my uncle." If there were a good semantic program, it would realize that the verb "sit" cannot be used with an inanimate object without a location specified. This would prevent the constituent "the typewriter sitting" from ever being parsed. Even if this does not happen, the program would fail to find a verb when it looked at the remaining sentence, "on the cake." By going through the cutting loop again, it would find the proper subject, "the typewriter," and would continue through the sentence.

Once a CUT point has been set for any active node, no descendant of that node can extend beyond that point until the CUT is moved. Whenever a PROGRAMMAR program is called, the variable END is set to the current CUT point of the node which called it. The CUT point for each constituent is initially set to its END. When the function PARSE is called for a word, it first checks to see if the current CUT has been reached (i.e., N and CUT are the same), and if so it fails. The third branch in a three-direction branch statement is taken if the current CUT point has been reached. The CUT pointer is set by evaluating (CUT X), where X is a pointer to a place in the sentence.

5.2.6 Messages

A good parsing program may at times need to know why a particular PROGRAMMAR program failed, or why a certain pointer command could not be carried out. To facilitate this, two message variables are kept at the top level of the system, MES, and MESP. Messages can be put on MES in two ways, either by using the special failure directions in the branch statements (see Section 5.1.4) or by using the functions M and MQ. When a unit returns either failure or success, MES is bound to the current value of ME, the message list, so the calling program can receive an arbitrary list of messages for whatever purpose it may want

them. MESP always contains the last failure message received from **
or *. (See Section 5.2.9.)

5.2.7 *The Form of the Parsing Tree*

Each node is actually a list structure with the following information:

FE   the list of features associated with the node
NB   the place in the sentence where the constituent begins
N   the place immediately after the constituent
H   the subtree below that node (actually a list of its daughters in
       reverse order, so that H points to the last constituent parsed)
SM   a space reserved for semantic information

These symbols can be used in two ways. If evaluated as variables, they
will always return the designated information for the currently active
node. C is always a pointer to that node. If used as functions of one
argument, they give the appropriate values for the node pointed to by
that argument; so (NB H) gives the location in the sentence of the first
word of the last constituent parsed, while (FE(NB H)) gives the feature
list of that word.

Each word in the sentence is actually a list structure containing the four
items:

FE   as above
SMWORD   the semantic definition of the word
WORD   the word itself (a pointer to an atom)
ROOT   the root of the word (e.g., "run" if the word is
            "running").

5.2.8 *Variables Maintained by the System*

There are two types of variables, those bound at the top level, and
those which are rebound every time a PROGRAMMAR program is called.
Variables bound at the top level:

N   Always points to next word in the sentence to be
             parsed
SENT   Always points to the entire sentence
PT PTW   Tree and sentence pointers. See Section 5.2.9
MES MESP   List of messages passed up from lower levels. See
             Section 5.2.6

Special variables bound at each level:

C FE NB SM H   See Section 5.2.7

NN CUT END	See Section 5.2.5. NN always equals (NOT(EQ N CUT))
UNIT	the name of the currently active PROGRAMMAR program
REST	the list of arguments for the call to PARSE (These form the initial feature list for the node, but as other features are added, REST continues to hold only the original ones.)
T1 T2 T3	Three temporary variables for use by the program in any way needed.
MVB	Bound only when a CLAUSE is parsed, used as a pointer to the main verb
ME	List of messages to be passed up to next level. See Section 5.2.6

5.2.9 *Pointers*

The system always maintains two pointers, PT to a place on the parsing tree, and PTW to a place in the sentence. These are moved by the functions * and **, respectively, as explained in Section 5.1.4. The instructions for PT are:

C	set PT to the currently active node
H	set PT to most recent (rightmost) daughter of C
DL	(down-last) move PT to the rightmost daughter of its current value
DLC	(down-last completed) like DL, except it only moves to nodes which are not on the push-down list of active nodes.
DF	(down-first) like DL, except the leftmost
PV	(previous) move PT to its left-adjacent sister
NX	(next) move PT to its right-adjacent sister
U	(up) move PT to parent node of its current value
N	Move PT to next word in sentence to be parsed

The pointer PTW always points to a place in the sentence. It is moved by the function ** which has the same syntax as *, and the commands:

N	Set PTW to the next word in the sentence
FW	(first-word) set PTW to the first word of the constituent pointed to by PT
LW	(last-word) like FW
AW	(after-word like FW, but first word after the constituent
NW	(next-word) Set PTW to the next word after its current value

PW   (previous-word) like NW

SFW   (sentence-first-word) set PTW to the first word in the sentence

SLW   (sentence-last-word) like SFW

Since the pointers are bound at the top level, a program which calls others which move the pointers may want to preserve their location. PTW is a simple variable, and can be saved with a SETQ, but PT operates by keeping track of the way it has been moved, in order to be able to retrace its steps. This is necessary since LISP lists are threaded in only one direction (in this case, from the parent node to its daughters, and from a right sister to its left sister). The return path is bound to the variable PTR, and the command (PTSV X) saves the values of both PT and PTR under the variable X, while (PTRS X) restores both values.

5.2.10 *Feature Manipulating*

As explained in Section 5.1.4, we must be able to attach features to nodes in the tree. The functions F, FQ, and TRNSF are used for putting features onto the current node, while R and RQ remove them. (F A) sets the feature list FE to the union of its current value with the list of features A. (FQ A) adds the single feature A (i.e., it quotes its argument). (TRNSF A B) was explained in Section 5.1.5. R and RQ are inverses of F and FQ. The functions IS, ISQ, CQ, and NQ are used to examine features. If A points to a node of the tree or word of the sentence, and B points to a feature, (IS A B) returns non-nil if that node has that feature. (ISQ A B) is equivalent to (IS A (QUOTE B)), (CQ B) is the same as (ISQ C B) (where C always points to the currently active node), and (NQ B) is the same as (ISQ N B) (N always points to the next word in the sentence left to be parsed).

The function NEXTW checks to see if the root of the next word matches the argument. (NEXTW BE) evaluates to non-NIL only if the next word is some form of the verb "be." PUTF and REMF are used to add and remove features from some node other than the current one. They are nonevaluating functions whose arguments are features, which are put on or removed from the node currently pointed to by the pointer PT.

5.3 *Following the Parser in Operation*

Let us follow the parser through two examples to see how the grammar is used in practice. We will not actually watch all of the details, or deal with the way semantic programs are intermixed with the grammar. Instead we will follow a somewhat reduced version, to get a feeling for the way the grammar works, and the way it interacts with the different features described above. We have chosen one very simple sentence, and another which is difficult enough to exercise some of the more complex features of the grammar.

5.3.1 Simple Sentences

The first sentence is the first sentence of our sample dialog (Section 1.3): "Pick up a big red block."

The system begins trying to parse a sentence, which, as explained above, means looking for a MAJOR CLAUSE. It activates the grammar by calling (PARSE CLAUSE MAJOR). Since CLAUSE is one of our units, there is a program defined for it. The CLAUSE program is called with an initial feature list of (CLAUSE MAJOR).

The CLAUSE program looks at the first word, in order to decide what unit the CLAUSE begins with. If it sees an adverb, it assumes the sentence begins with a single-word modifier. If it sees a preposition, it looks for an initial PREPG. If it sees a BINDER, it calls the CLAUSE program to look for a BOUND CLAUSE. In English (and possibly all languages) the first word of a construction often gives a very good clue as to what that construction will be. We have "advance notice" of what structures to look for, and this makes parsing much easier. Our grammar tries to make as much use as possible of these signals. In this case, the initial word is a verb, and this indicates that we may have an IMPERATIVE CLAUSE. The program calls (PARSE VG IMPER) to start the VG program with the initial VG feature list (VG IMPER), looking for a VG of the right type. The VG program checks this initial feature list, and sees that it is looking for an imperative VG. This must either begin with some form of the verb "do," or with the main verb itself. Since the next word is not "do," it calls (PARSE VB INF (MVB)). This is a different kind of call to PARSE, since VB is not a unit we have defined. It is a word class, and the call says to check the next word in the input (in this case still the first word) to see whether it is indeed the infinitive form of a verb. If so, it is to be attached to the parsing tree, and given the additional feature MVB (main verb). The current structure can be diagrammed as in Fig. 29.

We use several conventions for diagramming syntactic structures. For each node of the parsing tree, we display its list of syntactic features. Rather than using a tree format (which quickly grows off of the page),

```
(CLAUSE MAJOR)                                          (pick...)
    (VG IMPER)*                                         (pick...)
        (VB MVB INF TRANS VPRT)                           pick
```

Figure 29—Syntactic Structure 1

we use a format more like a traditional outline, with the sub-phrases of any phrase indicated immediately below it and indented. We use the symbol "*" following the feature list to indicate the program which is currently active. The actual words making up a constituent are shown to the right of its feature list, putting units larger than WORD in parentheses. A series of dots in the English words to the right of a unit indicates that the program for that unit has not yet finished.

Our diagram shows that we have a CLAUSE, with a constituent which is a VG, and that the VG program is active. The VG so far consists of only a VB. Notice that some new properties have appeared on the list for VB. We have not mentioned TRANS or VPRT. These came from the definition of the word "pick" when we called the function PARSE for a word (see Section 5.2.4 for details).

Ordinarily the VG program checks for various kinds of tense and number, but in the special case of an IMPER VB, it returns immediately after finding the verb. We will see other cases in the next example.

When the VG program succeeds, CLAUSE takes over again. Since it has found the right kind of VG for an imperative CLAUSE, it puts the feature IMPER on the CLAUSE feature list. It then checks to see whether the MVB has the feature VPRT, indicating it is a special kind of verb which takes a particle. It discovers that "pick" is such a verb, and next checks to see if the next word is a PRT, which it is. It then checks in the dictionary to see if the combination "pick up" is defined, and when it discovers this is true, it calls (PARSE PRT) to add "up" to the parsing tree. Notice that we might have let the VG program do the work of looking for a PRT, but it would have run into difficulties with sentences like "Pick the red block up." in which the PRT is displaced. By letting the CLAUSE program do the looking, the problem is simplified.

As soon as it has parsed the PRT, the CLAUSE program marks the feature PRT on its own feature list. It then looks at the dictionary entry for "pick up" to see what transitivity features are there. It is transitive, which indicates that we should look for one object—OBJ1. The dictionary entry does not indicate that this is a verb which can take special types of RSNG clauses as objects, so the object must be either a NG or a WHRS clause (which can appear wherever a NG can). If the object were a WHRS clause, it would begin with a relative pronoun, like "Pick up *what I told you to.*" Since the next word is "a", this is not the case, so the CLAUSE program looks for an object by calling (PARSE NG OBJ OBJ1), asking the NG program to find a NG which can serve as an OBJ1. The structure is shown in Fig. 30.

The NG program is started and notices that the upcoming word is a determiner, "a". It calls (PARSE DET) to add it to the parsing tree, then

```
(CLAUSE MAJOR IMPER PRT)              (pick up . . .)
   (VG IMPER )                           (pick)
      (VB MVB INF TRANS PRT)              pick
      (PRT)                               up
   (NG OBJ OBJ1)*                        (. . .)
```

Figure 30—Syntactic Structure 2

uses the function TRNSF to transfer relevant features from the DET to the entire NG. It is interested in the type of determination (DEF *vs.* INDEF *vs.* QNTFR), and the number (NS *vs.* NPL). It also adds the feature DET to the NG to indicate that it has a determiner. The feature list for the NG is now:

(NG OBJ OBJ1 DET INDEF NS)

since "a" is a singular indefinite determiner. The NG program then notices the feature INDEF, and decides not to look for a number or an ordinal (we can't say "a next three blocks"), or for the OF construction ("a of them" is impossible). It goes on immediately to look for an adjective by calling (PARSE ADJ). When this succeeds with the next word "big", a simple program loop returns to the (PARSE ADJ) statement, which succeeds again with "red". On the next trip it fails, and sends the program on to look for a classifier, since "block" isn't an ADJ. But "block" isn't a CLASF either in our dictionary, so the NG program goes on to look for a NOUN, by calling (PARSE NOUN). This succeeds with the NOUN "block", which is singular, and the program checks to see if it agrees with the number features already present from the determiner (to eliminate illegal combinations like "these boy"). In this case, both are singular (NS), so the program is satisfied. Ordinarily it would go on to look for qualifiers, but in this case there is nothing left in the sentence. Remember that we have an especially easy way of indicating in a PROGRAMMAR program what action should be taken at any point if the sentence runs out. We can do it by simply putting a third direction in any branch statement. In this case, since we have found all of the basic constituents we need for a NG, the "third branch" tells us that the NG program should return success. If we had run out after the determiner, it would have checked for an incomplete NG, while if we run out after an ADJ it would have entered a backup program which would check to see whether it had misinterpreted a NOUN as an ADJ.

In this case, the NG program returns, and the CLAUSE program notices that the sentence has ended. Since a TRANS verb needs only one object, and that object has been found, the CLAUSE program marks the feature TRANS, and returns, ending the parsing. In actual use, a semantic program would be called here to understand and execute the command—in fact, semantic programs would have been called at various points throughout the process. The final result looks like Fig. 31.

5.3.2 *Complex Sentences*

Now let us take a more complex sentence, like: "How many blocks are supported by the cube which I wanted you to pick up?"
We will not go into as much detail, but will emphasize the new features exhibited by this example. First, the parser recognizes that this sentence is a question by its punctuation. This "cheating" is not really necessary: the grammar could be revised to look for the other signals of a question (for example, beginning with a determiner like "how many" or "which").

In any event, the feature QUESTION is noted, and the program must decide what type of question it is. It checks to see if the CLAUSE begins with a QADJ like "why", "where", etc. or with a preposition which might begin a PREPG QUEST (like "In what year . . .").

All of these things fail in our example, so it decides the CLAUSE must have a NG as its question element, (called NGQ), marks this feature, and calls (PARSE NG QUEST). The NG program starts out by noticing QUEST on its initial feature list, and looking for a question determiner (DET QDET). Since there are only three of these ("which", "what", and "how many"), the program checks for them explicitly, parsing "how" as a QDET, and then calling (PARSE NIL MANY), to add the word "many" to the parsing tree, without worrying about its features. (The call (PARSE NIL X) checks to see if the next word is actually the word "x")).

Since a determiner has been found, its properties are added to the NG feature list, (in this case, (NUMDET INDEF NPL)), and the NG program goes on with its normal business, looking for adjectives, classifiers, and a noun. It finds only the NOUN "blocks" with the features (NOUN NPL). The word "block" appears in the dictionary with the

(CLAUSE MAJOR IMPER PRT TRANS)	(pick up a big red block)
(VG IMPER)	(pick)
(VB MVB INF TRANS VPRT)	pick
(PRT)	up
(NG OBJ OBJ1 DET INDEF NS)	(a big red block)
(DET INDEF NS)	a
(ADJ)	big
(ADJ)	red
(NOUN NS)	block.

Figure 31—Syntactic Structure 3

(CLAUSE MAJOR QUESTION NGQ)*	(how many blocks . . .)
(NQ QUEST DET NUMDET NPL INDEF)	(how many blocks)
(DET QDET NPL INDEF)	how
( )	many
(NOUN NPL)	blocks

Figure 32—Syntactic Structure 4

feature NS, but the input program which recognized the plural ending changed NS to NPL for the form "blocks". Agreement is checked between the NOUN and the rest of the NG, and since "how many" added the feature NPL, all is well. This time, there is more of the sentence left, so the NG program continues, looking for a qualifier. It checks to see if the next word is a preposition (as in "blocks *on* the table), a relative word ("blocks *which* . . .), a past participle ("blocks *supported* by . . .), an ING verb ("blocks *sitting* on . . .), a comparative adjective ("blocks *bigger* than . . .), or the word "as" ("blocks *as* big as . . .). If any of these are true, it tries to parse the appropriate qualifying phrase. If not, it tries to find an RSQ CLAUSE ("blocks *the block supports*). In this case, all of these fail since the next word is "are", so the NG program decides it will find no qualifiers, and returns what it already has. This gives us Fig. 32.

Next the CLAUSE program wants a VG, so it calls (PARSE VG NAUX). The feature NAUX indicates that we want a VG which does not consist of only an auxiliary verb, like "be" or "have". If we saw such a VG, it would indicate a structure like "How many blocks *are* the boxes supporting?", in which the question NG is the object of the CLAUSE. We are interested in first checking for the case where the question NG is the subject of the CLAUSE.

The VG program is designed to deal with combinations of auxiliary verbs like "had been going to be . . ." and notes that the first verb is a form of "be". It calls (PARSE VB AUX BE), assuming that "are" is an auxiliary rather than the main verb of the sentence (if this turns out wrong, there is backup). It transfers the initial tense and person features from this verb to the entire VG (The English VG always uses the leading verb for these features, as in "He *has* been . . .", where it is "has" which agrees with "he".) In this case "are" is plural (VPL) and present tense (PRES).

When "be" is used as an auxiliary, it is followed by a verb in either the ING or the EN form. Since "supported" is an EN form (and was marked that way by the input program), the VG program calls (PARSE VB EN (MVB)), marking "supported" as the main verb of the clause. The use of a "be" followed by an EN form indicates a PASV VG, so the feature PASV is marked, and the VG program is ready to check agreement. Notice that so far we haven't found a subject for this clause, since the question NG might have been an object, as in "*How many blocks* does the box support?" However the VG program is aware of this, and realizes that instead of checking agreement with the constituent marked SUBJ, it must use the one marked QUEST. It uses PROGRAMMAR's pointer-moving functions to find this constituent, and notes that it is NPL, which agrees with VPL. VG therefore returns its value. We now have Fig. 33.

The CLAUSE program resumes, and marks the feature SUBJQ, since it found the right kind of VG to indicate that the NG "how many blocks" is indeed the subject. It next checks to see if we have a PRT situation as we did in our first example. We don't, so it next checks to see if the VG is PASV, and marks the clause with the feature PASV. This indicates that there will be no objects, but there might be an AGENT phrase. It checks that the next word is "by", and calls (PARSE PREPG AGENT).

The PREPG program is fairly simple—it first calls (PARSE PREP), then (PARSE NG OBJ PREPOBJ). The word "by" is a PREP, so the first call succeeds and NG is called and operates as described before, finding the DET "the" and the NOUN "cube," and checking the appropriate number features.

The NG program next looks for qualifiers, as described above, and this time it succeeds. The word "which" signals the presence of a RSQ WHRS CLAUSE modifying "cube". The NG program therefore calls (PARSE CLAUSE RSQ WHRS). The parsing tree now looks like Fig. 34.

The CLAUSE program is immediately dispatched by the feature WHRS to look for a RELWD. It finds "which", and marks itself as NGREL. It then goes on to look for a (VG NAUX) just as our QUESTION NGQ clause did above. Remember that WH- questions and WHRS clauses share a great deal of the network, and they share much of the program as well. This time the VG program fails, since the next word is "I", so the CLAUSE program decides that the clause "which I . . ." is not a SUBJREL. It adds the temporary feature NSUBREL, indicating this negative knowledge, but not deciding yet just what we do have. It then

(CLAUSE MAJOR QUESTION NGQ)°   (how many blocks are supported . . .
   (NG QUEST DET NUMDET NPL INDEF)   (how many blocks)
      (DET QDET NPL INDEF)   how
      ( )   many
      (NOUN NPL)   blocks
   (VG NAUX VPL PASV (PRES))   (are supported)
      (VB AUX BE PRES VPL)   are
      (VB MVB EN TRANS)   supported

Figure 33—Syntactic Structure 5

(CLAUSE MAJOR QUESTION NGQ SUBJQ PASV)
                              (how many blocks are supported by the cube . . .)

    (NG QUEST DET NUMDET NPL INDEF)   (how many blocks)
        (DET QDET NPL INDEF)   how
        ( )   many
        (NOUN NPL)   blocks

    (VG NAUX VPL PASV (PRES))   (are supported)
        (VB AUX BE PRES VPL)   are
        (VB MVB EN TRANS)   supported

    (PREPG AGENT)   (by the cube . . .)
        (PREP)   by

        (NG OBJ PREPOBJ DET DEF NS)   (the cube . . .)
            (DET DEF NPL NS)   the
            (NOUN NS)   cube
            (CLAUSE RSQ WHRS)*   (. . .)

Figure 34—Syntactic Structure 6

goes to the point in the normal clause program which starts looking for the major constituents of the clause—subject, verb, etc. We call (PARSE NG SUBJ) and succeed with the PRONG "I". We then look for a VG, and find "wanted". In this case, since the verb is PAST tense, it doesn't need to agree with the subject (only the tenses beginning with PRES show agreement). The feature NAGR marks the nonapplicability of agreement. The parsing tree from the WHRS node on down is shown in Fig. 35.

The CLAUSE program notes that the MVB is TRANS and begins to look for an OBJ1. This time it also notes that the verb is a TOOBJ and a SUBTOBJ (it can take a TO clause as an object, as in "I wanted *to go*.", or a SUBTO, as in "I wanted *you to go*." Since the next word isn't "to", it decides to look for a SUBTO clause, calling (PARSE CLAUSE RSNG OBJ OBJ1 SUBTO). In fact, this checking for different kinds of RSNG clauses is done by a small function named PARSEREL, which looks at the features of the MVB, and calls the appropriate clauses. PARSEREL is used at several points in the grammar, and one of the main advantages

(CLAUSE RSQ WHRS NGREL NSUBREL)*   (which I wanted . . .)

    (RELWD)   which

    (NG SUBJ PRONG NFS)   (I)
        (PRON NFS)   I

    (VG NAGR (PAST))   (wanted)
        (VB MVB PAST TRANS TOOBJ SUBTOBJ)   wanted

Figure 35—Syntactic Structure 7

of writing grammars as programs is that we can write such auxiliary programs (whether in PROGRAMMAR or LISP) to make full use of regularities in the syntax.

The CLAUSE program is called recursively to look for the SUBTO clause "you to pick up". It finds the subject "you", and calls (PARSE VG TO) since it needs a verb group of the "to" type. The VG program notices this feature and finds the appropriate VG (which is again NAGR). The PRT mechanism operates as described in the first example, and the bottom of our structure now looks like Fig. 36.

Notice that we have a transitive verb–particle combination, "pick up", with no object, and no words left in the sentence. Ordinarily this would cause the program to start backtracking—checking to see if the MVB is also intransitive, or if there is some way to reparse the clause. However we are in the special circumstance of an embedded clause which is somewhere on the parsing tree below a relative clause with an "unattached" relative. In the clause "which I told you to pick up", I is the subject, and the CLAUSE "you to pick up" is the object. The "which" has not been related to anything. There is a small program named UP-CHECK which uses PROGRAMMAR's ability to look around on the parsing tree. It looks for this special situation, and when it finds it does three things: (1) Mark the current clause as UPREL, and the appropriate type of UPREL for the thing it is missing (in this case OBJ1UPREL). (2) Remove the feature NSUBREL from the clause with the unattached relative. (3) Replace it with DOWNREL to indicate that the relative has been found below. This can all be done with simple programs using the basic PROGRAMMAR primitives for moving around the tree (see Section 5.2.9) and manipulating features at nodes (see 5.2.10). The information

```
(CLAUSE RSQ WHRS NGREL NSUBREL)        (which I wanted you to pick up)
     (RELWD)                                which
     (NG SUBJ PRONG NFS)                     (I)
          (PRON NFS)                          I
     (VG NAGR (PAST))                        (wanted)
          (VB MVB PAST TRANS TOOBJ SUBTOBJ)  wanted

     (CLAUSE RSNG SUBTO OBJ OBJ1 PRT)°      (you to pick up)

          (NG SUBJ PRONG NPL)                (you)
               (PRON NPL)                     you

          (VG TO NAGR)                       (to pick)
               ( )                            to
               (VB MVB INF TRANS VPRT)        pick

          (PRT)                              up
```

Figure 36—Syntactic Structure 8

which is left in the parsing tree is sufficient for the semantic routines to figure out the exact relationships between the various pieces involved.

In this example, once the CLAUSE "to pick up" has been marked as OBJ1UPREL, it has enough objects, and can return success since the end of the sentence has arrived. The CLAUSE "which I want you to pick up" has an object, and has its relative pronoun matched to something, so it also succeeds, as does the NG "the cube . . .", the PREPG "by the cube . .", and the MAJOR CLAUSE. The final result is shown in Fig. 37.

(CLAUSE MAJOR QUESTION NGQ SUBJQ PASV AGENT)

    (NG QUEST DET NUMDET NPL INDEF)   (how many blocks)
        (DET QDET NPL INDEF)   how
        ( )   many
        (NOUN NPL)   blocks

    (VG NAUX VPL PASV (PRES))   (are supported)
        (VB AUX BE PRES VPL)   are
        (VB MVB EN TRANS)   supported

(PREPG AGENT)   (by the cube which I wanted you to pick up)
   (PREP)   by

  (NG OBJ PREPOBJ DET DEF NS)
                      (the cube which I wanted you to pick up)
     (DET DEF NPL NS)   the
     (NOUN NS)   cube

    (CLAUSE RSQ WHRS NGREL DOWNREL TRANS)
                     (which I wanted you to pick up)
       (RELWD)   which

      (NG SUBJ PRONG NFS)   (I)
         (PRON NFS)   I

      (VG NAGR (PAST))   (wanted)

        (VG MVB PAST TRANS TOOBJ SUBTOBJ)   wanted

      (CLAUSE RSNG SUBTO OBJ OBJ1 PRT
              TRANS UPREL OBJ1UPREL)   (you to pick up)

        (NG SUBJ PRONG NPL)   (you)
          (PRON NPL)   you

        (VG TO NAGR)   (to pick)
          ( )   to
         (VB MVB INF TRANS VPRT)   pick

       (PRT)   up

Figure 37—Syntactic Structure 9
"How many blocks are supported by the cube
which I wanted you to pick up?"

Even in this fairly lengthy description, we have left out much of what was going on. For example we have not mentioned all of the places where the CLAUSE program checked for adverbs (like "usually" or "quickly"), or the VG program looked for "not", etc. These are all "quick" checks, since there is a PROGRAMMAR command which checks the features of the next word. In following the actual programs, the course of the process would be exactly as described, without backups or other attempts to parse major structures.

6. DEDUCTION, PROBLEM SOLVING, AND PLANNER

6.1 *Representing Knowledge in PLANNER*

6.1.1 *Complex Information*

Section 1.5 described a formalism for representing assertions about particular objects, properties, and relationships. We also want to handle more complex information, involving logical relationships and procedures. The representation for this knowledge must be useable by a problem-solving system. This could be done using a formal language such as the predicate calculus. Basic logical relations such as implies, or, and, there exists, etc. would be represented symbolically, and information would be translated into a "formula". Thus if we wanted to represent the information "All humans are fallible," or "A thesis is acceptable if either it is long or it contains a persuasive argument." we might have the formulas in Fig. 38.

Several notational conventions are used. First, we need variables so that we can say things about objects without naming particular ones. This is done with the quantifiers FORALL and EXISTS. Second, we need logical relations like AND, OR, NOT, and IMPLIES. For easier reading,

```
(FORALL (X) (IMPLIES( #HUMAN X)( #FALLIBLE X)))
(FORALL (X)(IMPLIES
           (AND ( #THESIS X)
                (OR ( #LONG X)
                    (EXISTS (Y)
                            (AND ( #PERSUASIVE Y)
                                 ( #ARGUMENT Y)
                                 ( #CONTAINS X Y)))))
           ( #ACCEPTABLE X)))
```

Figure 38—Predicate Calculus Representation
"All humans are fallible."
"All objects which are theses, and either are long or contain a persuasive argument are acceptable."

indentation is used. Expressions beginning at the same point on the line are subparts of the same larger expression.

Using this formalism, we can represent a question as a formula to be "proved". To ask "Is Sam's thesis acceptable?" we could give the formula (#ACCEPTABLE :SAM-THESIS) to a theorem prover to prove by manipulating the formulas and assertions in the data base according to the rules of logic. We would need some additional theorems which would allow the theorem prover to prove that a thesis is long, that an argument is acceptable, etc.

In some theoretical sense, such predicate calculus formulas could express all of our knowledge, but in a practical sense there is something missing. A person would also have knowledge about how to go about doing the deduction. He would know that he should check the length of the thesis first, since he might be able to save himself the bother of reading it, and that he might even be able to avoid counting the pages if there is a table of contents. In addition to complex information about what must be deduced, he also knows a lot of hints and "heuristics" telling how to do it better for the particular subject being discussed.

Many "theorem-proving" systems (see Green, 1969) do not have any way to include this additional intelligence. Instead, they are limited to a kind of "working in the dark". A uniform proof procedure gropes its way through the collection of theorems and assertions, according to some general procedure which does not depend on the subject matter. It tries to combine any facts which might be relevant, working from the bottom up. In our example given above, we might have a very complex theorem for deciding whether an argument is persuasive. A uniform proof procedure might spend a great deal of time checking the persuasiveness of every argument it knew about, since a clause of the form (#PER-SUASIVE X) might be relevant to the proof. What we would prefer is a way to guide the process of deduction in an intelligent way. Toward this end, Hewitt (1971) has developed a theorem proving language called PLANNER. In PLANNER, theorems are programs. They can control how to go about proving a goal, or how to deduce consequences from an assertion.

In PLANNER, the rule for thesis evaluation could be represented as shown in Fig. 39.

This is similar in structure to the predicate calculus representation given above, but there are important differences. The theorem is a program, in which each logical operator indicates steps to be carried out. THGOAL will try to find an assertion in the data base, or prove it using other theorems. THUSE gives advice on what other theorems to use, and in what order. THAND and THOR are equivalent to the logical AND

(DEFTHEOREM EVALUATE
EVALUATE is the name we are giving to the theorem.
(THCONSE(X Y) (#ACCEPTABLE $?X)
This indicates the type of theorem, names its variables,
and states that we are trying to prove something acceptable.
    (THGOAL(#THESIS $?X))
Show that X is a thesis. The "$?" indicates a variable.
    (THOR
THOR is like "or", trying things in the order given until one works.
        (THGOAL(#LONG $?X)(THUSE CONTENTS-CHECK COUNTPAGES))
THUSE says to try the theorem named CONTENTS-CHECK first,
then if that doesn't work, try the one named COUNTPAGES.
        (THAND
THAND is like "and".
            (THGOAL(#CONTAINS $?X $?Y))
Find something Y which is contained in X.
            (THGOAL(#ARGUMENT $?Y))
Show that it is an argument.
            (THGOAL(#PERSUASIVE $?Y)(THTBF THTRUE))))))
Prove that it is persuasive, using any theorems which are applicable.

Figure 39—PLANNER Representation

and OR except that they give a specific order in which things should be
tried. (The initial "TH" in the names is to differentiate PLANNER
functions from the standard LISP functions AND and OR. This same
convention is used for all functions which have LISP analogs, since
PLANNER's backup system demands that the functions operate differently internally.)

The theorem EVALUATE says that to prove that a thesis is acceptable,
we should first make sure it is a thesis (by looking in the data base, since
there are no recommendations for theorems to be tried). Next, try to
prove that it is long, first by using the theorem CONTENTS-CHECK
(which would check the table of contents), and if that fails, by using a
theorem named COUNTPAGES. If both fail, then look in the data base
for something contained in the thesis, check that this something is an
argument, and then try to prove that this argument is persuasive. The
instruction (THTBF THTRUE) is PLANNER's way of saying "try anything you know which can help prove it". PLANNER then will search
through all of its theorems on persuasiveness, just as any other theorem
prover would. Note, however, that PLANNER never need look at
persuasiveness at all if it can determine that the thesis is long. Second, it
only looks at the persuasiveness of arguments that are a part of the
thesis. We do not get sidetracked into looking at the persuasiveness
theorems except for the cases we really want.

6.1.2 *Questions, Statements, and Commands*

PLANNER is particularly convenient for a language understanding system, since it can express statements, commands, and questions directly. We have already shown how assertions can be stated in simple PLANNER format. Commands and questions are also easily expressed. Since a theorem is written in the form of a procedure, we can let steps of that procedure actually be actions to be taken by a robot. The command "Pick up the block and put it in the box." could be expressed as a PLANNER program:

```
(THAND(THGOAL(#PICKUP :BLOCK23))
      (THGOAL(#PUTIN :BLOCK23 :BOX7)))
```

Remember that the prefix ":" and the number indicate a specific object. The theorems for #PICKUP and #PUTIN would also be programs, describing the sequence of steps to be done. Since the robot is the only thing in its world which can pick things up, we have chosen to always represent actions like #PICKUP and #PUTIN without explicitly mentioning the subject. In a more complex model, they would be expressed as two-place predicates.

Earlier we asked about Sam's thesis in predicate calculus. In PLANNER we can ask:

```
(THGOAL (#ACCEPTABLE :SAM-THESIS)
                            (THUSE EVALUATE))
```

Here we have specified that the theorem EVALUATE is to be used. If we evaluated this PLANNER statement, the theorem would be called and executed as described above. PLANNER would return one of the values "T" or "NIL" depending on whether the statement is true or false.

The function THFIND is used for many question-answering tasks. It finds all of the objects or assertions satisfying a given PLANNER condition. For example, if we want to find all of the red blocks, we can evaluate:

```
(THFIND ALL $?X (X)
        (THGOAL(#BLOCK $?X))
        (THGOAL(#COLOR $?X RED)))
```

THFIND takes four pieces of information. First, there is a parameter, telling it how many objects to look for. When we use ALL, it looks for as many as it can find, and succeeds if it finds any. If we use an integer, it succeeds as soon as it finds that many, without looking for more. If we want to be more complex, we can tell it three things: (*a*) how many it needs to succeed; (*b*) how many it needs to quit looking, and (*c*) whether to succeed or fail if it reaches the upper limit set in *b*.

Thus if we want to find exactly three objects, we can use a parameter of (3 4 NIL), which means "Don't succeed unless there are three, look for a fourth, but if you find it, fail".

The second bit of information tells it what we want in the list it returns. For our purposes, this will always be the variable name of the object we are interested in. The third item is a list of variables to be used in the process. This acts much like an existential quantifier in the predicate calculus notation.

The fourth item is the *body* of the THFIND statement. It is this body that must be satisfied for each object found. It is identical to the body of a theorem, giving a sequence of expressions to be evaluated in order.

For a question like "What nations have never fought a war?" we would ask:

(THFIND ALL $?X (X Y)
  (THGOAL(#NATION $?X))
  (THNOT
    (THAND(THGOAL(#WAR $?Y))
          (THGOAL(#PARTICIPATED $?X $?Y)))))

and PLANNER would return a list of all such countries. (The prefix characters $? indicate that X and Y are variables.) Using our conventions for giving names to relations and events, we could even ask:

(THFIND ALL $?X (X Y Z EVENT)
  (THGOAL(#CHICKEN $?Y))
  (THGOAL(#ROAD $?Z))
  (THGOAL(#CROSS $?Y $?Z $?EVENT))
  (THGOAL(#CAUSE $?X $?EVENT)))

6.2 *Operation of the Deductive System*

6.2.1 *Basic Operation of PLANNER*

The easiest way to understand PLANNER is to watch how it works, so in this section we will present a few simple examples and explain the use of some of its features.

First we will take the traditional deduction:

Turing is a human.

All humans are fallible.

so

Turing is fallible.

It is easy enough to see how this could be expressed in the usual logical notation and handled by a uniform proof procedure. Instead, let us express it in one possible way to PLANNER by saying:

(THASSERT (#HUMAN :TURING))

This asserts that Turing is human.
```
(DEFTHEOREM THEOREM1
   (THCONSE (X) (#FALLIBLE $?X)
                 (THGOAL (#HUMAN $?X))))
```
This is one way of saying that all humans
are fallible.

The proof would be generated by asking PLANNER to evaluate the expression:
```
(THGOAL (#FALLIBLE :TURING)  (THTBF THTRUE))
```
Remember that PLANNER is an evaluator which accepts input in the form of expressions written in the PLANNER language, and evaluates them, producing a value and side effects. THASSERT is a function which, when evaluated, stores its argument in the data base of assertions or the data base of theorems (which are cross-referenced to give the system efficient look-up capabilities). A theorem is defined using the function DEFTHEOREM.

In this example we have defined a theorem of the THCONSE type (THCONSE means consequent; we will see other types later). This states that if we ever want to establish a goal of the form (#FALLIBLE $?X), we can do this by accomplishing the goal (#HUMAN $?X), where, as before, the prefix characters $? indicate that X is a variable.

The third statement illustrates the function THGOAL, which calls the PLANNER interpreter to try to prove an assertion. This can function in several ways. If we had asked PLANNER to evaluate (THGOAL (#HUMAN :TURING)) it would have found the requested assertion immediately in the data base and succeeded (returning as its value some indicator that it had succeeded). However, (#FALLIBLE :TURING) has not been asserted, so we must resort to theorems to prove it.

Later we will see that a THGOAL statement can give PLANNER various kinds of advice on which theorems are applicable to the goal and should be tried. For the moment, (THTBF THTRUE) is advice that causes the evaluator to try all theorems whose consequent is of a form which matches the goal (i.e., a theorem with a consequent ($?Z :TURING) would be tried, but one of the form (#HAPPY $?Z) or (#FALLIBLE $?Y $?Z) would not). Assertions can have an arbitrary list structure for their format—they are not limited to two-member lists or three-member lists as in these examples.

In the present case, the theorem we have just defined would be found, and in trying it, the match of the consequent to the goal would cause the variable $?X to be assigned to the constant :TURING. Therefore, the theorem sets up a new goal (#HUMAN :TURING) and this succeeds immediately since it is in the data base. In general, the success of a theorem will depend on evaluating a PLANNER program of arbitrary complexity. In this case it contains only a single THGOAL statement, so its success causes the entire theorem to succeed, and the goal (#FALLIBLE :TURING) is proved.

Consider the question "Is anything fallible?", or in predicate calculus, (EXISTS (Y)(#FALLIBLE Y)). This requires a variable and it could be expressed in PLANNER as:

(THPROG (Y) (THGOAL (#FALLIBLE $?Y)
                                        (THTBF THTRUE)))

Notice that THPROG (PLANNER's equivalent of a LISP PROG, complete with GO statements, tags, RETURN, etc.) acts as an existential quantifier. It provides a binding-place for the variable Y, but does not initialize it—it leaves it in a state particularly marked as unassigned. To answer the question, we ask PLANNER to evaluate the entire THPROG expression above. To do this it starts by evaluating the THGOAL expression. This searches the data base for an assertion of the form (#FALLIBLE $?Y) and fails. It then looks for a theorem with a consequent of that form, since the recommendation (THTBF THTRUE) says to look at all possible theorems which might be applicable. When the theorem defined above is called, the variable X in the theorem is identified with the variable Y in the goal, but since Y has no value yet, X does not receive a value. The theorem then sets up the goal (#HUMAN $?X) with X as a variable. The data-base searching mechanism takes this as a command to look for any assertion which matches that pattern (i.e., an instantiation), and finds the assertion (#HUMAN :TURING). This causes X (and therefore Y) to be assigned to the constant :TURING, and the theorem succeeds, completing the proof and returning the value (#FALLIBLE :TURING).

6.2.2 Backup

So far, the data base has contained only the relevant objects, and therefore PLANNER has found the right assertions immediately. Consider the problem we would get if we added new information by evaluating the statements:

(THASSERT (#HUMAN :SOCRATES))
(THASSERT (#GREEK :SOCRATES))

Our data base now contains the assertions:

(#HUMAN :TURING)
(#HUMAN :SOCRATES)
(#GREEK :SOCRATES)

and the theorem:

```
(THCONSE (X) (#FALLIBLE $?X)
              (THGOAL (#HUMAN $?X)))
```

What if we now ask, "Is there a fallible Greek?" In PLANNER we would do this by evaluating the expression:

```
(THPROG (X) (THGOAL (#FALLIBLE $?X)
                    (THTBF THTRUE))
            (THGOAL (#GREEK $?X)))
```

THPROG acts like an AND, succeeding only if all of its terms are satisfied. Notice that the first THGOAL may be satisfied by the exact same deduction as before, since we have not removed information. If the database searcher happens to run into :TURING before it finds :SOCRATES, the goal (#HUMAN $?X) will succeed, assigning $?X to :TURING. After (#FALLIBLE $?X) succeeds, the THPROG will then establish the new goal (#GREEK :TURING), which fails since it has not been asserted and there are no applicable theorems. If we think in LISP terms, this is a serious problem, since the evaluation of the first THGOAL has been completed before the second one is called, and the "push-down list" now contains only the THPROG. If we try to go back to the beginning and start over, it will again find :TURING and so on, ad infinitum.

PLANNER has a "backup" control structure which remembers what the program has done, so that in case of failure, it can always back up to the last decision made. In this instance, the last decision was the selection of a particular assertion from the data base to match a goal. In other instances the decision might be the choice of a theorem to achieve a goal, or an explicit choice put into the program using the function THOR.

In our example the decision was made inside the theorem for #FALLIBLE, when the goal (#HUMAN $?X) was matched to the assertion (#HUMAN :TURING). PLANNER will retrace its steps, try to find a different assertion which matches the goal, find (#HUMAN :SOCRATES), and continue with the proof. The theorem will succeed with the value (#FALLIBLE :SOCRATES), and the THPROG will proceed to the next expression, (THGOAL (#GREEK $?X)). Since X has been assigned to :SOCRATES, this will set up the goal (#GREEK :SOCRATES) which will succeed immediately by finding the corresponding assertion in the data base. Since there are no more expressions in the THPROG, it will succeed, returning as its value the value of the last expression, (#GREEK :SOCRATES). The whole course of the deduction process depends on this mechanism for backing up in case of failure and trying different branches in the subgoal tree. The PLANNER interpreter keeps track of all the bookkeeping needed for this backup, and gives the user facilities to control when and how it will happen.

6.2.3 *Controlling the Data Base*

The statement that all humans are fallible, though unambiguous in a declarative sense actually is ambiguous in its imperative sense (i.e., the way it is to be used by the theorem prover). We can use it whenever we are faced with the need to prove (#FALLIBLE $?X), or we can watch for assertions of the form (#HUMAN $?X) and then immediately assert (#FALLIBLE $?X) as well. There is no abstract logical difference, but the difference in impact on the size and utility of the data base is tremendous. The more conclusions we draw right at the time information is asserted, the easier proofs will be, since they will not have to deduce these consequences over and over again. Not having infinite speed and size, however, we cannot deduce and then assert everything possible (or even everything interesting) about data as it is entered. When we assert (#LIKES $?X #POETRY), we may want to deduce and assert (#HUMAN $?X). In deducing things about an object, it will often be relevant whether that object is human, and we shouldn't need to deduce it each time. On the other hand, it would be silly to deduce and assert (#HAS-AS-PART $?X #SPLEEN). PLANNER must know which facts about a subject are important, and when to draw consequences from an assertion. This is done by having theorems of an antecedent type:

(DEFTHEOREM THEOREM2
   (THANTE (X Y) (#LIKES $?X $?Y)
      (THASSERT (#HUMAN $?X))))

This says that when we assert that X likes something, we should also assert (#HUMAN $?X). Such theorems need not be so simple. A THANTE theorem may activate an entire PLANNER program. In addition, whenever anything is asserted, it is possible to evaluate the current situation and decide which if any antecedent theorems to call.

6.2.4 *Events and States*

Another advantage in representing knowledge in an imperative form is in dealing with a sequence of events. Notice that a declarative theorem prover cannot accept a statement like (#ON :B1 :B2) at face value. It is not an axiom, since its validity will change as the process goes on. To become an axiom, it must be put in a form (#ON :B1 :B2 SO) where SO is a symbol for an initial state of the world. (See Green (1969) for a discussion of such "state" problems.) In a declarative theorem prover we need to create a function whose value is the state which results from putting X on Y. We run into a problem when we try to ask whether block Z is on block W after we put X on Y. It may take a complex deduction to decide whether we have moved Z and W, and even if we haven't, it will take a whole chain of deductions (tracing back through the time sequence) to prove they haven't been moved. In PLANNER, this problem can be handled in an intuitively more satisfactory way by using the primitive function THERASE.

Evaluating (THERASE (#ON $?X $?Y)) removes the assertion (#ON $?X $?Y) from the data base. If we think of theorem provers as working with a set of axioms, it seems strange to have a function whose purpose is to erase axioms. But, instead we think of the data base as the "state of the world" and the operation of the prover as manipulating that state. Now we can simply assert (#ON :B1 :B2) without any explicit mention of states. We can express the necessary theorem as:

```
(DEFTHEOREM THEOREM3
  (THCONSE (X Y Z) (#PUT $?X $?Y)
    (THGOAL (#ON $?X $?Z))
    (THERASE (#ON $?X $?Z))
    (THASSERT (#ON $?X $?Y)))))
```

This says that whenever we want to satisfy a goal of the form (PUT $?X $?Y), we should first find out what thing Z the thing X is sitting on, erase the fact that it is sitting on Z, and assert that it is sitting on Y. In a more complex case, for example, we might have thought it worthwhile to keep assertions of the form (#ABOVE $?X $?Y). We would need to delete those assertions which became false when we erased (#ON $?X $?Z) and add those which became true when we added (#ON $?X $?Y). ANTECEDENT theorems would be called by the assertion (#ON $?X $?Y) to take care of that part, and ERASING theorems can be called in an exactly analogous way when an assertion is erased, to derive consequences of the erasure.

<h3>7. THE BLOCKS WORLD</h3>

We need a subject to discuss with our language-understanding program—something about which we can carry on a discourse, with statements, questions, and commands. We have chosen to pretend we are talking to a simple robot (like the ones being developed in AI projects at Stanford and MIT) with only one arm and an eye. It can look at a scene containing toy objects like blocks and balls, and can manipulate them with its hand (see section 1.3). Since we are interested primarily in complex language activity, we have adopted a very simplified model of the world, and the "robot" exists only as a display on the CRT scope attached to the computer.

<h3>7.1 Objects</h3>

First we must decide what objects we will have in the world. The model begins with the two participants in the dialog of section 1.3, the robot (named :SHRDLU), and the person (called :FRIEND). The robot has a hand (:HAND), and manipulates objects on a table (:TABLE), which has on it a box (:BOX). The rest of the physical objects are toys—blocks, pyramids, and balls. We give them the names :B1, :B2, :B3, . . .

Next we must decide on the set of concepts we will use to describe these objects and their properties. We can represent these in the form of a tree as shown in Fig. 40. The symbol #PHYSOB stands for "physical object," and #MANIP for "manipulable object" (i.e., something the robot can pick up).

We could use these as simple predicates just like (#BLUE :B5), and have assertions like (#ROBOT :SHRDLU), (#HAND :HAND), and (#PYRAMID :B5) to say that Shrdlu is a robot, the hand is a hand, and :B5 is a pyramid. Instead, for reasons involving the generation of English responses, as described in Section 8.3, we set these apart from other predicates. We use the concept #IS to mean "has as its basic description", and write (#IS :SHRDLU #ROBOT), (#IS :HAND #HAND), and (#IS :B5 #PYRAMID). Looking at the tree, we see that the properties #PHYSOB and #MANIP cannot be represented in this fashion, since any object having them also has a basic description. We therefore write (#MANIP :B5) and (#PHYSOB :TABLE).

Next, we assign physical properties to these objects, such as size, shape, color, and location. Shape and color are handled with simple assertions like (#COLOR :BOX #WHITE) and (#SHAPE :B5 #POINTED). The possible shapes are #ROUND, #POINTED, and #RECTAN-GULAR, and the colors are #BLACK, #RED, #WHITE, #GREEN, and #BLUE. To introduce any other shape or color name we need only use it in an assertion, like (#COLOR :B11 #MAUVE), and add an assertion telling what type of thing it is. The property names themselves can be seen as objects, and we have the concepts #COLOR and #SHAPE, to make assertions like (#IS #BLUE #COLOR), and (#IS #RECTANGULAR #SHAPE).

For size and location we use a three-dimensional coordinate system, with coordinates ranging from 0 to 1200 in all three directions. (The

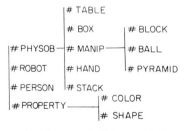

Fig. 40. Classification of Objects and Properties.

number 1200 was chosen for convenience in programming the display.) The coordinate point (0 0 0) is in the front lower left-hand corner of the scene. We assume that objects are not allowed to rotate, and therefore always kept their orientation aligned with the coordinate axes. We can represent the position of an object by the coordinates of its front lower left-hand corner, and its size by the three dimensions. We use the symbols #SIZE and #AT, and put the coordinate triples as a single element in the assertions. For example, we might have (#AT :B5 (400 600 200)), and (#SIZE :B5 (100 100 300)).

Since we assume that the robot has an eye, the system begins the dialog with complete information about the objects in the scene, their shapes, sizes, colors, and locations.

7.2 Relations

The basic relations we need are the spatial relations between objects, and, since we are interested in moving objects around, the #SUPPORT relation. The initial data base contains all of the applicable support relations for the initial scene, and every time an object is moved, an antecedent theorem removes the old assertion about what was supporting it, and puts in the correct new one. We have adopted a very simplified notion of support, in which an object is supported by whatever is directly below its center of gravity, at the level of its bottom face. Therefore, an object can support several others, but there is only one thing supporting it. Along with the #SUPPORT relations, we keep track of the property #CLEARTOP. The assertion (#CLEARTOP X) will be in the data base if and only if there is no assertion (#SUPPORT X Y) for any object Y. It is also kept current by antecedent theorems called whenever an object is moved. This happens automatically whenever an assertion of the form (#AT OBJ (X Y Z)) is made. The theorems check to see whether the #CLEARTOP status of any object has changed, and if so the necessary erasures and assertions are made.

Another relation kept in the data base is #CONTAIN. Information about what is contained in the box is kept current by an antecedent theorem. The relation #GRASPING is used to indicate what object (if any) the robot's hand is grasping. It is theoretically a two-place predicate, relating a grasper and a graspee, as in (#GRASPING :SHRDLU :B2). Since there is only one hand in our scene, it is clear who must be doing the grasping, so the assertion is reduced to (#GRASPING :B2). The same convention is followed for other relations involving :SHRDLU as a participant.

The #PART relation between an object and a stack is also stored in the data base. We can give a name to a stack, such as :S1, and assert

(#PART :B2 :S1). As objects are moved, the changes to the data base are again made by antecedent theorems which notice changes of location.

As explained in Section 6.2.3, we must decide what relations are useful enough to occupy space in our data base, and which should be re-computed from simpler information each time we need them. #SUP-PORT and #CONTAIN are often referenced in deciding how to move objects. Other relations, such as the relative position of two objects, are computed from their locations when needed. We represent these relations using the symbols #RIGHT, #BEHIND, and #ABOVE. (These represent the direction of the positive coordinate axes for X, Y, and Z, respectively). We do not need the converse relations, since we can represent a fact like ":B1 is below :B2" by (#ABOVE :B2 :B1), and our semantic system can convert what is said to this standard format. The symbol #ON is used to represent the transitive closure of #SUP-PORT. That is, Z is #ON A if A supports B, B supports C . . . supports Z.

The three spatial relations use a common consequent theorem called TC-LOC which decides if they are true by looking at the coordinates and sizes of the objects. The #ON relation has a consequent theorem TC-ON which looks for chains of support. (Notice that the prefix TC- stands for Theorem Consequent, and is attached to all of our consequent theorems. Similarly, TA- and TE- are used for antecedent and erasing theorems.)

#HEIGHT, #WIDTH, and #LENGTH are computed when needed from the #SIZE assertion, and can be accessed by using the theorem TC-MEASURE, or by using the name of the measure as a LISP function. The expression (#HEIGHT $?X) evaluates to the height of whatever object the variable X is bound to. If #SIZE is used in this way, it returns a measure of "overall size" to be used for comparisons like "bigger". Cur-rently it returns the sum of the X, Y, and Z coordinates, but it could be changed to a heuristic program more in accord with human judgments of size.

To compare measurements, we have the relation #MORE. The sentence ":B1 is shorter than :B2" is equivalent to the assertion (#MORE #HEIGHT :B2 :B1). Again, we do not need the relation "less" since we can simply reverse the order of the objects. #MORE, and the relation #ASMUCH, which expresses "greater than or equal", are computed as needed.

One final relationship is #OWN, which relates a person to any object. Knowledge about what the human user owns is gathered from his state-ments. The semantic programs can use statements about owning to generate further PLANNER theorems which are used to answer questions about what :FRIEND owns and make deductions needed to carry out commands.

7.3 Actions

Events in our world are actions taken by the robot. At the most basic level, there are only three actions which can occur: MOVETO, GRASP, and UNGRASP. These are the commands sent to the display routines, and could theoretically be sent directly to a physical robot system. MOVETO moves the hand and whatever it is currently grasping to a set of specified coordinates. GRASP sets an indicator that the grasped object is to be moved along with the hand, and UNGRASP unsets it. The robot grasps by moving its hand directly over the center of the object on its top surface, and turning on a "magnet". It can do this to any manipulable object, but can only grasp one thing at a time. Using these elementary actions, we can build a hierarchy of actions, including goals which may involve a whole sequence of actions. The result of calling a consequent theorem to achieve a goal requiring motion, like (#PUTON :B3 :B4), is not an action, but a plan—a list of instructions using the three elementary functions. For example, when PLANNER evaluates a statement like:

(THGOAL(#MOVEHAND (600 200 300)))

(THUSE TC-MOVEHAND))

nothing is actually moved. The theorem TC-MOVEHAND creates a plan to do the motion, but if necessary, the PLANNER backup mechanism can erase part or all of the plan.

The theorems also check to see if we are trying to do something physically impossible. For example, TC-MOVEHEAD makes sure the action would not involve placing a block where there is already an object, and TC-UNGRASP fails unless there is something supporting the object it wants to let go of. Conceptual impossibilities (like "Move an idea.") are handled by the semantic programs as explained in Section 8.

7.4 Carrying Out Commands

Some theorems, like TC-GRASP, are complex, as they can cause a series of actions. Figure 41 gives simplified definitions of various PLANNER theorems. Using these definitions, let us now follow PLANNER through a complex action in detail. If PLANNER tries the goal:

(THGOAL (#GRASP :B1)(THUSE TC-GRASP))

the theorem TC-GRASP can do a number of things. It checks to make sure :B1 is a graspable object by looking in the data base for (#MANIP :B1). If the hand is already grasping the object, it has nothing more to do. If not, it must first get the hand to the object. This may involve complications—the hand may already be holding something, or there may be objects sitting on top of the one it wants to grasp. In the first case, it must get rid of whatever is in the hand, using the command #GET-

```
(DEFTHEOREM TC-CLEARTOP
    (THCONSE (X Y) (#CLEARTOP $?X)
        GO    (THCOND ((THGOAL (#SUPPORT $?X $_Y))
                      (THGOAL (#GET-RID-OF $?Y)
                              (THUSE TC-GET-RID-OF))
                      (THGO GO))
                     ((THASSERT (#CLEARTOP $?X))))))

(DEFTHEOREM TC-GET-RID-OF
    (THCONSE (X Y) (#GET-RID-OF $?X)
        (THOR
            (THGOAL (#PUTON $?X :TABLE)(THUSE
                                        TC-PUTON))
            (THGOAL (#PUTON $?X $?Y)(THUSE TC-
                                        PUTON)))))

(DEFTHEOREM TC-GRASP
    (THCONSE (X Y) (#GRASP $?X)
        (THGOAL(#MANIP $?X))
        (THCOND ((THGOAL (#GRASPING $?X)))
                ((THGOAL (#GRASPING $_Y))
                 (THGOAL (#GET-RID-OF $?Y)
                         (THUSE TC-GET-RID-
                                        OF))))
            (T))
        (THGOAL (#CLEARTOP $?X) (THUSE TC-
                                        CLEARTOP))
        (THSETQ $_Y (TOPCENTER $?X))
        (THGOAL (#MOVEHAND $?Y)
                (THUSE TC-MOVEHAND))
        (THASSERT (#GRASPING $?X))))

(DEFTHEOREM TC-PUT
    (THCONSE (X Y Z) (#PUT $?X $?Y)
        (CLEAR $?Y (SIZE $?X) $?X)
        (SUPPORT $?Y (SIZE $?X) $?X)
        (THGOAL (#GRASP $?X) (THUSE TC-GRASP))
        (THSETQ $_Z (TCENT $?Y (SIZE $?X)))
        (THGOAL (#MOVEHAND $?Z) (THUSE
                                        TC-MOVEHAND))
        (THGOAL (#UNGRASP) (THUSE TC-
                                        UNGRASP))))

(DEFTHEOREM TC-PUTON
    (THCONSE (X Y Z) (#PUTON $?X $?Y)
        (NOT (EQ $?X $?Y))
        (THGOAL (#FINDSPACE $?Y $E (SIZE $?X)
                                        $?X $_Z)
                (THUSE TC-FINDSPACE TC-
                                        MAKESPACE))
        (THGOAL (#PUT $?X $?Z) (THUSE TC-PUT))))
```

Figure 41—Simplified PLANNER Theorems

RID-OF. The easiest way to get rid of something is to set it on the table, so TC-GET-RID-OF creates the goal (#PUTON $?X :TABLE), where the variable $?X is bound to the object the hand is holding. TC-PUTON after checking to see that it is not trying to put some object onto itself, must in turn find a big enough empty place to set down its burden. It uses the command #FINDSPACE, which performs the necessary calculations, using information about the sizes and locations of all the objects. TC-PUTON then creates a goal using #PUT, which calculates where the hand must be moved to get the object into the desired place, then calls #MOVEHAND to actually plan the move. If we look at the logical structure of our active goals at this point, assuming that we want to grasp :B1, but are presently grasping :B2, we see:

(#GRASP :B1)
    (#GET-RID-OF :B2)
        (#PUTON :B2 :TABLE)
            (#PUT :B2 (453 201 0))
                (#MOVEHAND (553 301 100))

After moving, TC-PUTON calls #UNGRASP, and we have achieved the first part of our original goal—emptying the hand. Now we must clear off the block we want to grasp. TC-GRASP sets up the goal:

(THGOAL(#CLEARTOP :B2)(THUSE TC-CLEARTOP))

This is a good example of the double use of PLANNER goals to both search the data base and carry out actions. If the assertion (#CLEAR-TOP :B1) is present, it satisfies this goal immediately without calling the theorem. However if :B1 is not already clear, this THGOAL statement calls TC-CLEARTOP which takes the necessary actions.

TC-CLEARTOP will try to #GET-RID-OF the objects on top of :B1. This will in turn use #PUTON, which uses #PUT. But TC-PUT may have more to do this time, since the hand is not already grasping the object it has to move. It therefore sets up a goal to #GRASP the object, recursively calling TC-GRASP again. Figure 42 lists the different action concepts more systematically, showing the form of the goal statements, and the actions taken by the theorems corresponding to them.

7.5 Memory

To answer questions about past events, the BLOCKS programs remember selected parts of their subgoal tree. They do this by creating objects called events, and putting them on an EVENTLIST. The system does not remember the detailed series of specific steps like #MOVE-HAND, but keeps track of the larger goals like #PUTON and #STACKUP. The time of events is measured by a clock which starts at 0 and is incremented by 1 every time any motion occurs. The theorems call the function MEMORY when the theorem is entered and MEMO-

Command	Effect
(#MOVEHAND (X Y Z))	Move the center of the hand to location (X Y Z). Anything being grasped goes along automatically.
(#UNGRASP)	Let go of whatever the hand is holding. Fails if the object is not supported.
(#GRASP X)	Grasp object X, doing any manipulations necessary to get to it.
(#PUT W (X Y Z))	Put W at location (X Y Z). Fails unless the space is empty.
(#RAISEHAND)	Raise the hand and whatever it holds as high as it will go.
(#PICKUP X)	Grasp X and raise the hand.
(#PUTON X Y)	Put object X on object Y. If there is not enough free space on Y, move objects to make it.
(#PUTIN X Y)	The same as #PUTON, except that Y must be a box, and different methods are used to find space.
(#GET-RID-OF X)	Try to put X on the table, and if that fails put it on anything else.
(#CLEARTOP X)	Get rid of everything which is on X.
(#STACKUP (X Y ...))	Stack X, Y, ... on top of each other, in order of size.
(#FINDSPACE A (X Y Z) B $_C)	This goal can be achieved by two different theorems. TC-FINDSPACE tries to find a space of size (X Y Z) on top of object A, counting any space occupied by B as empty. $ C is a variable binding used to return the answer. If this fails, TC-MAKESPACE can create the space by moving objects.

Figure 42—BLOCKS Commands.

REND when it exists. MEMOREND causes an event to be created, combining the original goal statement with an arbitrary name (chosen from E1, E2, . . .).

In addition to putting an assertion representing the event into the data base, MEMOREND puts information on the property list of the event name—the starting time, ending time, and reason for each event. The reason is the name of the event nearest up in the subgoal tree which is being remembered. The reason for goals called by the linguistic part of the system is a special symbol meaning "because you asked me to." MEMORY is called at the beginning of a theorem to establish the start time and declare that theorem as the "reason" for the subgoals it calls.

A second kind of memory keeps track of the actual physical motions of objects, noting each time one is moved, and recording its name and the location it went to. This list can be used to establish where any object was at any past time.

When we want to pick up block :B1, we can say: (THGOAL (#PICKUP :B1)), and it is interpreted as a command. We can also ask "Did you pick up :B1?", since when the robot picked it up, an assertion like (#PICKUP E2 :B1) was stored in the data base. If PLANNER evaluates:

(THPROG(X)
    (THGOAL (#PICKUP $?X :B1)))

it will find the assertion, binding the variable X to the event name E2. Since the property list of E2 gives its starting and ending times, and its reason, this is sufficient information to answer most questions.

If we want to ask something like "Did you pick up :B1 before you built the stack?" we need some way to look for particular time intervals. This is done by using a modified version of the event description, including a time indicator. The exact form of the time indicator is described in Section 8.1.8, but the way it is used to establish a goal is:

(THGOAL(#PICKUP $?X :B1 $?TIME)
    (THUSE TCTE-PICKUP))

The prefix TCTE- on the name of a theorem means that it includes a time and an event name. Ordinarily when such a theorem is entered, the variable TIME would have a value, while the variable X would not. The theorem looks through the data base for stored events of the form (#PICKUP $?X :B1) and checks them to see if they agree with the time TIME.

For some events, like #PUTON, this is sufficient since the system remembers every #PUTON it does. For others, like #PICKUP, less information is kept. When #PICKUP is called as a goal at the top level, it is remembered. But the system does not remember each time something was picked up in the course of moving the toys around. The fact that a block was picked up can be deduced from the fact that it was put somewhere, and the theorem TCTE-PICKUP actually looks at a number of different types of events (like #PUTON and #PUTIN) to find all the occasions on which an object was really picked up.

For spatial relations, we also need to be able to include time, for questions like, "Was the block behind the pyramid before . . .?" In this case, no assertions are stored, since the memory of motion events is sufficient to reconstruct the scene. There are special theorems with the prefix TCT- which try to verify a relation with a time condition. For example, we can ask "Is :B1 on :B2?" with the goal

(THGOAL(#ON :B1 :B2)(THUSE TC-ON))
To ask "Was :B1 on :B2 before . . .?" we bind the variable TIME to the
representation of the time we are interested in, and ask
(THGOAL(#ON :B1 :B2 $?TIME)(THUSE TCT-ON))
The theorem TCT-ON is the same as TC-ON except that it deals with
the specified time instead of the present. Similar TCT-theorems exist for
all of the spatial relations, and for properties which change in time, such
as #CLEARTOP and #AT.

Appendix C is a listing of parts of the BLOCKS program as it was used
in generating the sample dialog.

8. SEMANTICS

8.1 Semantic Structures

Section 1.6 outlined the structure of a semantic interpreter, and described the use of semantic "specialists," procedures for analyzing different
aspects of linguistic structure. These create parts of a complete description
of the meaning of the sentence by building complex list structures, which
we will call "semantic structures," to describe objects and relationships.
Events are a type of relationship involving time, and the class of "object"
includes anything which could be treated as an object in English grammar, even if it is as abstract as "truth". There are two basic types of
structures: an Object Semantic Structure, or OSS, and a Relation
Semantic Structure (RSS). In general, noun groups yield object structures,
and other groups and clauses form relationship structures. Words already
have semantic structures (their definition), which are used in building
up the structures for the larger units.

8.1.1 Object Semantic Structures

Let us first look at the semantic structures used to describe objects.
First, we need the actual PLANNER statements which will be used in
deducing things about the objects. An NG like "a red cube" can be described using the formalism of Sections 6 and 7 as in Fig. 43.

The variable "X1" represents the object, and this description says that
it should be a block, it should have equal dimensions, and it should be
red. (See Section 7 for the details of representation). A phrase such as
"a red cube which supports three pyramids but is not contained in a box"

```
(THPROG (X1)
   (THGOAL(#IS $?X1 #BLOCK))
   (#EQDIM $?X1)
   (THGOAL(#COLOR $?X1 #RED)))
```

Figure 43—Simple PLANNER Description

```
(THPROG(X1)
    (THGOAL( #IS $?X1 #BLOCK))
    ( #EQDIM $?X1)
    (THGOAL( #COLOR $?X1 #RED))
    (THFIND 3 $?X2 (X2) (THGOAL( #IS $?X2 #PYRAMID))
                        (THGOAL( #SUPPORT $?X1 $?X2)))
    (THNOT(THPROG(X3)
            (THGOAL( #IS $?X3 #BOX))
            (THGOAL( #CONTAIN $?X3 $?X1)))))
```

Figure 44—PLANNER Description

has a more complex description. This would be built up from the descriptions for the various objects, and would end up as in Fig. 44.

We can learn how the semantic specialists work by watching them build the pieces of this structure. First take the simpler NG, "a red cube". The first NG specialist doesn't start work until after the noun has been parsed. The PLANNER description is then built backwards, starting with the noun, and continuing in right-to-left order through the classifiers and adjectives. The beginning of the NG, with the determiner, number, and ordinal is handled by a part of the NG specialist described later. The first NG specialist is named SMNG1—all of the names begin with SM (for "semantic"), followed by the name of the unit they work with, followed by a number indicating the order in which they are called. SMNG1 sets up an environment (we will describe various parts of it as we go), then calls the definition of the noun. (Remember that definitions are in the form of programs). For simple nouns there is a standard function to define them easily. This includes, first, a way to indicate the PLANNER statements which are the heart of its meaning. The symbol "***" is used to represent the object, so our definition of "cube" contains the expression:

$$((\#IS *** \#BLOCK)(\#EQDIM ***))$$

The syntax of PLANNER functions such as THPROG and THGOAL will be added by the specialists, since we want to keep the definition as simple as possible.

There is one other part of the definition for a noun—the semantic markers, used to filter out meaningless interpretations of a phrase. The definition needs to attach these semantic markers to each OSS. The BLOCKS world uses the tree of semantic markers in Fig. 45.

As before, vertical bars represent choices of mutually exclusive markers, while horizontal lines represent logical dependency. The word "cube" refers to an object with the markers (#THING #PHYSOB #MANIP #BLOCK). We shouldn't need to mention all of these in the definition, since the presence of #BLOCK implies the others through the logical structure of the marker tree.

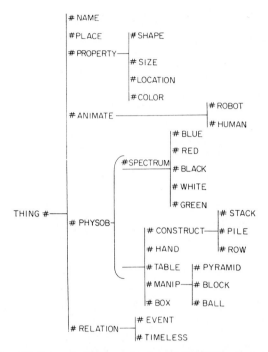

Fɪɢ. 45. Semantic Markers for the BLOCKS Vocabulary.

The definition of the noun "cube" is then:

(NMEANS((#BLOCK)((#IS *** #BLOCK)(#EQDIM ***))))

NMEANS is the name of the function for dealing with nouns, and it accepts a list of different meanings for a word. In this case, there is only one meaning. The first part of the definition is the marker list, followed by the reduced PLANNER definition. When NMEANS is executed, it puts this information onto the semantic structure which is being built for the object. It takes care of finding out what markers are implied by the tree, and deciding which predicates need to be in a THGOAL statement (like #IS), and which are LISP predicates (like #EQDIM). We will see later how it also can decide what recommendation lists to put onto the PLANNER goals, to guide the deduction.

SMNG1 then calls the definition for the adjective "red". We would like this definition to include the PLANNER assertion (#COLOR *** #RED), and indicate that it applies only to physical objects. We can use the same format used for nouns, defining "red" as:

(NMEANS((#PHYSOB)((#COLOR *** #RED))))

Notice that the same format is used to specify that #PHYSOB "applies only to physical objects" and that #BLOCK is part of the definition of "cube." This is because the marker list in a definition is interpreted to mean "this definition applies only if none of the markers here are in conflict with any of the markers already established for the object". Since the noun is the first thing interpreted, its markers cannot possibly conflict, and are simply entered as the initial marker list for the object. The marker programs permit us to classify objects along several dimensions, and set up separate marker trees for each. For example, we might classify objects both by their physical properties and by their use.

The order of analysis simplifies handling of "relative" modifiers. There is no absolute definition for "big" or "little"; a "big flea" is still not much competition for a "little elephant". The meaning of the adjective is relative to the noun it modifies, and it may also be relative to the adjectives following it as well, as in a "big toy elephant." Since our system analyzes the NG from right to left, the meaning of each adjective is added to the description already built up for the head and modifiers to the right. Since each definition is a program, it can just as well examine the description (both the semantic markers and the PLANNER description), and produce an appropriate meaning relative to the object being described. This may be an absolute measurement (e.g., a "big elephant" is more than 12 feet tall) or a relative PLANNER description of the form "the number of objects fitting the description and smaller than the one being described is more than the number of suitable objects bigger than it is".

In adding the meaning of "red" to the semantic structure, the specialist must make a choice in ordering the PLANNER expressions. We remember from Section 6.2.2 that the order of expressions can be important, since variable assignments are made in the order encountered. If we have the first sequence shown in Fig. 46, PLANNER will look through all of the blocks, checking until it finds one which is red. However if we have the second, it will look through all of the red objects until it finds one which is a block. In the robot's tiny world, this isn't of much importance, but if the data base took phrases like "a man in this room", we certainly would be better off looking around the room first to see what was a man, than looking through all the men in the world to see if one was in the room.

```
(THPROG(X)
        (THGOAL( #IS $?X  #BLOCK))
        (THGOAL( #COLOR $?X  #RED)))

(THPROG(X)
        (THGOAL( #COLOR $?X  #RED))
        (THGOAL( #IS $?X  #BLOCK)))
```

Figure 46—Ordering Goals

To make this choice we allow each predicate (like #IS or #COLOR) to have associated with it a program which knows how to evaluate its "priority" in any given environment. The program might be as simple as a single number, which would mean "this relation always has this priority". It might on the other hand be a complex heuristic program which takes into account the current state of the world and the discourse. The present system uses only the simpler alternative. By keeping track of the priority of the expression currently at the top of the PLANNER description, the function NMEANS can decide whether to add a new expression above or below it.

Figure 47 shows the structure which would be built up by the program.

Most of the parts of this structure have already been explained. The PLANNER description includes a variable list (we will see its use later), the priority of the first expression, and a list of PLANNER expressions describing the object. The "markers" position lists all of the semantic markers applicable to the object. The 0 at the beginning of the list is a place holder for a "plausibility value" for the interpretation of a unit. This value might be useful if we were faced with more than one possible interpretation of a word. The program includes mechanisms for carrying along with each semantic structure an accumulated plausibility rating. This remains 0 unless an ambiguity is detected. Since the present system involves only a single topic of discourse, no use is now made of this possibility.

The "systems" position is a list of all of the nodes in the set of marker trees (remember that there can be more than one) which have already had a branch selected. It is used in looking for marker conflicts. The "variable" is the variable name chosen to represent this object. The system generates it from the set X1, X2, X3 . . . , providing a new one for each new structure. The only two positions left are the determiner and the ordinal. These are explained in section 8.1.4.

```
( (  ((X1) 200 (THGOAL( #IS $?X1  #BLOCK))          PLANNER
              (THGOAL( #COLOR $?X1 #RED))           description
              ( #EQDIM $?X1))

      (0 #BLOCK  #MANIP  #PHYSOB  #THING)            markers

      ( #MANIP  #PHYSOB  #THING))                    systems

   X1                                               variable

   (NS INDEF NIL)                                   determiner

   NIL)                                             ordinal
```

Figure 47—OSS for "a red cube"

8.1.2 *Relative Clauses*

Let us now take a slightly more complicated NG, "a red cube which supports a pyramid," and follow the parsing and semantic analysis. First, the NG parsing program finds the determiner ("a"), adjective ("red"), and noun ("cube"). At this point SMNG1 is called and creates the structure described in the previous section. Notice that SMNG1 is called before the NG is finished, as soon as an initial semantic analysis is possible· At this point, the NG might be rejected without further parsing if the combination of noun, classifiers, and adjectives is contradictory to the system of semantic markers.

Next the NG program looks for a qualifier, and calls the CLAUSE part of the grammar by (PARSE CLAUSE RSQ). The feature RSQ (rank shifted qualifier) informs the CLAUSE program that it should look for a RELWD like "which". It does find the word, and then looks for a VG, succeeding with "supports." The VG program calls its own semantic specialist to analyze the time reference of the clause, but we will ignore this for now. Next, since "support" is transitive, the CLAUSE looks for an object, and calls the NG program once again. This operates in the same way as before, producing a semantic structure to describe "a pyramid". The definition of "pyramid" is:

(NMEANS((#PYRAMID)((#IS *** #PYRAMID))))

so the resulting structure is shown in Fig. 48.

At this point the first CLAUSE specialist is called to analyze the clause "which supports a pyramid." We want to define verbs in a simple way, as we do nouns and adjectives, saying something like "If the subject and object are both physical objects, then "support" means the relation #SUPPORT between them in that order." This is written formally using the function CMEANS, as:

(CMEANS((((#PHYSOB))((#PHYSOB)))

(#SUPPORT #1 #2)NIL))

The extra parentheses are there to leave room for options to be described later. The important parts are the semantic marker lists for the objects participating in the relationship, and the actual PLANNER expression naming it. The symbols "#1" and "#2" (and "#3" if necessary)

```
(    (    ((X2) 200 (THGOAL( #IS $?X2 #PYRAMID)))
          (O #PYRAMID #MANIP #PHYSOB #THING)
          (#MANIP #PHYSOB #THING))
     X2
     (NS INDEF NIL)
     NIL)
```

Figure 48—OSS for "a pyramid"

are used to indicate the objects, and the normal order is: (1) semantic subject (SMSUB); (2) semantic first object (SMOB1); (3) semantic second object (SMOB2). Notice that we have prefixed "semantic" to each of these, since they may not be the syntactic subject and objects of the clause. In this example, the SMSUB is the NG "a red cube" to which the clause is being related. SMCL1 knows this since the parser has noted the feature SUBJREL. Before calling the definition of the verb, SMCL1 found the OSS describing "a red cube" and set it as the value of the variable SMSUB. Similarly it put the OSS for "a pyramid" in SMOB1, since it is the object of the clause. The definition of the verb "support" is now called, and CMEANS uses the information in the definition to build up a Relation Semantic Structure. First it checks to make sure that both objects are compatible with their respective marker lists. The marker lists are in the same order as the symbols #1, #2, and #3. In this case, both the subject and object must be physical objects.

Next SMCL1 substitutes the objects into the relation. If it inserted the actual semantic structures, the result would be hard to read and time-consuming to print. Instead, the NG specialists assign a name to each OSS, from the set NG1, NG2, NG3, ... We therefore get (#SUPPORT NG1 NG2) as the description of the relationship. The final semantic structure for the clause (after a second specialist, SMCL2 has had a chance to look for modifiers and rearrange the structure into a convenient form) is in Fig. 49.

The position marked "rel" holds the name of the NG description to which this clause serves as a modifier. We will see later that it can be used in a more general way as well. The "relation" is the material PLAN-NER uses, and "neg" marks whether the clause is negative or not.

The last element is a set of semantic markers and a priority, just as we had with object descriptions. Relationships have the full capability to use semantic markers just as objects do, and at an early stage of building a relation structure, it contains a PLANNER description, markers, and systems in forms identical to those for object structures (this is to share some of the programs, such as those which check for conflicts between markers). We can classify different types of events and relationships (for example, those which are changeable, those which involve physical motion, etc.) and use the markers to help filter out interpretations of clause modifiers. For example, in the sentence "He left the house without the shopping list," the modifying PREPG "without the shopping list"

(NG1	(#SUPPORT NG1 NG2)	NIL)	(O))
rel	relation	neg	markers

Figure 49—Relation Semantic Structure 1

```
(  (     ((X1  X2)   200   (THGOAL(#IS  $?X1  #BLOCK))
                           (THGOAL(#COLOR  $?X1  #RED))
                           (#EQDIM  $?X1)
                           (THGOAL(#IS  $?X2  #PYRAMID))
                           (THGOAL(#SUPPORT  $?X1  $?X2)))
          (O  #BLOCK  #MANIP  #PHYSOB  #THING)
          (#MANIP  #PHYSOB  #THING))
    X1
    (NS  INDEF  NIL)
    NIL)
```

FIG. 50—OSS for "a red cube which supports a pyramid."

has a different interpretation from "without a hammer" in "He built the house without a hammer." If we had a classification of activities which included those involving motion and those using tools, we could choose the correct interpretation. A system can be constructed which operates much like Fillmore's (1968) case system, assigning classes of verbs according to the type of modification they take, and using this to find the correct relation between a verb and its modifying phrase.

In our limited world, we have not set up a marker tree for relationships and events, so we have not included any markers in the definition of "support". The marker list in the RSS therefore contains only the plausibility, 0. The "NIL" indicates that there are no markers, and would be replaced by a list of markers if they were used.

The clause is now finished, and the specialist on relative clauses (SMRSQ) is called. It takes the PLANNER descriptions of the objects involved in the relation, along with the relation itself, and puts the information onto the PLANNER description of the object to which the clause is being related. The procedure depends on the exact form of the different objects (particularly on their determiners). In this case, it is relatively easy, and the description of "a red cube which supports a pyramid" is shown in Fig. 50.

The only thing which has changed is the PLANNER description, which now holds all of the necessary information. Its variable list contains both X1 and X2, and these variable names have been substituted for the symbols NG1 and NG2 in the relation, which has been combined with the separate PLANNER descriptions for the objects. Section 8.1.4 describes how a relative clause works with other types of NG descriptions.

8.1.3 Preposition Groups

Comparing the phrase "a red cube which supports a pyramid" with the phrase "a red cube under a pyramid" we see that relative clauses and qualifying prepositional phrases are very similar in structure and meaning. In fact, their semantic analysis is almost identical. The definition of a preposition like "under" uses the same function as the definition of a verb like "support", saying "if the semantic subject and object are both physical objects, then the object is #ABOVE the subject" (Remember that in our BLOCKS world we chose to represent all vertical space relations using the concept #ABOVE). This can be formalized as:

(CMEANS((((#PHYSOB))((#PHYSOB))))

(#ABOVE #2 #1)NIL)

Again, the symbols #1 and #2 refer to the semantic subject and semantic first object, but in the case of a preposition group used as a qualifier, the SMSUB is the NG of which the PREPG is a part, while the SMOB1 is the object of the PREPG (the PREPOBJ). As with clauses, the situation may be more complex. For example, in a sentence like "Who was the antelope I saw you with last night?", the SMOBJ of the PREP "with" is the question element "who" in the MAJOR CLAUSE. However, the PREPG specialist (SMPREP) takes care of all this, and in defining a preposition, we can deal directly with the SMSUB and the SMOB1. Notice that if we had been defining "above" instead of "under", everything would have been the same except that the relation would have been (#ABOVE #1 #2) instead of (#ABOVE #2 #1). If the PREPG is an adjunct to a CLAUSE, the SMSUBJ is the RSS defining the CLAUSE. The definition of a preposition can then use the semantic markers which are included in an RSS.

8.1.4 Types of Object Descriptions

In the examples so far, all of the objects described have been singular and indefinite, like "a red cube", and the semantic system has been able to assign them a PLANNER variable and use it in building their properties into the description. Let us consider another simple case, a definite object, as in "a red cube which supports *the pyramid*".

The analysis begins exactly as it did for the earlier case, building a description of "red cube", then one of "pyramid." The "pyramid" description differs from OSS 2 in having DEF in place of INDEF in its determiner. This is noted at the very beginning of the analysis, but has no effect until the entire NG (including any qualifiers) has been parsed. At that time, the second NG specialist SMNG2 checks for a definite NG and tries to determine what it refers to before going on. The PLANNER description which has been built up is given to PLANNER in a THFIND ALL expression. The result is a list of all objects fitting the description. Presumably if the speaker used "the", he must be referring to a particular object he expects the listener to be aware of. If more than one object fits the description, there are various discouse heuristics used to find the reference (see Section 8.2.3), and if nothing succeeds, a failure message

```
( (X1) 200 (THGOAL( #IS $?X1 #BLOCK))
           ( #EQDIM $?X1)
           (THGOAL( #COLOR $?X1 #RED))
           (THGOAL( #SUPPORT $?X1 :B5)))
```

Figure 51—PLANNER Description 1
"a red cube which supports the pyramid"

is produced and the parser has to back up and try something else to parse the NG.

If SMNG2 is able to find the object being referred to, it puts it into the description (on the property list). When the Semantic Rank Shifted Qualifier specialist (SMRSQ) relates the descriptions to build the meaning of "a red cube which supports the pyramid" it takes advantage of this. The object found will have a proper name like :B5. Instead of building the PLANNER description of Fig. 50, it builds the one in Fig. 51. The object itself is used in the relation rather than dealing with its description.

What if we had asked about "a red cube which supports three pyramids"? In that case the PLANNER description would include an expression using the function THFIND with a numerical parameter, as shown in Fig. 52. If we had said "a red cube which supports at most two pyramids", a fancier THFIND parameter would have been used, as shown. Here, the parameter means "be satisfied if you don't find any,

```
(THGOAL( #IS   $?X2   #PYRAMID))
(THGOAL( #SUPPORT   $?X1   $?X2))
                    "which supports a pyramid"
(THGOAL( #SUPPORT   $?X1   :B3))
                    "which supports the pyramid"
(THFIND   3   $?X2   (X2).  (THGOAL( #IS   $?X2   #PYRAMID))
                           (THGOAL( #SUPPORT   $?X1   $?X2)))
                    "which supports three pyramids"
(THFIND   (O   3   NIL)   $?X2   (X2)
                           (THGOAL( #IS   $?X2   #PYRAMID))
                           (THGOAL( #SUPPORT   $?X1   $?X2)))
                    "which supports at most two pyramids"
(THNOT
    (THPROG   (X2)   (THGOAL( #IS   $?X2   #PYRAMID))
                     (THGOAL( #SUPPORT   $?X1   $?X2)))))
                    "which supports no pyramids"
(THNOT
    (THPROG   (X2)   (THGOAL( #IS   $?X2   #PYRAMID))
                     (THNOT
                         (THGOAL( #SUPPORT   $?X1   $?X2)))))
                    "which supports every pyramid"
```

FIG. 52—Quantifiers.

but if you find 3, immediately cause a failure." In addition to numbers, the SMNG1 and RSQ programs can work together to relate descriptions of quantified objects. "A red cube which supports *some* pyramid" is handled just like the original indefinite case. "A red cube which supports *no* pyramid" and "a red cube which supports *every* pyramid" are handled using the other PLANNER primitives. A universal quantifier is translated as "there is no pyramid which the red cube does not support". For the robot, "every" means "every one I know about". This is not a requirement of PLANNER, or even of the way we have set up our semantic programs. The system could be expanded to discuss universal statements as well as the specific commands and questions it now handles.

We similarly handle the whole range of quantifiers and types of numbers, using the logical primitives and THFIND parameters of PLANNER. The work is actually done in two places. SMNG1 takes the words and syntactic features, and generates the "determiner" which was one of the ingredients of our semantic structure for objects. The determiner contains three parts (see Fig. 53). First, the number is either NS (singular, but not with the specific number "one"), NPL (plural with no specific number), NS–PL (ambiguous between the two, as in "the fish"), or a construction containing an actual arithmetic number. This can either be the number alone, or a combination with ">", "<", or "exactly". Thus the two noun groups "at most 2 days" and "fewer than 3 days" produce the identical determiner, containing "(<3)". The second element of the determiner is either DEF, INDEF, ALL, NO, or NDET (no determiner at all—as in "We like *sheep*.") The third is saved for the question types HOWMANY and WHICH, so it is NIL in a NG which is not a QUEST or REL.

Other specialists such as SMRSQ and the answering routines use this information to produce PLANNER expressions like the ones described above. In addition, there are special programs for cases like the OF NG, as in "three *of* the blocks". In this case, the PREPOBJ following "of" is evaluated as a NG first. Since "the blocks" is definite, PLANNER is called to find out what it refers to. It returns a list of the blocks, (e.g., (:B1 :B4 :B6 :B7)). The OF specialist uses the PLANNER function THAMONG (which chooses its variable bindings from "among" a given list) to produce an expression like:

(THFIND 3 $?X1 (X1) (THAMONG X1
                      (QUOTE(:B1 :B4 :B6 :B7)))))

Ordinals are treated specially, along with superlative adjectives. If we have a NG like "the biggest block which supports a pyramid", it is impossible for SMNG1 to add the meaning of "biggest" to the description in the same way as it would add an expression for "big". The block is

Number

NS	an apple
NPL	some thoughts
7	seven sisters
(>2)	at least three ways
(<5)	fewer than five people
(EXACTLY 2)	exactly two minutes

Determiner

DEF	the law
INDEF	a riot
ALL	every child
NO	nothing
NDET	good intentions

Question Marker

HOWMANY	how many years
WHICH	which road

Figure 53—Examples of Determiner Elements

"biggest" with respect to a group of objects, and that group is not fully defined until the entire NG has been parsed, including the qualifiers. SMNG1 therefore does a partial analysis of the meaning, looking up the name of the measure the particular adjective refers to, then hangs the result in the last niche of the OSS described in Section 8.1.1. After all has been parsed, SMNG2 finds it there and creates a full logical description. In the case of "the biggest block which supports a pyramid", we would get the PLANNER description in Fig. 54. A similar type of description is generated for other superlatives and ordinals.

8.1.5 The Meaning of Questions

So far, we have discussed the semantics of objects and the relationships which are used to describe them in preposition groups and relative clauses. Now we will deal with the overall meaning of a sentence as an

```
((X1 X2 X3 X4 ) 200
    (THGOAL(#IS $?X1 #BLOCK))
    (THGOAL(#IS $?X2 #PYRAMID))
    (THGOAL(#SUPPORT $?X1 $?X2))
    (THNOT
        (THAND(THGOAL(#IS $?X3 #BLOCK))
              (THGOAL(#IS $?X4 #PYRAMID))
              (THGOAL(#SUPPORT $?X3 $?X4))
              (THGOAL(#MORE #SIZE $?X3 $?X1)))))))
```

Figure 54—PLANNER Description 2
"the biggest block which supports a pyramid"

utterance—as a statement, a question, or a command. The·sentence is analyzed into a relationship semantic structure, and the system must act on it by responding, taking an action, or storing some knowledge.

First let us look at questions. In describing the grammar of clauses (see Section 3.1) we pointed out the similarities between questions and relative clauses, which share a large part of the system network and the parsing program. They also have much in common on a semantic level. We can look at most questions as being a relative clause to some *focus* element in the sentence.

In the class of WH questions, this resemblance is easy to see. First we can take a NGQ question, whose question element is a NG. The question "Which red cube supports a pyramid?" is very closely related to the NG "a red cube which supports a pyramid." The system can answer such a question by relating the clause to the object, and building a description of "a red cube which supports a pyramid." It then takes this entire PLANNER description and puts it into a THFIND ALL statement, which is evaluated in PLANNER. The result is a list of objects fitting the description, and is in fact the answer to our question. Of course PLAN-NER might find several objects or no objects meeting the description. In this case we need answers like "none of them" or "two of them". Section 8.3 describes how responses to questions such as these are generated, depending on the relation between the specific question and the data found. If the question is "how many" instead of "which", the system goes through the identical process, but answers by counting rather than naming the objects found.

No matter what type of NGQ we have (there is a tremendous variety—see Section 3.1) the same method works. We treat the MAJOR clause as a relative clause to the NG which is the question element, and which we call the focus. This integrates the relationship intended by the clause into the description of that object. PLANNER then finds all objects satisfying the expanded description, and the results are used to generate an answer.

Next, we have the QADJ questions, like "when", "why", and "how". In these cases the focus is on an *event* rather than on one element of the relation. If we ask "Why did you pick up a block?", we are referring to an event which was stored in the system's memory as (#PICKUP E23 :B5) where :B5 is the name of the object picked up, and E23 is the arbitrary name which was assigned to the event (see Section 7.5 for a description of the way such information is stored.) We can ask in PLANNER:

```
(THFIND ALL $?EVENT ($?EVENT $?X)
    (THGOAL(#PICKUP $?EVENT $?X))
    (THGOAL(#IS $?X #BLOCK)))
```

In other words, "Find all of the events in which you picked up a block." This is clearly the first thing which must be done before we can answer "why". Once it has been done, answering is easy, since PLANNER will return as the value of THFIND a list of names of such events. On the property list of an event we find the name of the event for which it was called as a subgoal (the "reason"). We need only to describe this in English. Similarly if the question is "when", the property list of the event gives its starting and ending times. If the question is "how" it takes a little more work, since the subgoal tree is stored with only upward links. But by looking on the EVENTLIST, the system can generate a list of all those goals which had as their reason the one mentioned in the sentence.

This concept of a relation as a sort of object called an "event" is useful in other parts of the semantics as well—for instance in dealing with embedded clauses as in "the block which I told you to pick up". This is described in section 8.1.12.

"Where" is sometimes handled differently, as it may be either a constituent of a clause, such as a location object (LOBJ) (in "Where did you put it?") or an ADJUNCT (as in "Where did you meet him?"). The first case is handled just like the NG case, making the clause a relative, as if it were "the place where you put it", then asking in PLANNER:

(THFIND ALL $?PLACE (PLACE EVENT)
    (THGOAL (#PUT $?EVENT :OBJ $?PLACE)))

The ADJUNCT case involves a special #LOCATION assertion, as in:

(THFIND ALL $?PLACE (PLACE EVENT)
    (THGOAL(#MEET $?EVENT :YOU :HIM))
    (THGOAL(#LOCATION $?EVENT $?PLACE)))

In this example, we have moved away from the BLOCKS world, which does not contain in its vocabulary any actions that occur at a specific place without the place being mentioned in the event. However the semantic system is perfectly capable of handling such cases.

So far, we have seen that we can answer WH- questions by pretending they are a relative to some object, event, or place, and by adding the relationship to the description of this focus. It is an interesting fact about English that even in a YES-NO question, where there is no question element, there is usually a focus. Consider a simple question like "Does the box contain a block?" Someone might answer "Yes, a red one.", as if the question had been "Which block does the box contain?" Notice that "Yes, the box." would not have been an appropriate answer. Something about "the box" makes it obvious that it is not the focus. It is not its place as subject or object, since "Is a block in the box?" reverses these roles, but demands the same answer. Clearly it is the fact that "a block" is an indefinite NG.

The fact that a speaker says "a block" instead of "the block" indicates that he is not sure of a specific object referred to by the description. Even if he does not inquire about it specifically, the listener knows that the information will be new, and possibly of interest since he mentioned the object. In answering "Does the box contain a block?", our system does the same thing it would do with "How many blocks does the box contain?". It adds the relation "contained by the box" to the description of "a block", and finds all of the objects meeting this description. Of course the verbal answer is different for the two types of question. In one case, "Yes" is sufficient, while in the other "one" is. But the logical deduction needed to derive it is identical. In fact, our system uses this extra information by replying, "Yes, two of them: a red one and a green one." This may sometimes be verbose, but usually gives a natural sounding answer. It takes on the "intelligent" character of telling the questioner information he would be interested in knowing, even when he doesn't ask for it explicitly.

In YES-NO questions, it is not always easy to determine the focus. Only an INDEF NG which is not embedded in another NG can be the focus, but there may be several of them in a sentence. Sometimes there is no way to choose, but that is rare. In asking a question, people usually focus their attention on a particular object or event. There are a number of devices for indicating the focus. For example a quantifier, like "any" or a TPRON like "something" emphasizes the NG more than a simple determiner like "a". In both "Does anything green support a block?", and "Does a block support anything green?", the phrase "anything green" is the focus. When none of these cues are present, the syntactic function of the NG makes a difference. If we ask "Is there a block on a table", then "block" is the focus, since it is the subject while "table" is inside a PREPG. Our system contains a heuristic program which takes into account the kind of determiners, number features (singular is more likely than plural), syntactic position, and other such factors in choosing a focus. If it is in fact very difficult to choose in a given case, it is likely that the speaker will be satisfied with any choice.

For sentences in the past tense, which contain no focus NG, we can again have an event as a focus. If we ask, "Did Jesse James rob the stagecoach?", a possible answer, interpreting the event as the focus, is "Yes, three times: yesterday, last week, and a year ago." This is closely parallel to answering questions in which the focus is an object.

There are some questions which have no focus, such as present-tense clauses with only definite noun groups. These however, are even easier to answer, since they can be expressed in the form of a simple set of assertions with no variables. The NG analysis finds the actual objects referred to by a definite NG, and these are used in place of the variable in relationships. We can therefore answer "yes" or "no" by making a goal of the relationship and letting PLANNER evaluate it. The question "Does the red cube support the box?" would generate the simple PLANNER expression

(THGOAL (#SUPPORT :B3 :BOX))

if :B3 is the internal name for the red cube. PLANNER would return a non-NIL value only if the answer were "yes".

8.1.6 *Interpreting Imperatives*

The system can accept commands in the form of IMPERATIVE sentences. These are handled somewhat differently from questions. If they contain only definite objects, they can be treated in the way mentioned above for questions with no focus. The command "Pick up the red ball.", is translated into the relationship (#PICKUP :B7) which can be evaluated directly by putting it in a THGOAL statement which will carry out the action:

(THGOAL (#PICKUP :B7)(THUSE TC-PICKUP))

However, if we say "Pick up *a* red ball.", the situation is different. We could first use THFIND to find a red ball, then put this object in a simple goal statement as we did with "*the* red ball". This, however, might be a bad idea. In choosing a red ball arbitrarily, we may choose one which is out of reach or which is supporting a tower. The robot might fail or be forced to do a lot of work which it could have avoided with a little thought.

Instead, we send the theorem which works on the goal a description rather than an object name, and let the theorem choose the specific object to be used, according to the criteria which best suit it. Remember that each OSS has a name like "NG45". Before a clause is related to its objects, these are the symbols used in the relationship.

When we analyze "Pick up a red ball", it will actually produce (#PICKUP NG45), where NG45 names an OSS describing "a red ball." We use this directly as a goal statement, calling a special theorem which knows how to use these descriptions. The theorem calls a theorem named TC-FINDCHOOSE, which uses the description of the object, along with a set of "desirable properties" associated with objects used for trying to achieve the goal. #PICKUP may specify that it would prefer picking up something which doesn't support anything, or something near the hand's current location. Each theorem can ask for whatever it wants. Of course, it may be impossible to find an object which fits all of the requirements, and the theorem has to be satisfied with what it can get. TC-FIND-CHOOSE tries to meet the full specifications first, but if it can't find an object (or enough objects in the case of plural), it gradually removes the restrictions in the order they were listed in the theorem. It must always keep the full requirements of the description input in English in order to carry out the specified command. The robot simply tries to choose those objects which fit the command but are also the easiest for it to use.

8.1.7 Accepting Declarative Information

In addition to questions and commands, the system can accept declarative sentences. We have intentionally not emphasized them, as there are theoretical problems and dangers in designing a program to accept information in this way. In Section 1.5, we discussed the complex world-model a person has and explained why we felt that intelligence needed a highly structured and coordinated body of knowledge rather than a set of separate uniform facts or axioms. It is comparatively easy to get a program to add new information of the latter type, but very difficult to get it to add the former, since this involves understanding the relationship between the new information and whatever is already there.

Therefore, although we have included declarative sentences in our dialog (and they are fully handled in the grammar), we believe that before trying to "tell" many things to a program, we need to have a better idea of how knowledge should be structured; the program should approach new information as a problem solving activity rather than a clerical one.

When a human sees a new sentence, he does not simply store it away, but he relates it to what he already knows, perhaps changing his "programs", or ignoring the content of the sentence and interpreting something about the person who said it. A language understander needs to have an interpreter which looks at each new sentence and decides how to use it. This may include checking it for consistency with what it already knows, creating new data or types of data in its storage, modifying theorems, and many other possibilities.

In our system we have four different ways in which information can be accepted in a declarative sentence. The first is a simple word definition facility. If we say "A 'marb' is a red block which is behind a box.", the system recognizes that we are defining a new word. It currently recognizes this by the quote marks, but it could just as easily declare all unfamiliar words as possible new words. We have not done this as it would eliminate the feature that the system immediately recognizes typing errors without waiting to begin parsing the sentence.

In this kind of definition, the complement of the sentence is a noun group, which has an OSS. We save this OSS and generate a new dictionary entry for the word, defined syntactically as a noun, and with its semantic definition being the program "set the object description to this one we saved earlier." Remember that all definitions are programs, so this one fits in with no problem. When it is called on to build part of the description, it simply inserts the description used to define it. If we talk about "two big marbs", the system will build a description exactly like the one for "two big red blocks which are behind a box."

The second kind of information the system accepts is simple assertions involving a predicate for which it does not have complete knowledge. As we mentioned in Section 7, the system has complete data about the physical characteristics of the objects in the scene. We have selected #OWN as an arbitrary relation about which the system knows nothing except what it is told in the dialog. If we say "I own you." this produces the assertion· (#OWN :FRIEND :SHRDLU), which is simply added to the data base. The system also understands pronouns like "mine".

If we use an object which isn't definite, as in "I own red blocks.", the system uses the object description to generate a simple PLANNER consequent theorem. It creates a theorem of the form:
(THCONSE (X1)
  (#OWN :FRIEND $?X1)
            (THGOAL (#IS $?X1 #BLOCK))
            (THGOAL (#COLOR $?X1 #RED)))
This theorem says "Whenever you want to prove that the user owns something, you can do it by proving that it is a block and it is red." This is added to the theorem data base, and can be used to answer questions or carry out deductions. The system does not separate types of non-definite objects and assumes universal quantification. The results would have been the same if the sentence used "any red block", "every red block", "all red blocks", or (wrongly) "a red block." A more complete treatment is one of the possible extensions of the system.

It does notice the form "no red blocks" and uses this for the fourth kind of information. If we say "I own no red blocks.", it sets up the theorem:
(THCONSE (X1)
  (#OWN :FRIEND $?X1)
            (THGOAL (#IS $?X1 #BLOCK))
            (THGOAL (#COLOR $?X1 #RED)))
            (THFAIL THGOAL))
When the system is trying to prove that we own something, this theorem is called just like the one above. But this time, after it finds out that the object is a red block, it does not succeed. Instead, it uses the PLANNER function THFAIL, to cause not just that theorem but the entire goal to fail, regardless of what other theorems there are. We can

also accept a sentence like this with a positive NG but a negative clause, as in "I don't own the red block" or "I don't own any red blocks," producing a similar theorem.

8.1.8 *Time*

One of the most complex parts of English semantics is temporal relationships. It was pointed out earlier that one of the primary differences between the clause and other units such as the NG or PREPG is the special set of mechanisms within the clause for handling time. In this section we will describe how those mechanisms operate both within the clause and at other levels of syntax. The semantic programs for dealing with time can be described in three parts—the form of structures used to represent time, the way those structures are created, and the way they are used in understanding and deduction.

Time Semantic Structures (TSS). For the purposes of our BLOCKS world, we have treated only a simple part of the overall range of time references in English. In particular we have dealt only with references to actual events which happened in the past or are occurring in the present, not with the many varieties of future events, possible events, conditional events, etc. With this simplification the system can use a simple linear time scale (like a clock), relating all events to specific numerical times. This does not mean that a single event must occur at a single time—it may continue for a period of time during which other events are occurring.

English makes a clear distinction between events which are thought of as occurring at a particular time, and those which are pictured as continuing over an interval. This contrast is expressed both in the choice of verbs and in the shape of the VG containing the verb.

Verbs like "like", and "know", are inherently *progressive*. They express a relationship which continues over a period of time. Verbs like "hit", and "write" are not progressive, but indicate the completion of an action as a whole. Of course, this action also involves a process, and there is a way to express this aspect by using tenses whose first element is PRESENT such as PRESENT IN PAST. The sentence "I broke it." is not progressive, giving the feeling of a single momentary act. "I was breaking it." emphasizes the process of breaking, to which other events can be related.

In the present tense, the distinction is clear. The present of a progressive verb has the expected meaning, as in "I know your name." With a nonprogressive verb, there is a special meaning of habitual or repeated action, as in "I break bottles." In order to produce the meaning usually considered "present," the verb group must be PRESENT IN PRESENT, as in "I am breaking bottles."

Ambiguities can arise from verbs which are both progressive and non-

A supports B	(PRES) T :NOW :NOW
A supported B before time 23	(PAST) T NIL 23
A hit B before time 23	(PAST) NIL NIL 23
You built it after time 24	(PAST) NIL 24 NIL
You were building it after time 24	(PAST) T 24 NIL

Figure 55—Time Semantic Structures

progressive. The question "Did the red block touch the green one while you were building the stack?" has two interpretations. One means "Was it in contact during that time?", while the other asks "Did it make contact during that time?" If the verb were replaced by "support", only the analog of the first meaning would be valid, while "hit" would involve the second. The representation for time references must take this progressivity into account in trying to interpret time modifiers.

The representation used for time has four elements: the tense, an indicator for progressive, a starting time limit, and an ending time limit. Either or both of the limits may be omitted. Some examples of sentences and their corresponding structures are shown in Fig. 55.

The difference between the last two examples in Fig. 55 can be visualized by drawing a time line as in Fig. 56.

A nonprogressive action must begin after the start time, and end before the end time. A progressive one begins before the start time and ends after the end time. The TSS for "you hit it during event 23" (assuming event 23 began at time 3 and ended at 7) would be

(PAST) NIL 3 7

i.e., the hit began after event 23 started and ended before it ended. The sentence "you were hitting it during event 23" would be:

(PAST) T 7 3

i.e., the hitting began before event 23 was over, but ended after it had begun. This covers all ways of having the two events overlap. The

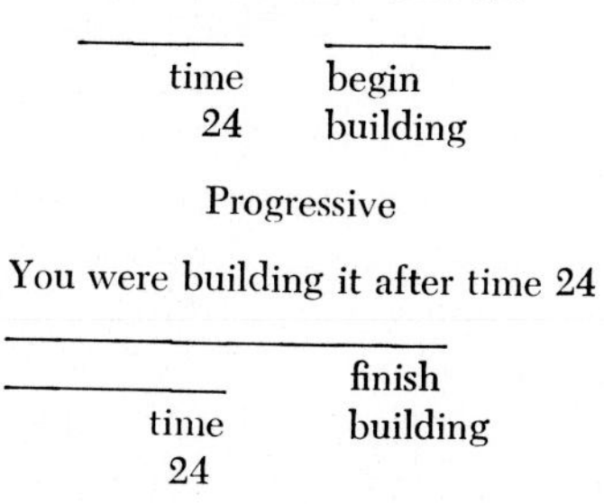

Non-Progressive

You built it after time 24

time	begin
24	building

Progressive

You were building it after time 24

	finish
time	building
24	

Figure 56—Progressive and non-Progressive Times

definitions of the relating words like "during" and "before" do not have explicit mention of this distinction, but the semantic analysis programs take into account whether the verb and VG are progressive in setting up the TSS.

Setting Up Time Structures. Time Semantic Structures are associated with clauses, and a new one is generated each time a clause is parsed. Its elements are determined by different aspects of the clause structure—the tense depends on the form of the VG, the progressivity depends on both the tense and the specific verb, and the limits are set by modifiers such as bound clauses, adverbs, and time noun groups as well as by the tense.

No analysis is done until after the VG is parsed and the tense established. Some types of secondary clauses such as ING, SUBING, TO, and SUBTO do not indicate a tense. There is a potential ambiguity in determining the time reference. "The man sitting on the table baked the bread." might indicate that the man was sitting on the table when he baked it, or that he is sitting on the table now.

Unless there is a specific reference (like "the man sitting on the table yesterday . . .") the system should take both possibilities into account and resolve them as it would an ambiguity caused by multiple senses of words. The current system does not do this, but uses a simplifying heuristic. If the secondary clause involves PAST, and is embedded in a PAST MAJOR CLAUSE, the two times are assumed the same unless specifically mentioned. If the secondary clause has no tense, it is assumed PRESENT. If it is PAST, but imbedded in a PRESENT MAJOR CLAUSE, the system checks the time reference of the previous sentence. If this is PAST, the new one is assumed to be the same (including whatever modifiers, limits, etc. applied). If not it sets up a general time structure for PAST, with no beginning limit, and an end limit of :NOW. A PRESENT tense TSS is represented by the single atom :NOW, which is treated specially by the programs, and is often deleted from relations which interrogate the current state of the data base (see below). It can be applied only to progressive verbs and tenses (no provision now exists for understanding habitual action). Modals are treated like the present tense in establishing time references. A more complete system would account for future tenses, different types of modals, and more complex tenses.

The start and end limits are set by modifiers. Adverbs like "yesterday" and TIME NG's like "the week he arrived" set both limits. This can also be done by bound clauses like "while you were building the stack" or preposition groups like "during the flood". Other clauses, prepositions, and groups set only the start limit (like "after you hit it", "after the war") while others (like "before" and "until") set the end limit. In the current system the event being referred to in the modifier is assumed to be known along with its exact time (it must be in the past.) The exact beginning and ending time are used in setting the limits.

The question "Did you pick it up while you were building the stack?" is answered by first finding the event of building the stack (using a TSS for PAST tense with no other limits), then using the beginning and ending of that event as limits for the TSS in the relation #PICKUP.

There are discourse phenomena which involve time reference. First, there are specific back-references with words like "then" and phrases like "at that time." The system keeps track of the major time reference of the previous sentence, and substitutes it in the current sentence whenever such phrases are used. This time is also carried forward implicitly. Consider "Did you pick up a red block while you were building the tower?" "No." "Did you pick up a green one?" In this sequence, the second question involves a specific time interval although it is not mentioned again. Whenever there are two successive PAST sentences and the second does not have any explicit time reference, the previous TSS is used. Long dialogs can appear in which the same time interval is used throughout, but is mentioned only in the first sentence.

Use of TSS. So far, all of our discussion has involved the clause with its verb group and time modifiers. But in making use of time information we must handle other units as well. The sentence "The man sitting on the table baked the bread." has two meanings, but the point would have been identical for "The man on the table baked the bread." The qualifying prepositional phrase "on the table" does not refer to time, but can be interpreted either as meaning "on the table now" or "on the table then." Adjectives can be affected similarly. Consider the sentences:

a. Many rich men made their fortunes during the depression.
b. Many rich men lost their fortunes during the depression.
c. Many rich men worked in restaurants during the depression.

The first clearly means "men who are now rich", the second "men who were rich", and the third might have either interpretation. The adjective "rich" involves an implicit time reference, as does any adjective which describes a state which can be true of an object at one time, but false at another. Nouns can also involve states which are changeable, and the problem would be identical if "rich men" were replaced by "millionaires".

In a traditional transformational approach, this would be used to show that even a simple phrase such as "a rich man" or "millionaires" is generated by a series of transformations. The possibility of two meanings is accounted for by two different deep structures, involving sentences corresponding to "The men were rich." and "The men are rich." This leads to a syntactic theory in which the simplest sentence may involve dozens of such transformations, to account for each noun, adjective, preposition, etc. The parser must be able to handle all of these details using syntactic information.

In our approach, these can be seen as semantic ambiguities which arise within a single syntactic structure. Part of the semantic definition of the word "millionaire" (or "student", "bachelor", etc.) involves a reference to time. Within the language for writing semantic definitions, there is a special symbol *TIME. Whenever the program for the meaning of a word in the dictionary is called, the semantic system will have determined the appropriate Time Semantic Structure (or structures) and have assigned a value to this symbol accordingly. If the time reference is ambiguous, the definition will be called once for each possibility. The noun "millionaire" might be defined:

(NMEANS ((#PERSON) ((#IS *** #PERSON)
                    (#POSSESS *** $1,000,000 *TIME))))

Notice that not every relation involves time. Being a #PERSON is assumed to be a permanent characteristic. If the time is PRESENT (indicated by the TSS :NOW), the system deletes the time reference, so PLANNER will receive the expression (THGOAL (#POSSESS $?X1 $1,000,000)), where $?X1 is the variable assigned to the object being described. If the sentence were "During the war, many millionaires worked in restaurants.", the time reference of the sentence would be a structure like ((PAST) NIL 1941 1945), and the PLANNER expression for "millionaire" would include:

(#POSSESS $?X1 $1,000,000 ((PAST) NIL 1941 1945))

A different theorem would be used for this case, since it cannot look directly into the data base to see what the person has, but must look into its past "records" to reconstruct the information. In our programs, a record is kept of when and where objects have been moved, so theorems can determine the location of any object at any time in the past.

Since adjectives can be defined with NMEANS, they are treated identically. Prepositions and verbs are usually defined with CMEANS, which has the same conventions. The symbol *TIME can appear in the definition, and is deleted if the applicable time is :NOW, and replaced with the TSS otherwise. The time applicable to anything but a clause is that of the clause closest above it in the parsing tree. This is only an approximation, and does not take into account ambiguities such as illustrated in sentence c above. In fact, a PREP or NG can have its own time reference, as in "a *former* millionaire", "many *future* students", "my roommate *last year*", "the man on the table *yesterday*". This is one of many places where the current semantic system needs to be extended by making the analysis more general.

8.1.9 *Semantics of Conjunction*

The semantic system does not handle conjunction as generally as does the parser. A few cases have been dealt with in a simplified way—noun groups, adjectives, RSQ clauses, and MAJOR clauses which are not questions. The distinction between "and" and "but" is ignored.

With MAJOR clauses, the conjunction must be "and", and the components are processed as if they were completely separate sentences, except that the response ("ok." for imperatives, and "I understand." for declaratives) is suppressed for all but the last. The system will not accept sentences joined with "or", or "nor", and will misunderstand compounds which cannot be separated into individual actions (e.g., "Build a stack *and* use three cubes in it.")

Noun groups can be connected with "and" wherever they appear, and with "or" if they are part of an argument to a command (like "Pick up a cube *or* a pyramid."). An OSS is built with the semantic markers of the first constituent NG, the conjunction itself, and a list of the OSS for the components. If all of the components are definite and the conjunction is "and", the conjoined NG is definite, and its referent is the union of the referents.

The use of the conjoined OSS depends on its place in the sentence. If it is the object or subject of a verb or preposition, the definition of that verb or preposition can check explicitly for conjoined structures and treat them specially. For example, "touch" can be defined so that the sentence "A and B are touching." will be represented as (THGOAL (#TOUCH :A :B)). If there is no special check, the system assumes that the desired object is the list of referents. "A and B support C." would produce (THGOAL (#SUPPORT (:A :B) :C)). If the first element of the PLANNER expression (usually the name of a predicate) has a property MULTIPLE on its property list, the system modifies this to create the expression:

(THAND(THGOAL(#SUPPORT :A :C))
(THGOAL(#SUPPORT :B :C)))

If the conjoined NG is one of the arguments to a command, the theorem TC-CHOOSE will choose the specific referents. If the conjunction is "and", it will combine the referents for each of the components in a single list. If it is "or", it will first choose according to the first constituent, then if a failure backs up to the choice, it will try the second, third, etc. It does not look at the various choices in advance to decide which is most appropriate for the task being done.

The other units which can be combined with "and" and "or" are the adjective and RSQ clause. The semantic structure for the conjoined unit is a list whose first element is the conjunction, and the rest are the individual interpretations for the constituents. In using these to modify an OSS, the system combines all of the descriptions with THOR or implicit THAND. For example, "a block which is in the box *and* is red" becomes:

    (THGOAL(#IS $?X #BLOCK))
    (THGOAL(#IN $?X :BOX))
    (THGOAL(#COLOR $?X #RED))

while "a red *or* green block" becomes:

    (THGOAL(#IS $?X #BLOCK))
    (THOR(THGOAL(#COLOR $?X #RED))
        (THGOAL(#COLOR $?X #GREEN)))

This could easily be extended to other modifiers such as preposition groups. Many other types of conjunction could be handled without major changes to the system, usually by adding two bits of program. One would create a conjoined semantic structure appropriate to the unit, and the other would recognize it and take the appropriate action for its use.

8.1.10 *More on Ambiguity*

Section 8.1.1 described the OSS as having a position to mark the "plausibility" of its interpretation. As a semantic structure is built, it takes on the sum of the plausibilities of its components. If the sentence is a command, the system tries to carry out the most plausible interpretation. If that fails, it tries the next, and so on until one succeeds or a total failure causes the system to respond "I can't." Questions are handled more completely. The system orders the interpretations by plausibility and finds the answer for the most plausible. It then tries again to answer it, using only information mentioned in the previous sentence and its answer. If it succeeds in finding the same answer, it reduces the plausibility, since it is unusual to ask a question to which the answer was just given, either explicitly or implicitly. If the information in the previous sentence is not sufficient to answer it, the system then tries to answer using only information which has been mentioned previously in the discourse. If the plausibility is higher than that of the next interpretation by a large enough margin (a factor set by the user and called TIMID) it gives the answer as found. If not, it saves the answer and repeats the process for the next interpretation. After all interpretations have been processed, the answers are checked to see if they are identical. In this case it doesn't matter which interpretation is intended, and the system simply gives the answer. Finally, if there are differing answers, the user must be asked what he meant. Associated with each interpretation is a list of those places where it differed from others. This is produced automatically by each program which accepts multiple definitions (such as NMEANS and CMEANS).

Faced with an unresolvable ambiguity, the system looks through the list of interpretations for a conflict, then generates a response like:

I'm not sure what you mean by "on top of" in the phrase "on top of green cubes".

do you mean:

1 - directly on the surface

2 - anywhere on top of?

The response (a typed number) indicates which is meant, and all interpretations which involve the other meanings (there can be more than two associated with a single ambiguity) are eliminated. If there are still conflicting interpretations, another ambiguity is selected and the process is repeated until all those which have not been eliminated give the same answer, and it can be used as a response.

8.1.11 *To Be and To Have*

The verbs "be" and "have" have a complex variety of uses, and they appear in the system in two ways. First, in the syntax they are treated specially since they can occur as auxiliary verbs, as in "I would *have been* going". In this use, they do not add any semantic information except for helping to determine features of the VG, such as its tense. Their other use is as main verbs in clauses like "Do you *have* a match?" and "He *is* wrong." As a main verb, "be" is handled specially in the syntax since it can enter into constructions such as "there is" which do not appear with any other verb. However, the semantic analyzer does not know anything special about "be" and "have".

Be. The use of "be" depends on the specific constellation of objects and complements in the clause. The definition of its meaning is a LISP program of about 40 lines, which handles those meanings relevant to the BLOCKS world (for example, it cannot deal with a "role-playing" meaning, like "Laurence Olivier *was* Hamlet.")

Sentences with the feature THERE, involving a construction like "there is," are represented by the concept #EXISTS, which involves an object and a time. This is necessary for objects which can be created and destroyed, as in "Was there a stack . . .?".

The other meanings of "be" involve intensive clauses which contain an object and a complement. One definition checks for COMPQ questions like "What color is the block?", to generate a PLANNER expression (#COLOR :BLOCK $?X1). If the complement is a definite NG, as in "Is the green block *the biggest object?*" or "What is *the biggest object?*", the referent will have already been determined, and is inserted in a PLANNER expression (THAMONG *** (QUOTE(:OBJ))), where :OBJ is the referent. This can function in two ways. If the subject is also definite, as in the first example, the *** will be replaced by its referent, and the statement will succeed only if the two are identical. If the subject is indefinite, the THAMONG statement will cause it to be assigned to the same referent as the complement.

If the complement is a PREPG or a complex ADJG, like "bigger than a breadbox", "be" is only serving as a place-holder which can accept a time reference. The semantic interpreter in dealing with a phrase like "on the table" in "Is the block on the table?" has already set up a relation of the form (#ON :BLOCK :TABLE) which includes the appropriate time reference. In this case, the "be" program simply takes the RSS produced for the complement, and uses it as the semantic interpretation of the clause.

The other possibilities for the complement are an indefinite NG, a simple ADJG (e.g., a single adjective), or a new word. In the case of a NG, the complement NG contains additional information to be ascribed to the subject, as in "a large object which is *a red block*". The PLANNER description of the complement is stripped from its OSS, and appended to the PLANNER description of the subject. If the subject is definite, as in "Is *the biggest thing* a red block?", the referent is known, and can be plugged into the PLANNER description of the complement to see if the description applies.

If the complement is a simple ADJG, the ADJG semantic specialist creates its OSS by taking the OSS for the subject, stripping away the PLANNER description, and using the rest as a skeleton on which to place the PLANNER expression produced by the adjective. Once this is done, it can be treated exactly like an indefinite NG.

Finally, if the subject or complement is a new word (as in "A frob is a big red cube." or "A big red cube is a frob.") a new definition is created as described in 8.1.7.

Have. The definition of "have" is also used to handle the possessive. For the limited subject matter (and for much of English) this is a good approximation. There are cases where it does not apply—"the painting which John has" is not necessarily the same as "John's painting." The preposition "of" also makes use of the same definition. A more complete treatment would distinguish between the three, and this would involve only simple changes to the semantic programs.

The interesting thing about "have" is that it is not used to indicate a few different relationships, but is a place-marker used to create relationships dependent on the semantic types of the objects involved. "Sam has a mother." can be represented (#MOTHER-OF X SAM), "Sam has a friend." is (#FRIEND X SAM), "Sam has a car." is (#OWN SAM CAR), "Sam has support." is (#SUPPORT X SAM), "Sam has a hand." is (#PART SAM HAND), etc. The definition of "have" (or the possessive, or "of") does not include within itself all of these different relations. A few interpretations (like have-as-part, owning, or having in physical possession) can be reasonably considered distinct meanings of "have", and are included in its definition. The others, such as "mother" and "support" really are determined by the subject and object. Some systems use this fact to find the meaning of special phrases like "client's lawyer" without doing syntactic analysis. Our system uses a different method, allowing a word to be defined as a #ROLE. "Mother" might be defined as:

```
(NMEANS((#PERSON #ROLE)
        ((#PERSON ***)
         (#MOTHER-OF *** ?)
         (#ROLE((#PERSON))(#MOTHER-OF
                                    #1 #2)))
```

There are two new things in this definition. First, the semantic marker #ROLE is added to indicate the type of definition. Second, a role definition is included. It contains a semantic filter for objects which can be used in the relation (in this case those which could have a mother), and a PLANNER statement indicating the relation (in the same syntax used by CMEANS). If the word "mother" is used in a phrase like "Carol's mother" or "Carol has a mother" or "the mother of Carol", the system will insert the right OSS to produce the PLANNER description (#MOTHER-OF $?X1 CAROL) If "mother" appears in any other form, the OSS will contain (#MOTHER-OF $?X1 ?) which uses the PLANNER symbol "?", which matches anything. This goal will be satisfied if X1 is the mother of anyone at all.

Through the #ROLE mechanism, various arbitrary relationships can be expressed with "have" (or "of", or possessives). There could be more than one #ROLE assigned to a word as well. For example "painting" would involve different roles for "Rembrandt's painting" "George Washington's painting by Stuart", "the Modern Museum's painting.", etc.

8.1.12 Additional Semantic Information

Using Clauses as Objects. In order to interpret a sentence like "Find a block which is taller than the one I told you to pick up." the system must use a clause ("you to pick up") as the object of a verb ("tell"). It generates a pseudo-object of the type #EVENT, and creates an OSS for that object. In the example mentioned, the clause "you to pick up" would have produced the RSS in Fig. 57.

NG1 is an OSS describing the object "the one", which the system has set up as the object of the clause, and has interpreted as "block". The

((NG1 (#PICKUP NG1 ((PAST) NIL NIL NIL)) NIL) (0))
   rel   PLANNER expression   neg markers

Figure 57—RSS for "you to pick up"

program SMCL4 takes this structure and produces a corresponding OSS
shown in Fig. 58.

A variable is generated for the event, of the form EVXn, and a new
PLANNER expression for the event is generated, including the event
name as the second element. In the expression, the name of the OSS is
replaced with its associated variable (in this case $?X1) since the new
structure will be used as part of the description of that object. The recommendation list includes a theorem added by the system which deals
with expressions involving time and event-names. The resultant OSS
can be used just like any other OSS, as an object of a verb, preposition,
etc. When PLANNER evaluates the expression, it may have the event
already stored away, or it may have to deduce it from other events, using
the theorem TCTE-PICKUP. The name of the resultant event is assigned
to the variable EVX1.

Types of Modification. There are a variety of ways in which a modifier
can affect the meaning of the phrase or clause it modifies. A time modifier
like "now" or "then" will modify the Time Semantic Structure associated
with the clause; an adverb like "quickly" may set up a new relation such
as (#SPEED $?EV1 #FAST) using the name of the event; others may
change the relation being constructed, using arbitrary functions, suiting
the meanings of the modifiers. One special facility exists for making
substitutions within an expression. If the PLANNER expression of a
CMEANS or NMEANS definition is of the form (#SUBST a1 a2 b1
b2 . . .), the effect will be to modify the existing semantic structure by
substituting the atom a2 for a1, b2 for b1, etc. No new expression is
added to the PLANNER description. The word "move" might be defined
using:

  (CMEANS((((#ANIMATE))((#MANIP)))
                         (#PUT #2 LOC °TIME) (#MOVE)))

((((EVX1) 0 (THGOAL (#PICKUP $?EVX1 $?X1 ((PAST) NIL NIL
                                                  NIL))
               (THUSE TCTE-PICKUP)))
   (0 #EVENT #THING)
   (#THING))
  EVX1
  (1 INDEF NIL)
  NIL)

Figure 58—OSS for "you to pick up"

This indicates that moving is done by an animate object to a manipulable object, and involves putting it at the place "LOC." The atom LOC would be given a OSS indicating an unknown place. The resulting RSS has the semantic marker #MOVE. The sentence "Move a block." would create a goal (#PUT NG1 LOC), where NG1 is a description of "a block". The theorem for #PUT could then choose a block and place. If the sentence is "Move a block into the box.", the final result should be (#PUTIN NG1 :BOX). The modifying phrase makes a major change in the internal representation of the meaning. This can be done by defining "into" to include among its meanings:

(CMEANS((((#MOVE))((#BOX))) (#SUBST #PUTIN
#MOVE #2 LOC) NIL))

If a PREPG with the preposition "into" modifies a clause with the semantic marker #MOVE, and the object of the preposition has the marker #BOX, then the definition applies. The RSS for the clause is changed by substituting #PUTIN for #MOVE, and the object of the preposition for #LOC. The special symbols #1, #2, #3, ***, and *TIME are treated as they would be in a normal CMEANS or NMEANS definition, being replaced by the appropriate object.

Using Evaluation in CMEANS and NMEANS. Although every definition has the power to use programs, definitions using the standard forms CMEANS and NMEANS are forced into a rather rigid syntax which does not have a procedural character. To give them more flexible possibilities, there is an extra level of evaluation. If the PLANNER portion of a definition is of the form (#EVAL S) where S is any LISP atom or list structure, the form will be evaluated by LISP before the description is used in the definition, and its value used instead. This value will undergo the usual substitutions for #1, #2, *TIME, etc. This feature is of particular use in capturing the semantic regularities of the language by using auxiliary functions in defining words. For example, color adjectives like "red" and "blue" share most of their characteristics. They apply to physical objects, involve a relation with #COLOR, etc. Rather than define them separately, we would like a single function #COLOR which needs only to have the exact color specified. The dictionary definition of blue would then be (#COLOR #BLUE). The function #COLOR can be defined in LISP:

(DEFUN #COLOR FEXPR (A)
  (NMEANS((#PHYSOB)
             (#EVAL (LIST(LIST (QUOTE #COLOR)
                                 (QUOTE ***)
                                 (CAR A)))))))

When (#COLOR #BLUE) is evaluated, the #EVAL will produce

the form $((\#COLOR *** \#BLUE))$, which will then be used by NMEANS in the usual way.

As another example, the word "grasp" can be used to mean #GRASPING (an object being held) or #GRASP (the action of closing the fingers around it). The difference depends on whether the VG is progressive or not. The function (PROGRESSIVE) finds out whether the clause is progressive, by looking at the verb and the tense. The definition of "grasp" can be:

```
(CMEANS((((#ANIMATE))((#MANIP)))
   (#EVAL (COND ((PROGRESSIVE) (QUOTE
                             (#GRASPING #2 *TIME)))
          (T (QUOTE (#GRASP #2
                             *TIME))))) NIL))
```

8.1.13 Some Interesting Problems

There are many areas in which the semantic analysis needs to be refined and expanded. The system primarily illustrates how a number of aspects of semantics could be handled. This section describes a few places where modification might begin.

Definite Determiners. In our system, a definite noun phrase is interpreted as referring to a unique object or set of objects known to the hearer. In more general language use, definiteness is often used to convey new information. The phrase "my brother who lives in Chicago" can be said to someone who is not aware I have a brother, and the effect is to inform him that indeed I do, and to tell him where this brother lives. Other nouns can describe "functions", so that "the title of his new book," or "my address", are allowable even if the hearer has not heard the title or address, since he knows that every book has a unique title, and every person an address. Superlative phrases like "the tallest elephant in Indiana" also refer to a unique object, even though the hearer may not have seen or heard of this object before.

Cases such as these can lead to problems of referential opacity. If your name is "Seymour", and I say "Excuse me, I've never heard your name.", it does not imply that I have never heard the name Seymour. The sentence "I want to own the fastest car in the world." does not have the same meaning if we replace the NG with its current referent—I don't want whichever car it is that happens to be fastest right now.

Verb Tenses. The current system implements only a few of the possible tenses—PRESENT, PAST, PRESENT IN PRESENT, PRESENT IN PAST, PAST IN PAST, and an elementary form of the MODAL "can." A deeper analysis is needed to account for interactions between the order of phrases and the possibilities for time reference. The modals, conditionals, subjunctives, etc. need to be handled. This may demand a version of PLANNER which can temporarily move into a hypothetical world, or which has more power to analyze its own theorems to answer questions involving modals like "can" and "must".

Conjunction. Only the most elementary problems in conjunction are dealt with in the current system. For example, it does not know that "and" can be used to indicate temporal sequence ("We went to the circus and came home.") causality ("We saw him and understood."), as a type of conditional ("Do that again and I'll clobber you!"), how to do something ("Be a friend and help me."), etc. These uses relate to the discourse problem of the ordering of sentences. For example, "The light is on. He's there." indicates a chain of reasoning.

In addition, no attempt has been made to disambiguate nested structures like "A and B or C", or "the old men and women." Syntactic criteria are not sufficient for these distinctions, and a more powerful semantic program will be required for such cases.

Nonsyntactic Relations. There are some places in English where the relation between a set of words is not indicated by syntactic clues, but is largely based on semantics. One example is chain of classifiers before a noun. In "strict gun law", the law is strict, but in "stolen gun law", the gun is stolen. It is possible to combine long strings like "an aluminum soup pot cover clearance sale", in which a large amount of semantic information must be combined with the ordering to find the correct interpretation. The current system handles classifiers by assuming that they all separately modify the head. This needs to be changed, to use both the semantic markers and complex deductions to find the real relationships.

8.2 *The Semantics of Discourse*

In Section 1.6, we discussed the different types of context which can affect the way a sentence is interpreted. This section describes the mechanisms used by our program to include context in its interpretation of language. We have concentrated on the "local discourse context," and the ways in which parts of the meaning of a sentence can be referred to by elements of the next sentence. For example, pronouns like "it" and "they" can refer to objects which have been previously mentioned or to an entire event, as in "Why did you do *it*?". The words "then" and "there" refer back to a previous time and place, and words like "that" can be used to mean "the one most recently mentioned," as in "Explain *that* sentence."

In addition to referring back to a particular object, we can refer back to a description in order to avoid repeating it. We can say: "Is there a small grey elephant from Zanzibar next to a big *one?*". Sometimes instead of using "one" to avoid repetition, we simply omit part of a phrase or sentence. We can reply to "Would you like a corned-beef sandwich?" with "Bring me *two.*" or we can respond to almost anything with "Why?" In these examples, the second sentence includes by implication a part of the first.

These features can appear just as well in a single sentence. In fact, some sentences would be difficult to express without these mechanisms, for example: "Find a block which is bigger than anything which supports *it.*" These mechanisms can refer back to anything mentioned previously, whether in an earlier sentence of the speaker, a reply, or something earlier in the same utterance.

8.2.1 *Pronouns*

First we will look at the use of pronouns to refer back to objects. Our robot has no trouble with the pronouns "you" and "I", which always refer to the two objects :SHRDLU and :FRIEND. A more general program would keep track of who was talking to the computer in order to find the referent of "I".

When the NG program used by the parser finds a NG consisting of a pronoun, it calls the program which is the definition of that pronoun. The definitions of "it" and "they" use a special heuristic program called SMIT, which looks into the discourse for all of the different things they might refer to, and assigns a plausibility value to each interpretation, according to factors such as its position in the syntactic structure, and the form of its determiner. If more than one is possible, they are carried along simultaneously through the rest of the sentence, and the ambiguity mechanism decides at the end which is better, including the last-resort effort of printing out a message asking for clarification. If SMIT finds two different interpretations, and one is chosen because of a higher plausibility, the system types out a message to inform us of the assumption made in choosing one interpretation, as in Sentence 3 of Section 1.3, we get:

BY "IT", I ASSUME YOU MEAN THE BLOCK WHICH IS TALLER THAN THE ONE I AM HOLDING.

If a response from the user is needed, the request is typed in the same format as the message used for other ambiguities, as described in Section 8.3.1.

In our discussion of pronouns, we will use "it" as typical. In most cases, "they" (or "them") is treated identically except for checking for agreement with plural rather than singular. "He" and "she" never occur in our limited subject matter, but they would be treated exactly like "it", except for an extra check that their referent is animate and of the right gender.

The first thing checked by SMIT is whether "it" has already appeared in the same sentence. We seldom use the same pronoun to refer to two different objects in the same sentence, so it is generally safe to adopt the same interpretation we did the first time. If there were several possible interpretations, the system is careful not to match up one interpretation from one occurrence of "it" with a different one from another occurrence in building an overall interpretation of the sentence.

Similarly, if "it" was used in the previous sentence, it is likely that if used again it will refer to the same thing. In either of these cases, SMIT simply adopts the previous interpretation.

Next, a pronoun may be inside a complex syntactic construction such as "a block which is bigger than anything which supports it." English uses the reflexive pronouns, like "itself" to refer back to an object in the same sentence. However, if it is necessary to pass through another NG node in going from the pronoun to the referent on the parsing tree, an ordinary pronoun like "it" is used, since "itself" would refer to the intermediate NG. Notice that if we replaced "it" by "itself" in our sentence, it would no longer refer to the block, but to "anything".

SMIT looks for this case and other related ones. When such a situation exists, the program must work differently. Ordinarily, when we refer to "it" we have already finished finding the referent of the NG being referred back to, and "it" can adopt this referent. In this case, we have a circle, where "it" is part of the definition of the object it is referring to. The part of the program which does variable binding in relating objects and clauses recognizes this, and uses the same variable for "a block" and "it".

The pronoun may also refer to an object in an embedded clause appearing earlier in the same clause, as in "Before you pick up the red cube, clear it off." SMIT looks through the sentence for objects in such acceptable places to which "it" might refer. If it doesn't find them there, it begins to look at the previous sentence. The pronoun may refer to any object in the sentence, and we cannot eliminate any possibilities on syntactic grounds. Some may be more plausible, however. For example, in Section 8.1.5 we discussed the importance of a "focus" element in a clause. We assume that "it" is more likely to refer to the previous focus than to other elements of the clause. Similarly, the subject is a more likely candidate than an object, and both are more likely than a NG appearing embedded in a PREPG or a secondary clause.

The system keeps a list of all of the objects referred to in the previous sentence, as well as the entire parsing tree. By using PROGRAMMAR'S functions for exploring a parsing tree, SMIT is able to find the syntactic position of all the possible references and to assign each a plausibility, using a fairly arbitrary but hopefully useful set of values. To keep the list of the objects in the last sentence, the semantic system has to do a certain amount of extra work. If we ask the question: "Is any block supported by three pyramids?", the PLANNER expression produced is:

```
(THFIND ALL  $?X1 (X1)
          (THGOAL(#IS $?X1 #BLOCK))
          (THFIND 3 $?X2 (X2)
                     (THGOAL(#IS $?X2 #PYRAMID))
                     (THGOAL(#SUPPORT $?X2 $?X1)))))
```

Once this is evaluated, it returns a list of all the blocks satisfying the description, but no record of what pyramids supported them. If the next sentence asked "Are they tall?", we would have no objects for "they" to refer to. Special instructions are inserted into our PLANNER descriptions which cause lists like this to be saved. The actual PLANNER expression produced would be:

```
(THPUTPROP (QUOTE X1)
         (THFIND ALL $?X1 (X1)
             (THGOAL (#IS $?X1 #BLOCK))
             (THPUTPROP (QUOTE X2)
                     (THFIND 3 $?X2 (X2)
                                (THGOAL(#IS $?X2
                                               #PYRAMID))
                                (THGOAL(#SUPPORT $?X2
                                                  $?X1))
                     (QUOTE BIND)))
         (QUOTE BIND))
```

This only occurs when the system is handling discourse.

Finally, "it" can be used in a phrase like "Do it!" to refer to the entire main event of the last sentence. This LASTEVENT is saved, and SMIT can use it to replace the entire meaning of "do it" with the description generated earlier for the event.

When "that" is used in a phrase like "do that", it is handled in a similar way, but with an interesting difference. If we have the sequence "Why did you pick up the ball?" "To build a stack." "How did you do it?", the phrase "do it" refers to "Pick up a ball". But if we had asked "How did you do that?", it would refer to building a stack. The heuristic is that "that" refers to the event most recently mentioned by anyone, while "it" refers to the event most recently mentioned by the speaker.

In addition to remembering the participants and main event of the previous sentence, the system also remembers those in its own responses so that it can use them when they are called for by pronouns. It also remembers the last time reference, (LASTTIME) so the word "then" can refer back to the time of the previous sentence.

Special uses of "it" (as in "It is raining.") are not handled, but could easily be added as further possibilities to the SMIT program.

8.2.2 Substitutes and Incompletes

The next group of things the system needs to interpret involves the use of substitute nouns like "one", and incomplete noun groups like "Buy me *two.*" Here we cannot look back for a particular object, but must look for a description. SMIT looks through a list of particular objects for its meaning. SMONE (the program used for "one") looks back into the input sentence instead, to recover the English description. "One" can be used to stand for part or all of that description.

As with "it", "one" can refer back to something in a previous sentence, the previous reply, or earlier in the same sentence. Here though, there are no restrictions about where in the parsing tree the description can be. "One" depends more on surface characteristics than on structural differences. For example, it cannot refer back to a NG which is a pronoun or uses a TPRON like "anything". Our program for "one" is not as complex as the one for "it". It is primarily based on the heuristic of "contrast". People often use "one" to contrast two characteristics of basically similar objects, for example, "the big red block and the little *one.*" The program must understand these contrasts to know that "the little one" means "the little red block", not "the little big red block" or "the little block". To do this, the system has as part of its semantic knowledge a list of contrasting adjectives. This information is used not only to decide how much of the description is to be borrowed by "one", but also to decide which description in a sentence "one" is referring to. If we say "The green block supports the big pyramid but not the little one." it is fairly clear that "one" refers to "pyramid". But if we say "The big block supports the green pyramid but not the little one.", then "one" might refer to "block". The only difference is the change of adjectives—"big" and "little" contrast, but "green" and "little" do not. The program looks for such contrasts, and if it finds one, it assumes the most recent contrasting description is the referent. If there is no contrast between the phrase being analyzed and any NG in the same sentence, previous answer, or previous sentence, it then looks for the most recent NG which contains a noun.

It is interesting to note that SMONE causes the system to do a simplified parse of some of its own output. In order to use the fragment of a NG it finds, SMONE must know which elements it can use (such as noun, adjective, and classifier) and which it cannot (such as number and determiner). For the noun groups in previous inputs, the parsing is available, but for the reply, only the actual words are available and parsing is necessary.

An incomplete NG, containing only a number or quantifier, is used in much the same way as "one". In fact, if we look at the series "Buy me three." "Buy me two." "Buy me one.", we see they are nearly identical, and the program handles such noun groups accordingly.

8.2.3 Overall Discourse Context

One way of using overall discourse context is to keep track of what has been mentioned earlier in the discourse. This is not the same as looking back in the previous sentence for pronoun references, as it may involve objects several sentences back or occurring in separate sentences. If there are many blocks are on the table, we can have a conversation: "What is in the box?" "A block and a pyramid." "What is behind it?" "A red block and another box." "What color is the box?" "Green." "Pick up the two blocks."

The phrase "the two blocks" is to be interpreted as a particular pair of blocks, but there may be others in the scene, and nowhere in the dialog were two blocks mentioned together. The system needs to keep track of when things were mentioned, in order to interpret "the" as "the most recently mentioned" in cases like this. To do so, we use PLANNER'S facility for giving properties to assertions. When we mention a "green block", the semantic system builds a PLANNER description which includes the expressions:

$$(THGOAL(\#IS \ \$?X1 \ \#BLOCK))$$
$$(THGOAL(\#COLOR \ \$?X1 \ \#GREEN))$$

After the sentence containing this phrase has been interpreted, the system goes back to the PLANNER descriptions and marks all of the assertions which were used, by putting the current sentence number on their property lists. This is also done for the assertions used in generating the descriptions of objects in the answer.

When the semantic programs find a definite NG like "the two red blocks", the second NG specialist (SMNG2) uses PLANNER to make a list of all of the objects which fit the description. If there are the right number for the NG, these are listed as the referents of the NG, and the interpretation of that NG is finished. If there are fewer than called for by the determiners and numbers, SMNG2 makes a note of the English phrase which was used to build the description, and returns a message to the parser that something has gone wrong. If the parser manages to parse the sentence differently, all is well. If not, the system assumes that the NG interpretation was the reason for the failure, and the system uses the stored phrase to print out a message, "I don't understand what you mean by . . ."

However, if there are too many objects which match the description, SMNG2 tries to find out which were mentioned most recently. If an appropriate number cannot be found by looking farther and farther back in the discourse, a message of failure is returned to the parser as before, but a marker is set so that in case the sentence cannot be understood, the message returned is "I don't know which . . . you mean."

8.3 Generation of Responses

In this section we will describe how our language understanding system generates its linguistic responses. The system is not a general theory of discourse generation. The programs produce simple behavior which seems reasonable for carrying on a dialog about the robot world. In particular we dealt with four aspects of discourse production—patterned responses, appropriate answers to questions, generating descriptions of objects and events, and the production of fluent discourse.

8.3.1 Patterned Responses

The easiest way to get language behavior from a computer program is to include a set of fixed responses which are appropriate for the situations it will encounter. These responses can be made as complex and varied as we want, since they are created by the programmer, and the program only repeats them. Many language systems make heavy use of these fixed responses, and they are useful when the program has to indicate that something has happened, or that it has reached a certain point in its analysis.

Our system uses several types of patterned response. First there is a set of simple responses for specific situations, e.g., "ok." when a command is carried out, and "I understand." when a declarative sentence is analyzed. A slightly more complex type of response involves "filling in the blank" with a phrase borrowed from the input. The simplest example in our system is "sorry, I don't know the word . . .". Slightly more complex types of response involve manipulating the determiners of the phrase which was input. For example, if the user types something like "the three green pyramids", and the system cannot figure out what he is referring to, it types "I don't know which three green pyramids you mean." It has simply replaced "the" with "which" before filling the blank. The "I assume" mechanism does the opposite, replacing an indefinite determiner or quantifier with "the". If we talk about "some green pyramid" or "a green pyramid", then later refer to that pyramid as "it", the system can notify us of its interpretation of "it" by saying "by 'it' I assume you mean the green pyramid."

Our most complex "blank-filling" response is the one which handles ambiguity. It uses parts of the input sentence and pieces of the definitions of words stored in the dictionary. In the response to the sentence, "How many things are on top of green cubes?" the system typed:

I'M NOT SURE WHAT YOU MEAN BY "ON TOP OF" IN THE PHRASE "ON TOP OF GREEN CUBES".

1 - DIRECTLY ON THE SURFACE

2 - ANYWHERE ON TOP OF?

The two phrases "on top of" and "on top of green cubes" were taken directly from the input, and the paraphrases "directly on the surface" and "anywhere on top of" were part of the dictionary definition provided for "on". If the ambiguity is caused by multiple interpretations for a pronoun, the English phrases originally used to refer to the objects are used in the response choices.

8.3.2 Answering Questions

In order to carry on a discourse, we need to know what types of responses people expect to different types of questions. In Section 3.1 we classified various types of questions syntactically, and we can use this classification to select appropriate answers. No attempt is made to produce full sentences, since in fact people rarely answer questions with sentences. The natural response to "Which block is in the box?" is "the red block", or "the red one", certainly not "The red block is in the box."

The first case is the WH- question, and within that class, the NGQ (see Section 3.1), involving a question NOUN GROUP, such as "which block", "who", "how many pyramids", or "what". We can divide these into three classes—"how many", "vague", and "specific". If asked "What is in the box?", we can answer "a blue block and a pyramid" without being more specific at identifying them. If instead we are asked "Which block is in the box?" we must use a more specific description like "the large blue cube which supports a pyramid." The program, which must generate both definite and indefinite English descriptions of particular objects, is described in the next section. The use of its results is straightforward for NGQ questions. If the NG is "what", we generate indefinite descriptions of the object or objects. If it is "which . . .", we generate a definite description. "Who" is never a problem, since the system only knows of two people, "you", and "I". There are also default responses, so that a question like "Which block supports the table?" can be answered with "none of them."

HOWMANY questions are answered with the number of appropriate objects, followed by "of them" to make the discourse smoother.

The next type of question is the QADJ. The only three which have been implemented so far are "why" "when", and "how", but the others could be done in an analogous fashion. A "why" question is answered using the system's memory of the subgoals it used in achieving its goals. If we can decide what event is being referred to in the question, we can see what goal called it as a subgoal, and answer by describing the higher goal in English. If the event was itself a top-level goal, it must have been requested as a command, then the response is "because you asked me to.". "How" questions are answered using a program, described below, that creates an English description of an event from its PLANNER description. In general, it describes all of the events which were subgoals used in achieving the event mentioned. It says "by . . .", then lists each event in an "ing" form, as in: "by picking up a red block and putting it in the box."

"When" questions are answered similarly. In general, a time is specified by describing the top-level goal which was being carried out at the time, saying "while I was . . ." and using the "ing" form to describe the event.

Finally we come to YES-NO questions which, paradoxically, are the most complicated. A one word answer is often impossible and rarely the best way to respond. If we ask "Does the block support three pyramids?", and in fact it supports four, what is the correct answer? The system could ask for clarification of the implicit ambiguity between "at least three" and "exactly three", then answer "yes" or "no". But it is more efficient and helpful to answer "four of them", leaving the speaker to interpret his own question. If there were only two pyramids, the system could respond "no", but it would be more informative to say "no, only two of them". In any of these cases, we might be even more complete, and say something like "four of them: a blue one, two red ones, and a large green one."

There are three parts we can include in the answer—"yes" or "no", a number, and a description of the objects. Remember that whenever possible a YES-NO question is treated like a NG question by looking for a focus element (an indefinite NG in the question). A question like "Does the pyramid support a block?" is treated logically like the question "Which block does the pyramid support?", or "How many blocks does the pyramid support?" All three send a THFIND ALL request to PLANNER, asking for all of the objects fitting the description:

```
(THPROG (X)
    (THGOAL (#IS $?X #BLOCK))
    (THGOAL (#SUPPORT :B5 $?X)))
```

where :B5 is the system's internal name for the pyramid being referred to by "the pyramid" (this would be determined in separate calls to PLANNER). In the case of the HOWMANY question we answer with the number of objects found. For the "which" question, we name the objects. In the case of a YES-NO question, we answer with all three kinds of information, saying "yes, two of them: a large red one and the green one."

The first element is "yes" if the answer is clearly yes (for example if the number is matched exactly, or the number in the original question was indefinite as in this example), "no" if it is clearly no (for example if there are fewer than requested, none at all, or the request was of a form "exactly . . ." "at least . . ." "more than . . ." etc. and was not met), and is omitted if there is a question about its interpretation (as described above).

The second element, the number, is omitted if the number found matches the request (For example, "Are there three blocks?" is not answered redundantly, "yes, three of them: a green one and two large red ones."). The phrase "of them" following the number is changed to "things" if the focus contains a TPRON like "anything", or "something". If the number found is less than that in the focus, it is preceded by "only . . .", so the answer comes out "no, only two of them: . . .")

At the end of a response, we put the description of the objects found, unless the request used a special number format such as "exactly . . .", "at least . . ." etc. in which case the system assumes the number is more important than the specific objects. We use the object-naming program in its indefinite mode. If the focus originally appeared as the object of a preposition, we repeat that preposition before the description to clarify the answer. Thus, "Is the pyramid on a block?" is answered "yes, on a large green one." The unknown agent of a passive like "Is it supported?" is implicitly the object of "by", so the answer is "yes, by the table." If a YES–NO question contains no possible focus since all of its noun groups are definite, as in "Does the table support the box?", the system answers simply "yes" or "no".

8.3.3 Naming Objects and Events

The previous section covers the questions the system can handle, and the types of phrases it uses in response. We have not yet explained how it names an object or describes an event. This is done with a set of PLANNER and LISP functions which examine the data base and find relevant information about objects. These programs are limited. A description should depend on what the person being spoken to is interested in and what he already knows. In the present system, however, certain features of objects, such as their color and size, are used in all contexts. First we need to know how the object is basically classified. In the BLOCKS world, the concept #IS represents this, as in (#IS :HAND #HAND), (#IS :B1 #BLOCK), and (#IS #BLUE #COLOR). The naming program for objects first checks for the unique objects in its world, "I", "you", "the table", "the box", and "the hand". If the object is one of these, these names are used. Next it checks to see if it is a color or shape, in which case the English name is simply the concept name without the "#". The question "What shape is the pyramid?" is answered "pointed." since it has the shape #POINTED. If the object is not one of these and is not a #BLOCK, #BALL, or a #PYRAMID the program gives up. If it is one of those three, the correct noun is used (including a special check of dimensions to see if a #BLOCK is a "cube"), and a description is built of its color and size. As it is built, the description is checked to see if it refers uniquely to the object being described. If so, the determiner "the" is put on, and the description is used without further addition. If there is only one ball in the scene, it will always be referred to as "the ball".

If the description includes color and size, but still fits more than the desired object, the outcome depends on whether a specific description or a nonspecific one is called for. If it is nonspecific, the program puts the indefinite pronoun "a" or "an" on the beginning and produces something like "a large green cube". If it is specific, more information is needed. If the object supports anything, the program adds the phrase "which supports . . ." then includes the English descriptions (indefinite) of all the objects it supports. If the object supports nothing, the program adds "Which is to the right of . . ." and names all of the objects to the left of the desired one. This still may not characterize the object uniquely in some situations, but the system assumes that it does. If at any point in the dialog, an object is given a proper name, it is referred to using only the noun and the phrase "named . . .", as in "The block named superblock."

Naming events is relatively straightforward. With each event type (such as #PUTON or #STACKUP) we associate a small program which generates an English name for the event and combines it properly with the names of the objects involved. For example, the definition for #PUTON is:

(APPEND (VBFIX (QUOTE PUT))

OBJ1 (QUOTE (ON)) OBJ2)

VBFIX is a program which puts the verb into the right form for the kind of clause needed to answer the question (for example, "-ing" for answering "how", or infinitive for answering "why"). It takes into account the changes in spelling involved in adding endings. OBJ1 and OBJ2 are bound by the system to the English names of the objects involved in the event, using the object-naming program described above. APPEND is the LISP function which puts together the four ingredients end to end. We therefore get descriptions like "by putting a large red cube on the table". There is a special check for the order of particles and objects, so that we output "to pick up the small blue pyramid.", but, "to pick it up" rather than, "to pick up it".

8.3.4 Generating Discourse

The previous sections described a generating capability which can produce reasonable English answers to different types of questions, but used by themselves, the features described would produce awkward and stilted responses which would at times be incomprehensible. Even though we have mentioned some discourse-like patterns (like ". . . of them" following a number), we have not yet discussed the real problems of discourse. The system uses three different discourse devices in producing its answers. These are much more limited than the range of discourse features it can understand, but they are sufficient to produce fluent dialog.

The first problem involves lists of objects. Our initial way of naming more than one object is to simply string the descriptions together with commas and "and". We might end up with an answer like "yes, four of them: a large blue block, a small red cube, a small red cube, and a small red cube." To avoid this redundancy, the object-namer looks for identical descriptions and combines them with the appropriate number to get "a large blue block and three small red cubes." (Note that it also must change the noun to plural).

The next problem is the use of substitute nouns. We would like to respond to "Is there a red cube which supports a pyramid?" by "yes, a large one." instead of "yes, a large red cube." By comparing the English descriptions of the objects with the wording of the focus in the input sentence, we can omit those nouns and adjectives they share and replace them by "one".

The third problem is more serious, as ignoring it can lead to incomprehensible responses. Consider the answer to question 30 in the dialog ("How did you do it?"). If we did not use the pronoun "it" or the determiner "that", the response would be:

By putting a large red block on the table, then letting go of a large red block, then putting a large green cube on a large red block, then letting go of a large green cube, then putting the red cube on a large green cube, then letting go of the red cube.

How many different blocks and cubes are involved? In describing events, we must have some way to indicate that we are referring to the same object more than once. We can do this using "it" and "that", and at the same time can use these words to improve the smoothness of the discourse in other ways. The system has heuristics which lead it to use "it" to refer to an object in an event it is describing whenever: (1) the same object was called "it" in the question; (2) the object was called "it" in the question preceding the current one, and "it" was not used in the current one; (3) the object has already been named in the current answer, and was the first object in the answer; or (4) no objects have yet been named in the current answer, and the object was the only one named in the previous answer.

To refer to an object already named in the current answer, other than the first, the program applies the determiner "that" to the appropriate noun, to get a phrase like "by putting a green block on a red cube then putting that cube in the box."

REFERENCES

BAR-HILLEL, J. *Language and information.* Reading, Mass.: Addison Wesley, 1964.

BLACK, F. A deductive question answering system. In M. Minsky (Ed.), *Semantic information processing.* Cambridge: M.I.T., 1968. Pp. 354–402.

BOBROW, D. G. Syntactic theory in computer implementations. In H. Borko (Ed.), *Automated language processing.* New York: Wiley, 1967. Pp. 217–252.

BOBROW, D. G. Natural language input for a computer problem solving system. In M. Minsky (Ed.), *Semantic information processing.* Cambridge: M.I.T., 1968. Pp. 133–215.

BOBROW, D. G., AND FRASER, J. B. An augmented state transition network analysis procedure. *Proceedings of the International Joint Conference on Artificial Intelligence.* Bedford, Mass: Mitre Corp., 1969. Pp. 557–568.

BORKO, H. (Ed.). *Automated language processing.* New York: Wiley, 1967.

CHARNIAK, E. Computer solution of calculus word problems. *Proceedings of the International Joint Conference on Artificial Intelligence.* Bedford, Mass: Mitre Corp., 1969. Pp. 303–316.

CHOMSKY, N. *Syntactic structures.* The Hague: Mouton, 1957.

CHOMSKY, N. *Aspects of the theory of syntax.* Cambridge: M.I.T., 1965.

COLES, L. S. An on-line question-answering system with natural language and pictorial input. *Proceedings of 23rd National Conference of Association for Computing Machinery,* 1968, 157–167.

DARLINGTON, J. Translating ordinary language into symbolic logic. Memo MAC-M-149 Project MAC, M.I.T., 1964.

EARLEY, J. C. Generating a recognizer for a BNF grammar. Computing Center Paper, Carnegie-Mellon University, 1966.

FEIGENBAUM, E. A., AND FELDMAN, J. (Eds.), *Computers and thought.* New York: McGraw-Hill, 1963.

FILLMORE, C. The case for case. In E. Bach and R. T. Harms (Eds.), *Universals in Linguistic Theory.* New York: Holt, Rinehart, & Winston, 1968. Pp. 1–88.

Fodor, J. A., and Katz, J. J. (Eds.), *The structure of language*. Englewood Cliffs, New Jersey: Prentice-Hall, 1964.

Garvin, O. L., *et al.* A syntactic analyzer study—final report Bunker-Ramo Corporation, Rome Air Development Center, RADC-TT-65-309, December, 1965.

Green, C., and Raphael, B. The use of theorem proving techniques in question-answering systems. *Proceedings of the 23rd National Conference of the Association for Computing Machinery.* Washington, D. C., Thompson Book Co., 1968.

Green, C. Application of theorem proving to problem solving. *Proceedings of the International Joint Conference on Artificial Intelligence.* Bedford, Mass.: Mitre Corp., 1969. Pp. 219–240.

Green, P. F., Wolf, A. K., Chomsky, C., and Laugherty, K. BASEBALL: An automatic question answerer. In, E. A. Feigenbaum and J. Feldman (Eds.), *Computers and thought.* New York: McGraw-Hill, 1963.

Halliday, M. A. K. The English verbal group: A specimen of a manual of analysis. Nuffield Programme in Linguistics and English Teaching, Work Paper VI, University College, London, 1966.

Halliday, M. A. K. Notes on transitivity and theme in English. *Journal of Linguistics,* 1967, 3, 37–81 and 1968, 4, 179–215.

Halliday, M. A. K. Functional diversity in language as seen from a consideration of modality and mood in English. *Foundations of Language,* 1970, 6, 322–361.

Hewitt, C. PLANNER: A language for proving theorems in robots. *Proceedings of the International Joint Conference on Artificial Intelligence.* Bedford, Mass.: Mitre Corp., 1969. Pp. 295–301.

Hewitt, C. Description and theoretical analysis (using schemas) of PLANNER: A language for proving theorems and manipulating models in a robot. Unpublished Doctoral dissertation, Massachusetts Institute of Technology, 1971.

Katz, J. J., and Fodor, J. A. The Structure of a semantic theory. In J. A. Fodor and J. J. Katz (Eds.), *The structure of language.* Englewood Cliffs, New Jersey: Prentice-Hall, 1964.

Kellogg, C. A natural language compiler for on-line data management. *Proceedings of Fall Joint Computer Conference.* New York: Spartan, 1968. Pp. 473–492.

Klima, E. S. Negation in English. In J. A. Fodor, and J. J. Katz (Eds.), *The structure of language.* Englewood Cliffs, New Jersey: Prentice-Hall, 1964.

Kuno, S. The predictive analyzer and a path elimination technique. *Communications of the Association for Computing Machinery,* 1965, 8, 687–698.

Lindsay, R. K. Inferential memory as the basis of machines which understand natural language. In E. A. Feigenbaum and J. Feldman (Eds.), *Computers and thought.* New York: McGraw-Hill, 1963. Pp. 217–236.

McCarthy, J., Abrahams, P., Edwards, D., Hart, T., and Levin, M. *LISP 1.5 Programmer's Manual.* Cambridge: M.I.T., 1962.

McConlogue, K. L., and Simmons, R. Analyzing English syntax with a pattern-learning parser. *Communications of the Association for Computing Machinery,* 1965, 8, 687–698.

Michie, D. (Ed.). *Machine Intelligence 3.* New York: American Elsevier, 1968.

Minsky, M. Matter, mind, and models. In M. Minsky (Ed.), *Semantic information processing.* Cambridge: M.I.T., 1968. Pp. 425–432.

Minsky, M. Form and content in computer science. *Journal of the Association for Computing Machinery,* 17:2 April 1970.

Newell, A., and Simon, H. A. GPS, a program that simulates human thought. In

E. A. Feigenbaum and J. Feldman (Eds.), *Computers and thought.* New York: McGraw-Hill, 1963. Pp. 279–293.

PETRICK, S. A recognition procedure for transformational grammars. Unpublished Doctoral dissertation, Massachusetts Institute of Technology, 1965.

QUILLIAN, M. R. Semantic memory. In M. Minsky (Ed.), *Semantic information processing.* Cambridge: M.I.T., 1968. Pp. 216–270.

QUILLIAN, M. R. The teachable language comprehender. *Communications of the Association for Computing Machinery,* 1969, **12,** 459–475.

RAPHAEL, B. SIR: A computer program for semantic information retrieval. In M. Minsky (Ed.), *Semantic information processing.* Cambridge: M.I.T., 1968. Pp. 33–134.

ROBINSON, J. A. A machine-oriented logic based on the resolution principle. *Journal of the Association for Computing Machinery,* 1965, 8, 536–541.

SHAPIRO, S. C., AND WOODMANSEE, G. H. A net structure based relational question answerer: Description and examples. *Proceedings of the International Joint Conference on Artificial Intelligence.* Bedford, Mass: Mitre Corp., 1969. Pp. 325–346.

SIKLOSSY, L. Natural language learning by computer. Unpublished Doctoral dissertation, Carnegie-Mellon University, 1968.

SIMMONS, R. F. Storage and retrieval of aspects of meaning in directed graph structures. *Communications of the Association for Computing Machinery,* 1966, 9, 211–214.

SIMMONS, R. F., BURGER, J. F., AND LONG, R. E. An approach toward answering English questions from text. *Proceedings of Fall Joint Computer Conference.* New York: Spartan, 1966. Pp. 357–363.

SIMMONS, R. F., BURGER, J. F., AND SCHWARCZ, R. A computational model of verbal understanding. *Proceedings of Fall Joint Computer Conference.* New York: Spartan, 1968. Pp. 441–456.

SLAGLE, J. R. Experiments with a deductive question-answering program. *Communications of the Association for Computing Machinery,* 1965, 8, 792–798.

SUSSMAN, G., WINOGRAD, T., AND CHARNIAK, E. Micro-planner reference manual. AI Memo 203, Artificial Intelligence Laboratory, M.I.T., July, 1970.

THARP, A. L., AND KRULEE, G. K. Using relational operators to structure long-term memory. *Proceedings of the International Joint Conference on Artificial Intelligence.* Bedford, Mass: Mitre Corp., 1969. Pp. 579–586.

THOMPSON, F. B. English for the computer. *Proceedings of Fall Joint Computer Conference.* New York: Spartan, 1968. Pp. 349–356.

THORNE, J., BRATLEY, R., AND DEWAR, H. The syntactic analysis of English by machine. In D. Michie (Ed.), *Machine Intelligence 3.* New York: American Elsevier, 1968. Pp. 281–309.

THORNE, J. A. program for the syntactic analysis of English sentences. *Communications of the Association for Computing Machinery,* 1969, **12,** 476–480.

WEISSMAN, C. *LISP 1.5 Primer.* Belmont, California: Dickenson, 1967.

WEIZENBAUM, J. ELIZA. *Communications of the Association for Computing Machinery,* 1966, 9, 36–45.

WEIZENBAUM, J. Contextual understanding by computers. *Communications of the Association for Computing Machinery,* 1967, **10,** 474–480.

WHITE, J. L. Interim LISP progress report. AI Memo 190, Artificial Intelligence Laboratory, M.I.T., 1970.

WINOGRAD, T. Linguistics and the computer analysis of tonal harmony. *Journal of Music Theory*, 1968, **12**(1), 2–49.

WINOGRAD, T. Procedures as a representation for data in a computer program for understanding natural language. MAC-TR-84, Artificial Intelligence Laboratory, Massachusetts Institute of Technology, February 1971.

WOODS, W. A. Procedural semantics for a question-answer machine. *Proceedings of Fall Joint Computer Conference*. New York: Spartan, 1968. Pp. 457–471.

WOODS, W. A. Augmented transition networks for natural language analysis. Report No. CS-1, Aiken Computation Laboratory, Harvard University, December, 1969.

ZWICKY, A. M., FRIEDMAN, J., HALL, B. C., AND WALKER, D. E. The MITRE syntactic analysis procedure for transformational grammars. *Proceedings of Fall Joint Computer Conference*. New York: Spartan, 1965. Pp. 317–326.

Appendix A

INDEX OF SYNTACTIC FEATURES

Italicized number indicates primary reference for that feature.

-OB, 71
-OB2, 71
ACTV, 54, 55, 65
ADJ, 56, 62, *66*
ADJG, 57, *61–62*, 66
ADJQ, 48, 49
ADJREL, 48, 51, 53
ADJUNCT, 48, 50, 60, 61, 62
ADV, *66*
ADVADV, 66
ADVMEASQ, 48, 49
ADVMEASREL, 48, 51
AGENT, 54, 56, 60, 61
AND, 72
AS, 61, 62
AUX, 70, 71
BE, 54, 70
BINDER, *66*
BOTH, 72
BOUND, 48, 50
BUTNOT, 72
CLASF, 56, 57, *66–67*
CLAUSE, 47–56, 57, 70, 71
CLAUSEADV, 66
COMP, 48, 49, 54, 55, 58, 60, 61
COMPAR, 57, 61, 66
COMPONENT, 72
COMPOUND, *71–73*
COMPQ, 48, 49
COMPREL, 48, 51, 53
DANGLING, 48, 49, 51, 53, 61
DECLARATIVE, 48, 67, 68
DEF, 58, 67
DEFPOSS, 58, 60, 69
DEM, 58, 68, 69
DET, 56, 57, 58, *67–68*
DOWNQ, 48, 50
DOWNREL, 48, 52, 53
DPRT, 54, 55
EN, 48, 51, 64, 65, 70
FINITE, 64, 65
FUTURE, 62, 63
IMPERATIVE, 47, 48, 65
INCOM, 58, 59, 68

INDEF, 58, 59, 68
ING, 48, 50, 51, 52, 64, 65, 70
INGOB2, 70
INT, 54, 71
IT, 54, 56
ITRNS, 54, 70, 71
ITRNSL, 54, 55, 70, 71
ITSUBJ, 48, 53, 56
LIST, 72
LISTA, 72
LOBJ, 48, 55, 60, 61
LOBJQ, 48
LOBJREL, 48
MAJOR, 48, 49
MASS, 68
MEASQ, 48, 50
MEASREL, 48, 51
MODAL, 62, 63, 64, 70, 71
NDET, 58
NEED2, 69
NEG, 58, 65, 68
NFS, 58, 60, 69
NG, *56–60*, 61, 62
NGQ, 48, 49
NGREL, 48
NONUM, 68
NOR, 72
NOUN, 56, 57, *68–69*
NPL, 58, 60, 68, 69, 70
NS, 58, 60, 68, 69, 70
NUM, 56, 57, *69*
NUMD, 58, 59, *69*
NUMDALONE, 69
NUMDAN, 69
NUMDAS, 69
NUMDAT, 69
NUMD, 58, 59
OBJ, 48, 58, 59
OBJ1, 48, 53, 55, 58
OBJ1Q, 48, 50
OBJ1REL, 48, 51
OBJ1UPREL, 53
OBJ2, 48, 58
OBJ2Q, 48, 50

OBJ2REL, 48, 51
OBJQ, 48
OBJREL, 48
OF, 58, 59, 60, 61
OFD, 68
OFOBJ, 58, 59
OR, 72
ORD, 56, 57, 69
PAST, 62, 63, 64, 71
PASV, 54, 55, 64, 65
POSES, 58, 59
POSS, 58, 59
PREP, 60, 69
PREP2, 69
PREPADV, 66
PREPG, 57, 60–61
PREPOBJ, 48, 52, 58, 59, 60
PREPQ, 48, 49
PREPREL, 48, 51, 53, 61
PRESENT, 62, 63, 64
PRON, 69
PRONG, 58, 59, 60
PRONREL, 69
PROPN, 70
PROPNG, 58, 59
PRT, 54, 55, 70
Q, 56, 57, 60, 61
QADJ, 70
QAUX, 70, 71
QDET, 67
QNTFR, 58, 59, 67, 68
QUEST, 58, 61, 69
QUESTION, 48, 49, 70, 71
RELDEL, 48, 52
RELPREPG, 60, 61
REPOB, 71
REPORT, 48, 52, 71
RSNG, 48, 50, 52, 56, 60, 71
RSQ, 48, 51, 57
SEC, 48
SHORT, 48, 49, 61
SHORTREL, 51, 53

SUBING, 48, 52, 71
SUBJ, 48, 52, 54, 58, 59
SUBJFORK, 73
SUBJQ, 48, 49
SUBJREL, 48, 51
SUBJT, 54, 58
SUBJTQ, 48, 49
SUBJTREL, 48, 51, 53
SUBQ, 48
SUBREL, 48
SUBTO, 48, 52, 71
SUBTOB, 71
SUP, 57, 66
THAN, 62, 63
THAT, 48, 52
THERE, 49, 54
TIM1, 66
TIME, 58, 59, 66
TIMEQ, 48, 50
TIMEREL, 48, 52
TO, 48, 50, 51, 52, 53, 65, 71
TODEL, 65
TPRON, 57, 70
TPRONG, 57, 58
TRANS, 54, 55, 71
TRANS2, 54, 71
TRANS2TOQ, 48, 50
TRANS2TOREL, 48, 51, 52
TRANSL, 54, 55
UPQUEST, 61
UPREL, 48, 53, 61
V3PS, 70
VB, 70–71
VBAD, 66
VBFORK, 73
VFS, 70
VG, 62–65, 71
VPRT, 71
WH–, 48, 49, 51
WHRS, 48, 51
WORD, 66–71
YES–NO, 48

Appendix B - Sample Parsings

(((HOW MANY EGGS WOULD YOU HAVE BEEN GOING TO USE IN THE
    CAKE IF YOU HADN'T LEARNED YOUR MOTHER'S RECIPE WAS
    WRONG)
(CLAUSE MAJOR QUEST NGQUES POLR2 ACTV OBJ1Q TRANS)
(((HOW MANY EGGS)
  (NG QUEST HOWMANY NDEF NPL DET)
  ((HOW (QDET)) (MANY (QDET)) (EGGS (NOUN NPL))))
  (WOULD (VB AUX MODAL QAUX))
  ((YOU) (NG SUBJ DEF NS NPL) ((YOU (PRON NPL NS SUBJ OBJ))))
  ((HAVE BEEN GOING TO USE) (VG MODAL NAGR (FUT PAST MODAL))
                          ((WOULD (VB AUX MODAL QAUX))
                          (HAVE (HAVE VB AUX INF TRANS))
                          (BEEN (AUX VB BE EN))
                          (GOING (VB ITRNS ING))
                          (TO (TO))
                          (USE (VB INF TRANS MVB))))
  ((IN THE CAKE) (PREPG)
                ((IN (PLACE PREP PLACE))
                ((THE CAKE)
                (NG OBJ DET NS DEF)
                ((THE (DET NPL NS DEF)) (CAKE (NOUN NS))))))
  ((IF YOU HADN'T LEARNED YOUR MOTHER'S RECIPE WAS WRONG)
  (CLAUSE BOUND DECLAR ACTV TRANS)
  ((IF (BINDER))
  ((YOU) (NG SUBJ DEF NS NPL) ((YOU (PRON NPL NS SUBJ OBJ))))

```
((HADN'T LEARNED)
 (VG VPL V3PS NEG (PAST PAST))
 ((HADN'T (HAVE VB AUX TRANS PAST VPL V3PS VFS NEG))
  (LEARNED (VB TRANS REPOB PAST EN MVB))))
((YOUR MOTHER'S RECIPE WAS WRONG)
 (CLAUSE RSNG REPORT OBJ OBJ1 DECLAR BE INT)
 (((YOUR MOTHER'S RECIPE)
   (NG SUBJ NS DEF DET POSES)
   (((YOUR MOTHER'S)
     (NG SUBJ NS DEF DET POSES POSS)
     (((YOUR) (NG SUBJ POSS)
              ((YOUR (PRON NPL NS SUBJ OBJ POSS))))
      (MOTHER'S (NOUN NS POSS))))
    (RECIPE (NOUN NS))))
  ((WAS) (VG V3PS VFS (PAST))
         ((WAS (AUX VB BE V3PS VFS PAST MVB))))
  ((WRONG) (ADJG Q COMP) ((WRONG (ADJ)))))))))))
```

PICK UP ANYTHING GREEN, AT LEAST THREE OF THE BLOCKS, AND
EITHER A BOX OR A SPHERE WHICH IS BIGGER THAN ANY BRICK ON THE
TABLE.


```
(((PICK UP ANYTHING GREEN /, AT LEAST THREE OF THE BLOCKS /, AND
    EITHER A BOX OR A SPHERE WHICH IS BIGGER THAN ANY BRICK ON
    THE TABLE)
  (CLAUSE MAJOR IMPER ACTV TRANS)
  (((PICK) (VG IMPER) ((PICK (VPRT VB INF TRANS MVB)))))
  (UP (PRT))
  ((ANYTHING GREEN /, AT LEAST THREE OF THE BLOCKS /, AND
    EITHER A BOX OR A SPHERE WHICH IS BIGGER THAN ANY
    BRICK ON THE TABLE)
  (NG OBJ OBJ1 EITHER COMPOUND LIST NS)
  (((ANYTHING GREEN) (NG OBJ OBJ1 TPRON)
                  ((ANYTHING (NS TPRON)) (GREEN (ADJ))))
    ((AT LEAST THREE OF THE BLOCKS)
    (NG OBJ OBJ1 COMPONENT NUMD NUM NPL DET OF)
    ((AT (AT))
     (LEAST (NUMD NUMDAT))
     (THREE (NUM))
     ((OF THE BLOCKS)
      (PREPG OF)
      ((OF (PREP))
       ((THE BLOCKS)
        (NG OBJ DET NPL DEF)
        ((THE (DET NPL NS DEF)) (BLOCKS (NOUN NPL)))))))))
```

```
((A BOX OR A SPHERE WHICH IS BIGGER THAN ANY BRICK ON THE
    TABLE)
(NG OBJ OBJ1 COMPONENT OR COMPOUND BOTH NS)
(((A BOX) (NG OBJ OBJ1 COMPONENT DET NS INDEF)
            ((A (DET NS INDEF)) (BOX (NOUN NS))))
  ((A SPHERE WHICH IS BIGGER THAN ANY BRICK ON THE TABLE)
   (NG OBJ OBJ1 COMPONENT DET NS INDEF)
   ((A (DET NS INDEF))
    (SPHERE (NOUN NS))
    ((WHICH IS BIGGER THAN ANY BRICK ON THE TABLE)
     (CLAUSE RSQ SUBREL BE INT)
     (((WHICH) (NG RELWD DEF NPL) ((WHICH (NPL))))
      ((IS) (VG V3PS (PRES))
            ((IS (AUX VB BE V3PS PRES MVB))))
      ((BIGGER THAN ANY BRICK ON THE TABLE)
       (ADJG Q COMP COMPAR THAN)
       ((BIGGER (ADJ COMPAR))
        (THAN (THAN))
        ((ANY BRICK ON THE TABLE)
         (NG SUBJ COMPAR DET NS QNTFR)
         ((ANY (DET NS NPL QNTFR))
          (BRICK (NOUN NS))
          ((ON THE TABLE)
           (PREPG Q)
           ((ON (PREP PLACE))
            ((THE TABLE)
             (NG OBJ DET NS DEF)
             ((THE (DET NPL NS DEF))
              (TABLE (NOUN NS)))))))))))))))))))))
```

Appendix C - Sample BLOCKS Theorems

```
(DEFTHEOREM TA-CONTAIN
        (THANTE (X Y Z)
              (#AT $?X ?)
              (THGOAL (#MANIP $?X))
              (THGOAL (#SUPPORT $?Y $?X))
              (THOR (THAND (THGOAL (#IS $?Y #BOX))
                          (THVSETQ $_Z $?Y))
                    (THGOAL (#CONTAIN $?Z $?Y)))
              (THASSERT (#CONTAIN $?Z $?X))))
```

```
(DEFTHEOREM TC-MAKESPACE
        (THCONSE (SURF SIZE OBJ SPACE X (WHY (EV)) EV)
                (#FINDSPACE $?SURF $?SIZE $?OBJ $?SPACE)
                (THNOT (THGOAL (#IS $?SURF #BOX)))
                (MEMORY)
                TAG
                (THAND (THGOAL (#SUPPORT $?SURF $_X))
                       (THGOAL (#GET-RID-OF $?X)
                               (THUSE TC-GET-RID-OF)))
                (THOR (THGOAL (#FINDSPACE $?SURF
                                          $?SIZE
                                          $?OBJ
                                          $?SPACE)
                              (THUSE TC-FINDSPACE))
                      (THGO TAG))
                (MEMOREND (#MAKESPACE $?EV $?SURF)))))


(DEFTHEOREM TC-MORE
        (THCONSE (MEASURE X Y)
                (#MORE $?MEASURE $?X $?Y)
                (THVSETQ $_MEASURE
                        (GET $?MEASURE (QUOTE MEASFN)))
                (GREATERP ($?MEASURE $?X)
                          ($?MEASURE $?Y))))
```

```
(DEFTHEOREM TC-ON
            (THCONSE (X Y Z)
                     (#ON $?X $?Y)
                     (THOR (THGOAL (#SUPPORT $?Y $?X))
                           (THAND (THASVAL $?X)
                                  (THGOAL (#SUPPORT $_Z $?X))
                                  (THGOAL (#ON $?Z $?Y)
                                          (THUSE TC-ON))))))


(DEFTHEOREM TC-PICKUP
            (THCONSE (X (WHY (EV)) EV)
                     (#PICKUP $?X)
                     (MEMORY)
                     (THGOAL (#GRASP $?X) (THUSE TC-GRASP))
                     (THGOAL (#RAISEHAND)
                             (THNODB)
                             (THUSE TC-RAISEHAND))
                     (MEMOREND (#PICKUP $?EV $?X))))


(DEFTHEOREM TCT-PICKUP
            (THCONSE (X EV TIME)
                     (#PICKUP $?X $?TIME)
                     (THOR (THAND (THGOAL (#PICKUP$?EV $?X))
                                  (TIMECHK $?EV $?TIME))
                           (THGOAL (#PICKUP $?EV $?X $?TIME)
                                   (THUSE TCTE-PICKUP))))
```

```
(DEFTHEOREM TCTE-PICKUP
        (THCONSE (X EV EVENT TIME)
                (#PICKUP $?EV $?X $?TIME)
                (THOR (THAND (THGOAL (#PICKUP $?EV $?X))
                            (TIMECHK $?EV $?TIME)))
                (THSUCCEED))
        (THAMONG $?EVENT EVENTLIST)
        (MEMQ (GET $?EVENT (QUOTE TYPE))
                (QUOTE (#PUTON #GET-RID-OF)))
        (TIMECHK $?EVENT $?TIME)
        (THOR (THGOAL (#PUTON $?EVENT $?X ?))
                (THGOAL (#GET-RID-OF $?EVENT $?X)))
        (THVSETQ $_EV (MAKESYM (QUOTE E)))
        (AND (PUTPROP $?EV
                        (PUTPROP $?EV
                                (GET $?EVENT (QUOTE END))
                                (QUOTE START))
                        (QUOTE END))
                (PUTPROP $?EV (QUOTE #PICKUP) (QUOTE TYPE))
                (PUTPROP $?EV $?EVENT (QUOTE WHY))
                (SETQ EVENTLIST (CONS $?EV EVENTLIST))
                (THASSERT (#PICKUP $?EV $?X)))))


(DEFTHEOREM TE-CONTAIN (THERASING (X Y)
                        (#AT $?X ?)
                        (THGOAL (#CONTAIN $_Y $?X))
```

Appendix D - Sample PROGRAMMAR Program

Excerpt from Noun Group Parser

```
DET1
(COND ((ISQ H NS) (FQ NS)) (T (FQ NPL)))
(OR NN (AND (FQ NUMBER) (GO INCOM)))
NUMBER
(FQ DET)
((NQ OF) OF ADJ)
QNUM
((ISQ H NONUM) OF NIL)
((AND (PARSE NUM) (FQ NUM)) NIL OF)
((COND ((EQ (SM H) 1) (AND (CQ NS) (RQ NPL)))
        ((CQ NPL) (RQ NS)))
 NIL
 (NUMD)
 INCOM)
((EQ (CADDR (NB H)) (Q NO)) ADJ NIL)
OF
((AND (NQ OF) (PARSE PREPG OF)) SMOF NIL)
((EQ (CADDR (NB H)) (Q NONE)) INCOM ADJ)
SMOF
(FQ OF)
((OR SMN (SMNGOF) (NOT (POP))) RETSM INCOM)
ADJ
((PARSE ADJ) ADJ CLASF NIL)
EPR
((OR (ISQ H SUP) (ISQ H COMPAR)) NIL REDUC)
```

```
(FQ ADJ)
(AND (EQ (CADDAR N) (Q OF))
     (PARSE PREPG OF)
     (OR SMN (SMNGOF) (AND (ERT NOUN SMNGOF3) (GO FAIL)))
     (FQ OF)
     (GO RETSM))
(GO INCOM)
CLASF
((OR (PARSE VB ING (CLASF)) (PARSE VB EN (CLASF)) (PARSE CLASF))
 CLASF
 NIL
 REDUC)
NOUN
((PARSE NOUN) NIL RED2)
((AND (CQ TIME) (NOT (ISQ H TIM1))) RED1 NIL)
(SETQ T1 FE)
(COND ((AND (ISQ H MASS) (OR (CQ PART) (NOT (CQ DET))))
        (FQ MASS)))
(COND ((NOT (ISQ H NPL)) (RQ NPL PART)))
(COND ((NOT (ISQ H NS)) (RQ NS)))
(COND ((AND (NOT (CQ DET)) (NOT (CQ NUMD))) (* H)
                                   (TRNSF NPL MASS)))
((MEET FE (Q (NS NPL PART MASS))) NIL REDO)
SMNG
((OR (NOT (CQ OFOBJ)) (CQ DET)) NIL FAIL)
(OR SMN (SMNG1) (AND (ERT NOUN SMNG1) (GO FAIL)))
((NOT (ISQ H POSS)) NIL POSS RETSM)
```

```
((AND (NEXTW TO)
      (MEET FE (Q (COMP SUBJ)))
      (PARSE CLAUSE RSQ TO)
      (OR SMN (SMRSQ (SM H) SM) (GO POPRET)))
 RETSM
 NIL)
((AND (OR (NEXTW AS) (NQ COMPAR))
      (PARSE ADJG THANNEED)
      (OR SMN
          (AND (NULL N)
               (CQ SUBJ)
               (ISQ (* C PV) AUX)
               (ISQ PT BE)
               (GO POPRET))
          (SMPREP (QUOTE ADJ))
          (GO POPRET)))
 RETSM
 NIL)
```

Appendix E - Sample Dictionary Entries

Syntactic Definitions

```
(DEFLIST WORD

        (LITTLE (ADJ))

        (LONG (ADJ))

        (MAKE (VB INF TRANS))

        (MOVE (VB INF TRANS))

        (NAME (NOUN NS VB INF TRANS))

        (NARROW (ADJ))

        (NICE(ADJ))

        (OBJECT (NOUN NS))

        (OFF (PRT))

        (OUT (PRT))

        (PICK (VPRT VB INF TRANS))

        (PUT (INF PAST VB TRANSL VPRT))

        (POINTED (ADJ))

        (PYRAMID (NOUN NS))

        (RED (ADJ))

        (RELEASE (VB TRANS INF))

        (RIGHT (NOUN NS))

        (ROUND (ADJ)))


(DEFLIST WORD1

        (BEGAN (BEGIN (PAST) (INF)))

        (GAVE (GIVE (PAST) (INF)))

        (SAW (SEE (PAST) (INF)))

        (TOLD (TELL (PAST) (INF))))
```

Semantic Definitions


```
(DEFLIST SMNTC

        (A ((DET T)))

        (ABOVE ((PREP ((T (#LOC #ABOVE T))))))

        (AFTER ((BINDER (END NIL))))

        (ALL ((DET (COND ((CQ OF) (Q ALL))

                        ((MEET (Q (NUM DEF)) FE) (Q DEF))

                        ((Q NDEF))))))

        (BALL ((NOUN (NMEANS ((#MANIP #ROUND)

                                ((#IS *** #BALL)))))))

        (BIG ((MEASURE ((#SIZE (#PHYSOB) T)))

            (ADJ (NMEANS ((#PHYSOB #BIG)

                        ((#MORE #SIZE *** (200 200

                                            200)))))))))

        (BLACK ((ADJ (#COLOR #BLACK))))

        (BLOCK ((NOUN (NMEANS ((#MANIP #RECTANGULAR)

                                ((#IS *** #BLOCK)))))))

        (BLUE ((ADJ (#COLOR #BLUE))))

        (BY ((PREP ((T (CMEANS ((((#PHYSOB)) ((#PHYSOB)))

                                (#NEXTO #1 #2 *TIME)

                                NIL)))))))

        (COLOR ((NOUN (NMEANS ((#COLOR) ((#IS *** #COLOR)))))))

        (CONTAIN ((VB ((TRANS (CMEANS ((((#BOX)) ((#PHYSOB)))

                                        (#CONTAIN #1 #2 *TIME)
                                        NIL)
```

```
                              (((((#CONSTRUCT))

                                ((#THING)))

                                (#PART #2 #1 *TIME)

                                NIL)))))))

          (CUBE ((NOUN (NMEANS (((#MANIP #RECTANGULAR)

                                ((#IS *** #BLOCK)

                                (#EQDIM ***)))))))

          (EVERYTHING ((TPRON (QUOTE ALL))))

          (FEWER ((NUMD (LIST (Q <) NUM))))

          (FOUR ((NUM 4)))

          (FRIEND ((NOUN (NMEANS ((#PERSON)

                                ((#IS *** #PERSON)))))))

          (GRAB ((VB ((TRANS (#GRASP))))))

          (GRASP ((VB ((TRANS (#GRASP))))))

          (I ((PRON (SETQ SM (Q (FRIEND))))))

          (IT ((PRON (SMIT (Q IT)))))

          (NICE ((ADJ (NMEANS ((#THING)

                                ((#LIKE :FRIEND ***)))))))

          (NOW ((ADV (OR (EQ (CADR (ASSQ (QUOTE TIME) FE))

                                (QUOTE :NOW))

                                (ERT NOW DEFINITION)))))

          (THE ((DET T)))

          (THEY ((PRON (SMIT (Q THEY)))))

          (THICK ((ADJ (NMEANS ((#PHYSOB) ((#MORE #THICKNESS

                                ***

                                (0 200 0)))))))

          (MEASURE ((#THICKNESS (#PHYSOB) T)))))
```

```
(THIN ((ADJ (NMEANS ((#PHYSOB) ((#MORE #THICKNESS
                                 (0 200 0)
                                 ***)))))
       (MEASURE ((#THICKNESS (#PHYSOB) NIL)))))
(THING ((NOUN (NMEANS ((#THING #VAGUE #PHYSOB)
                       ((#IS *** ?)))))))
(WHO ((PRONREL (SETQ SM (QUOTE (ANIMATE))))
      (PRON (SETQ SM (QUOTE (ANIMATE))))))
(WHY ((QADJ (FQ WHY)))))
```

Appendix F - PLANNER Data for Dialog in Section 1.3

```
(#IS :B1 #BLOCK)              (#MANIP :B6)
(#IS :B2 #PYRAMID)            (#MANIP :B7)
(#IS :B3 #BLOCK)              (#MANIP :B10)
(#IS :B4 #PYRAMID)            (#SUPPORT :TABLE :B1)
(#IS :B5 #PYRAMID)            (#SUPPORT :TABLE :B3)
(#IS :B6 #BLOCK)              (#SUPPORT :BOX :B4)
(#IS :B7 #BLOCK)              (#SUPPORT :TABLE :B10)
(#IS :B10 #BLOCK)             (#SUPPORT :TABLE :B6)
(#IS #RED #COLOR)             (#SUPPORT :TABLE :BOX)
(#IS #BLUE #COLOR)            (#AT :BOX (600 600 0))
(#IS #GREEN #COLOR)           (#IS :BOX #BOX)
(#IS #WHITE #COLOR)           (#IS :TABLE #TABLE)
(#IS #BLACK #COLOR)           (#CONTAIN :BOX :B4)
(#IS #RECTANGULAR #SHAPE)     (#SHAPE :B1 #RECTANGULAR)
(#IS #ROUND #SHAPE)           (#SHAPE :B3 #RECTANGULAR)
(#IS #POINTED #SHAPE)         (#SHAPE :B2 #POINTED)
(#IS :SHRDLU #ROBOT)          (#SHAPE :B4 #POINTED)
(#IS :FRIEND #PERSON)         (#SHAPE :B5 #POINTED)
(#IS :HAND #HAND)             (#SHAPE :B6 #RECTANGULAR)
(#AT :B1 (100 100 0))         (#SHAPE :B7 #RECTANGULAR)
(#AT :B2 (100 100 100))       (#SHAPE :B10 #RECTANGULAR)
(#AT :B3 (400 0 0))           (#COLOR :B1 #RED)
(#AT :B4 (640 640 1))         (#COLOR :B2 #GREEN)
(#AT :B5 (500 100 200))       (#COLOR :B3 #GREEN)
(#AT :B6 (0 300 0))           (#COLOR :B4 #BLUE)
```

```
(#AT :B7 (0 240 300))          (#COLOR :B5 #RED)



(#AT :B10 (300 640 0))         (#COLOR :B6 #RED)
(#SUPPORT :B1 :B2)             (#COLOR :B7 #GREEN)
(#SUPPORT :B3 :B5)             (#COLOR :B10 #BLUE)
(#SUPPORT :B6 :B7)             (#COLOR :BOX #WHITE)
(#CLEARTOP :B2)                (#COLOR :TABLE #BLACK)
(#CLEARTOP :B4)                (#CALL :SHRDLU SHRDLU)
(#CLEARTOP :B5)                (#CALL :FRIEND YOU)
(#CLEARTOP :B7)
(#CLEARTOP :B10)
(#MANIP :B1)
(#MANIP :B2)
(#MANIP :B3)
(#MANIP :B4)
(#MANIP :B5)
```